# CLASSIC CRIME AND SUSPENSE WRITERS

Writers of English: Lives and Works

# CLASSIC CRIME AND SUSPENSE WRITERS

Edited and with an Introduction by

Harold Bloom

CHELSEA HOUSE PUBLISHERS
New York    Philadelphia

**Jacket illustration:** Edward Hopper (1882–1967), detail from *Nighthawks* (1942) (oil, 76.2 x 144 cm). Friends of American Art Collection, photo copyright © 1994 by The Art Institute of Chicago.

CHELSEA HOUSE PUBLISHERS

**Editorial Director** Richard Rennert
**Executive Managing Editor** Karyn Gullen Browne
**Picture Editor** Adrian G. Allen
**Copy Chief** Robin James
**Art Director** Robert Mitchell
**Manufacturing Director** Gerald Levine

Writers of English: Lives and Works

**Senior Editor** S. T. Joshi
**Series Design** Rae Grant

Staff for CLASSIC CRIME AND SUSPENSE WRITERS

**Assistant Editor** Mary Sisson
**Research** Stefan Dziemianowicz, Robert Green
**Picture Researcher** Matthew Dudley

© 1995 by Chelsea House Publishers, a division of Main Line Book Co.

Introduction © 1995 by Harold Bloom

Printed and bound in the United States of America.

First Printing

1 3 5 7 9 8 6 4 2

Library of Congress Cataloging-in-Publication Data

Classic crime and suspense writers / edited and with an introduction by Harold Bloom.
   p.   cm.—(Writers of English)
   Includes bibliographical references (p.).
   ISBN 0-7910-2206-4.—ISBN 0-7910-2231-5 (pbk.)
   1. Detective and mystery stories, English—Bio-bibliography. 2. English fiction—20th century—Bio-bibliography. 3. Detective and mystery stories, American—Bio-bibliography. 4. Detective and mystery stories, American—Dictionaries. 5. Detective and mystery stories, English—Dictionaries. 6. American fiction—20th century—Bio-bibliography. 7. Novelists, American—Biography—Dictionaries. 8. Novelists, English—Biography—Dictionaries. I. Bloom, Harold. II. Series.
PR888.D4C53 1995                                                    93-22607
823'.087209'03—dc20                                                       CIP

# ◩ Contents

# ◈ User's Guide

THIS VOLUME PROVIDES biographical, critical, and bibliographical information on the thirteen most significant crime and suspense writers of the first half of the twentieth century. Each chapter consists of three parts: a biography of the author, a selection of brief critical extracts about the author, and a bibliography of the author's published books.

The biography supplies a detailed outline of the important events in the author's life, including his or her major writings. The critical extracts are taken from a wide array of books and periodicals, from the author's lifetime to the present, and range in content from biographical to critical to historical. The extracts are arranged in chronological order by date of writing or publication, and a full bibliographical citation is provided at the end of each extract. Editorial additions or deletions are indicated within carets.

The author bibliographies list every separate publication—including books, pamphlets, broadsides, collaborations, and works edited or translated by the author—for works published in the author's lifetime; selected important posthumous publications are also listed. Titles are those of the first edition; if a work has subsequently come to be known under a variant title, this title is supplied within carets. In selected instances dates of revised editions are given where these are significant. Pseudonymous works are listed, but the pseudonyms under which these works were published are not. Periodicals edited by the author are listed only when the author has written most or all of the contents. For plays we have listed date of publication, not date of production; unpublished plays are not listed. Titles enclosed in square brackets are of doubtful authenticity. All works by the author, whether in English or in other languages, have been listed; English translations of foreign-language works are not listed unless the author has done the translation.

# The Life of the Author

## Harold Bloom

NIETZSCHE, WITH EXULTANT ANGUISH, famously proclaimed that God was dead. Whatever the consequences of this for the ethical life, its ultimate literary effect certainly would have surprised the author Nietzsche. His French disciples, Foucault most prominent among them, developed the Nietzschean proclamation into the dogma that all authors, God included, were dead. The death of the author, which is no more than a Parisian trope, another metaphor for fashion's setting of skirt-lengths, is now accepted as literal truth by most of our current apostles of what should be called French Nietzsche, to distinguish it from the merely original Nietzsche. We also have French Freud or Lacan, which has little to do with the actual thought of Sigmund Freud, and even French Joyce, which interprets *Finnegans Wake* as the major work of Jacques Derrida. But all this is as nothing compared to the final triumph of the doctrine of the death of the author: French Shakespeare. That delicious absurdity is given us by the New Historicism, which blends Foucault and California fruit juice to give us the Word that Renaissance "social energies," and not William Shakespeare, composed *Hamlet* and *King Lear*. It seems a proper moment to murmur "enough" and to return to a study of the life of the author.

Sometimes it troubles me that there are so few masterpieces in the vast ocean of literary biography that stretches between James Boswell's great *Life* of Dr. Samuel Johnson and the late Richard Ellmann's wonderful *Oscar Wilde*. Literary biography is a crucial genre, and clearly a difficult one in which to excel. The actual nature of the lives of the poets seems to have little effect upon the quality of their biographies. Everything happened to Lord Byron and nothing at all to Wallace Stevens, and yet their biographers seem equally daunted by them. But even inadequate biographies of strong writers, or of weak ones, are of immense use. I have never read a literary biography from which I have not profited, a statement I cannot make about any other genre whatsoever. And when it comes to figures who are central to us—Dante, Shakespeare, Cervantes, Montaigne, Goethe, Whitman, Tolstoi, Freud, Joyce, Kafka among them—we reach out eagerly for every scrap that the biographers have gleaned. Concerning Dante and Shakespeare we know much too little, yet when we come to Goethe and Freud, where we seem to know more than everything, we still want to know more. The death of the author, despite our current resentniks, clearly was only a momentary fad. Something vital in every authentic lover of literature responds to Emerson's battle-cry sentence: "There is no history, only biography." Beyond that there is a deeper truth, difficult to come at and requiring a lifetime to understand, which is that there is no literature, only autobiography, however mediated, however veiled, however transformed. The events of Shakespeare's life included the composition of *Hamlet,* and that act of writing was itself a crucial act of living, though we do not yet know altogether how to read so doubled an act. When an author takes up a more overtly autobiographical stance, as so many do in their youth, again we still do not know precisely how to accommodate the vexed relation between life and work. T. S. Eliot, meditating upon James Joyce, made a classic statement as to such accommodation:

> We want to know who are the originals of his characters, and what were
> the origins of his episodes, so that we may unravel the web of memory
> and invention and discover how far and in what ways the crude material
> has been transformed.

When a writer is not even covertly autobiographical, the web of memory and invention is still there, but so subtly woven that we may never unravel it. And yet we want deeply never to stop trying, and not merely because we are curious, but because each of us is caught in her own network of memory and invention. We do not always recall our inventions, and long before we age we cease to be certain of the extent to which we have invented our memories. Perhaps one motive for reading is our need to unravel our own webs. If our masters could make, from their lives, what we read, then we can be moved by them to ask: What have we made or lived in relation to what we have read? The answers may be sad, or confused, but the question is likely, implicitly, to go on being asked as long as we read. In Freudian terms, we are asking: What is it that we have repressed? What have we forgotten, unconsciously but purposively: What is it that we flee? Art, literature necessarily included, is regression in the service of the ego, according to a famous Freudian formula. I doubt the Freudian wisdom here, but indubitably it is profoundly suggestive. When we read, something in us keeps asking the equivalent of the Freudian questions: From what or whom is the author in flight, and to what earlier stages in her life is she returning, and why?

Reading, whether as an art or a pastime, has been damaged by the visual media, television in particular, and might be in some danger of extinction in the age of the computer, except that the psychic need for it continues to endure, presumably because it alone can assuage a central loneliness in elitist society. Despite all sophisticated or resentful denials, the reading of imaginative literature remains a quest to overcome the isolation of the individual consciousness. We can read for information, or entertainment, or for love of the language, but in the end we seek, in the author, the person whom we have not found, whether in ourselves or in others. In that quest, there always are elements at once aggressive and defensive, so that reading, even in childhood, is rarely free of hidden anxieties. And yet it remains one of the few activities not contaminated by an entropy of spirit. We read in hope, because we lack companionship, and the author can become the object of the most idealistic elements in our search for the wit and inventiveness we so desperately require. We read biography, not as a supplement to reading the author, but as a second, fresh attempt to understand what always seems to evade us in the work, our drive towards a kind of identity with the author.

This will-to-identity, though recently much deprecated, is a prime basis for the experience of sublimity in reading. *Hamlet* retains its unique position in the Western canon not because most readers and playgoers identify themselves with the prince, who clearly is beyond them, but rather because they find themselves again in the power of the language that represents him with such immediacy and force. Yet we know that neither language nor social energy created Hamlet. Our curiosity about Shakespeare is endless, and never will be appeased. That curiosity itself is a value, and cannot be separated from the value of *Hamlet* the tragedy, or Hamlet the literary character. It provokes us that Shakespeare the man seems so unknowable, at once everyone and no one as Borges shrewdly observes. Critics keep telling us otherwise, yet something valid in us keeps believing that we would know Hamlet better if Shakespeare's life were as fully known as the lives of Goethe and Freud, Byron and Oscar Wilde, or best of all, Dr. Samuel Johnson. Shakespeare never will have his Boswell, and Dante never will have his Richard Ellmann. How much one would give for a detailed and candid *Life of Dante* by Petrarch, or an outspoken memoir of Shakespeare by Ben Jonson! Or, in the age just past, how superb would be rival studies of one another by Hemingway and Scott Fitzgerald! But the list is endless: think of *Oscar Wilde* by Lord Alfred Douglas, or a joint biography of Shelley by Mary Godwin, Emilia Viviani, and Jane Williams. More than our insatiable desire for scandal would be satisfied. The literary rivals and the lovers of the great writers possessed perspectives we will never enjoy, and without those perspectives we dwell in some poverty in regard to the writers with whom we ourselves never can be done.

There is a sense in which imaginative literature *is* perspectivism, so that the reader is likely to be overwhelmed by the work's difficulty unless its multiple perspectives are mastered. Literary biography matters most because it is a storehouse of perspectives, frequently far surpassing any that are grasped by the particular biographer. There are relations between authors' lives and their works of kinds we have yet to discover, because our analytical instruments are not yet advanced enough to perform the necessary labor. Perhaps a novel, poem, or play is not so much a regression in the service of the ego, as it is an amalgam of *all* the Freudian mechanisms of defense, all working together for the apotheosis of the ego. Freud valued art highly, but thought that the aesthetic enterprise was no rival for psycho-analysis, unlike religion and philosophy. Clearly Freud was mistaken; his own anxieties about his indebtedness to Shakespeare helped produce the weirdness of his joining in the lunacy that argued for the Earl of Oxford as the author of Shakespeare's plays. It was Shakespeare, and not "the poets," who was there before Freud arrived at his depth psychology, and it is Shakespeare who is there still, well out ahead of psychoanalysis. We see what Freud would not see, that psychoanalysis is Shakespeare prosified and systematized. Freud is part of literature, not of "science," and the biography of Freud has the same relations to psychoanalysis as the biography of Shakespeare has to *Hamlet* and *King Lear,* if only we knew more of the life of Shakespeare.

Western literature, particularly since Shakespeare, is marked by the representa-tion of internalized change in its characters. A literature of the ever-growing inner self is in itself a large form of biography, even though this is the biography of imaginary beings, from Hamlet to the sometimes nameless protagonists of Kafka and Beckett. Skeptics might want to argue that all literary biography concerns imaginary beings, since authors make themselves up, and every biographer gives us a creation curiously different from the same author as seen by the writer of a rival *Life.* Boswell's Johnson is not quite anyone else's Johnson, though it is now very difficult for us to disentangle the great Doctor from his gifted Scottish friend and follower. The life of the author is not merely a metaphor or a fiction, as is "the Death of the Author," but it always does contain metaphorical or fictive elements. Those elements are a part of the value of literary biography, but not the largest or the crucial part, which is the separation of the mask from the man or woman who hid behind it. James Joyce and Samuel Beckett, master and sometime disciple, were both of them enigmatic personalities, and their biographers have not, as yet, fully expounded the mystery of these contrasting natures. Beckett seems very nearly to have been a secular saint: personally disinterested, heroic in the French Resistance, as humane a person ever to have composed major fictions and dramas. Joyce, self-obsessed even as Beckett was preternaturally selfless, was the Milton of the twentieth century. Beckett was perhaps the least egoistic post-Joycean, post-Proustian, post-Kafkan of writers. Does that illuminate the problematical nature of his work, or does it simply constitute another problem? Whatever the cause, the question matters. The only death of the author that is other than literal, and that matters, is the fate only of weak writers. The strong, who become canonical, never die, which is what the canon truly is about. To be read forever is the Life of the Author.

# ◈ Introduction

BY ANY AESTHETIC STANDARD WHATSOEVER, Graham Greene is the most eminent writer discussed in this volume, but not because of his supposed "major" novels: *The Power and the Glory, The Heart of the Matter, The End of the Affair*. These have not endured even the half-century or so since their publication, and increasingly seem inadequate imitations of Greene's masters, Joseph Conrad and Henry James. Yet Greene's "entertainments," his suspense adventures, reread as freshly as ever, particularly *This Gun for Hire, Brighton Rock, The Confidential Agent*, and *The Ministry of Fear*, all of them enhanced by their half-century of currency. John Buchan and Eric Ambler in Great Britain, and the classic American foursome of Cain, Chandler, Hammett, and Ross Macdonald may rival the Greene of the "entertainments" in vividness and in a sense of social reality, and they are free of Greene's characteristic theological tendentiousness, which disfigures his "serious" novels and darkens even *Brighton Rock*. Still, *The Confidential Agent* and *The Ministry of Fear* have a moral complexity and a depth of characterization unique in the entire subgenre of crime and suspense narratives. Greene's disciple, John le Carré, and the American Elmore Leonard, the best of our contemporaries in this mode, also have not yet equaled Greene's artistry in creating protagonists who are more than the sum of their circumstances and their perplexities.

Greene's unheroic heroes recognizably descend from Conrad's Lord Jim and Nostromo, and they have set a pattern that modern suspense writers seem fated to keep repeating. D. in *The Confidential Agent* and Arthur Rowe in *The Ministry of Fear* manifest the enduring strength of a thoughtful humility, and they are undefeatable primarily because they never cease to regard themselves as failures, as men without hope. Their dark doubles are Pinkie in *Brighton Rock* and Raven in *This Gun for Hire*, twentieth-century versions of the Jacobean hero-villains of John Webster and Cyril Tourneur. Greene's suspense protagonists all suggest dialectical versions of Decadence: in Pinkie and Raven, the desire to be damned arises out of a horror of life, a horror indeed of the female as the source of life, while in the agent D. and in Rowe a fundamental love of natural existence and a quest for the female have been dimmed by a complex inability always to know the difference between humility and despair. The superiority, in my judgment, of *The Confidential Agent* and *The Ministry of Fear* over all other suspense narratives (since Robert Louis Stevenson, anyway) has everything to do with the difficult version of heroism that Greene embodies in D. and in Arthur Rowe. In a swerve away from the Conradian negative hero, Greene declines to let moral cowardice be the issue (or the horror) that animates his characters. Moral pride takes the place of cowardice as the supreme vice, and the suspense hero prevails in defiance of that pride, and in the power of an invigorating humility alone.

—H. B.

⊠ ⊠ ⊠

# Eric Ambler
## *b. 1909*

ERIC AMBLER was born in London on June 28, 1909, the son of two music hall entertainers, Amy Madeline Andrews and Alfred Percy Ambler. After attending Colfe's Grammar School and the University of London, he became an engineering apprentice in 1928, but the next year turned to acting and then to writing advertising copy. In 1936 he wrote his first novel, *Dark Frontier;* the following year he was successful enough to abandon his copy-writing job for full-time authorship. He married Louise Smith Crombie, an American, on October 5, 1939, then left to serve in North Africa and Italy in the Royal Artillery (1940–46), where he earned the Bronze Star.

Having made army films toward the end of the war, Ambler turned to producing and writing screenplays for many films from 1944 to 1977; his screenplay for *The Cruel Sea* (1953) was nominated for an Academy Award. Ambler later confessed, however, that he disliked screenwriting because he was never in total control of the finished product; it was, moreover, a hindrance to his own writing.

Many of Ambler's prewar novels—*The Dark Frontier, Uncommon Danger* (1937), *Epitaph for a Spy* (1938), *Cause for Alarm* (1938), *The Mask of Dimitrios* (1939), and *Journey into Fear* (1940)—showed his left-leaning political sentiments, a factor that helped to intellectualize the thriller and to bring it more critical attention. Ambler's left-wing sympathies were modified somewhat by the course of socialist and communist governments in the postwar period. His later novels, however, retained a political current. Contemporary world events frequently provided a political setting for Ambler's intrigues, as in *The Levanter* (1972), *Dr. Frigo* (1974), and *The Care of Time* (1981). Some critics went so far as to say that *The Levanter* left the genre of the thriller and entered the realm of the political novel. And though *The Levanter* was well received, *Dr. Frigo* was considered the least exciting of all Ambler's work. With *The Care of Time*, however, Ambler returned to techniques that popularized his earlier thrillers.

1

Ambler has been awarded many honors for his suspense novels, including the Crime Writers Association Award (1959), the Mystery Writers of America's Edgar Award (1963), and their Grand Master Award (1975). He received an OBE in 1981. In May 1958 he divorced his wife, Louise, and later that year married the writer and producer Joan Harrison. They now live in Switzerland.

# ▣ Critical Extracts

**JOSEPH WOOD KRUTCH**        Eric Ambler, whose *A Coffin for Dimitrios* is usually regarded as one of the undisputed masterpieces of the genre, adds a footnote of three pages to this first American edition of *Epitaph for a Spy*, one of his earlier stories. He is concerned chiefly with the question why the sub-species called "spy story" should have been late in developing, but he reveals nevertheless the characteristic uneasyness ⟨of defending this genre⟩. And just to set everybody's mind at rest the present writer would like to offer his explanation of the whole phenomenon: it is simply that detective stories are extremely popular because they, almost alone among contemporary works of fiction, do not try to do anything except please their readers.

In the beginning all novels were looked upon with disfavor as trivial productions unworthy of the attention of anyone who took seriously either art or morals. Before the middle of the nineteenth century they had begun to be respectable and during the twentieth the novelist took on Social Significance as well as Art. Finally it has got to the point where almost nobody except the mystery writer will demean himself so far as to consider chiefly the innocent expectations of the reader in such elementary matters as the Happy Ending or the Triumph of Virtue.

Mr. Ambler's spy stories represent one of the more successful attempts to introduce new elements—realism, excitement and a touch of social significance—into a form which is always tending to become stereotyped. And Mr. Ambler is more successful than some others who have attempted the same thing because his modifications are not too radical. Written just before World War II, *Epitaph for a Spy* takes advantage of our sense that Nazi intrigue represents unequivocal evil on a scale grander than that of individual criminality. Its hero, a simple "common man" who blunders into an intrigue which he cannot escape from, is a personage with whom it is easy to identify ourselves because we are aware of the uneasy feeling that in a world like the present monstrous events may any moment involve us. There is, as reviewers will be sure to point out, even a suggestion of Kafkaesque anxiety in the effect which Mr. Ambler produces.

> Joseph Wood Krutch, "Mr. Ambler's Spies," *New York Times Book Review*, 16 March 1952, p. 4

---

**C. DAY LEWIS**     In recent years the pure detection novel and the thriller have pooled their forces, producing a hybrid—the novel of suspense, it has been called. Eric Ambler's *A Coffin for Dimitrios* was a notable early product of this alliance. Mr. Ambler is not an original writer; but he gives a new twist to an old formula—a turn of the screw: indeed, he can be a master of tension. His first four books showed an unusual flair for creating alarm, if not despondency, in the gentle reader. Their atmosphere is one of disquiet, of the restive, exasperated, treacherous calm before a storm. Things, they disturbingly make us feel, are not what they seem. This ordinary little man in the hotel—what desperate secrets may he have under his derby hat. Will that innocent façade suddenly unmask a battery of menace? Whose side is X really on? *What side am I on?* We are in the twilit, illusionist world of espionage and counter-espionage, where such questions have a nightmare importance, a heart-searching urgency. It is a world to which we uneasily respond; for it is after all, the world of our own time.

Since the war, Mr. Ambler has written eight film scripts but only two novels: so we take up with *The Schirmer Inheritance* with considerable expectations. It is another variation on the chase. ⟨. . .⟩

What *The Schirmer Inheritance* lacks in suspense and—till its last chapters—physical excitement, it makes up for in expertise and verisimilitude. Fiction, as Scott well knew, is always better for solid, factual trimmings. Mr. Ambler's familiarity with, for example, the intestacy laws in Pennsylvania, the organization of the Komitajis, and the post-war political set-up in Greece, throws the glamour of reality over the features of romance.

We are, most of us, data-snobs, impressed by the general knowingness of a Kipling, or by the expertise of a Forester in writing an account of a cruiser action which even Royal Navy officers could not fault. Another skill Mr.

Ambler commands is in the pushing of a decent, civilized, conventional man into situations where the values and conventions he has lived by do not hold good at all. George Carey has to learn the truth of what the judge had told him—that "no case, however matter-of-fact it might seem, could be considered entirely proof against the regrettable tendency of reality to assume the shape and proportions of melodrama."

This setting of ordinary individuals against abnormal circumstances is, of course, a basis of the best crime fiction too. And it raises a crucial question for the writer. We shall never return to the classic detection novel, where the characters were only ciphers in a complicated puzzle. But the genre remains a fairy-tale one, dependent upon the suspension of disbelief and a sort of plausible unrealism: If the characters are too solid, too well-rounded, they will break through this delicate web of fantasy and ruin it. As every comedian wants to play Hamlet, so the detection or thriller novelist must resist the temptation to write another *Crime and Punishment*. It is one of Mr. Ambler's merits that he finely adjusts his characters to his medium, giving them reality enough, but never that mite too much which would destroy the airy fabric of the illusion.

> C. Day Lewis, "With a Flair for Creating Alarm," *New York Times Book Review*, 26 July 1953, p. 5

---

**ALFRED HITCHCOCK**      His heroes suffer precisely the sort of emotions that you yourself would suffer in similar circumstances. *Journey into Fear* is the story of a man afraid. He is afraid because someone took a shot at him for no reason that he could readily grasp and he was now informed that the same man would take another shot at him and this time he would try not to miss. The following one hundred and forty-five pages compose a hypnotically fascinating study in fear. If you were that man— an engineer with an attractive wife and pleasant home and a low handicap at golf—you would be afraid too. But do you realize that in the traditional spy novel you would not be afraid? You would be very busy trying to turn the tables on your unknown assailant—and, of course, the result would be a trite story with no genuine suspense.

So much for Mr. Ambler's "heroes." Consider the subsidiary characters. The "villains" are a strange motley crew indeed. There are big business men and bankers; the cheap scum of the low cafés of the ancient Continental cities; the professional, suave, well-heeled gangsters whom we have learned to recognize as the incipient chiefs of Gestapos and fascist conspiracies. In brief, they are not only real people, they are actually the kind of people who have generated violence and evil in the Europe of our time. And the wise men—the clever ones, the ones who solve or help to solve the riddles in these stories—they are not the traditional old-school-tie officers of British Military Intelligence. In two of these novels they are Soviet agents operating in Italy and Austria just before the outbreak of the war; in the other two they are Turkish political police. Again, people you can believe in—above all, the kind of people who really were clever in the corrupt and stupid years of the past decade.

Which leads to a consideration of the kind of material that Mr. Ambler deals with. It is the material of reality. The crimes grow out of fascist intrigues and the greed of big business; they grow out of a Europe run down, decadent, dirty, rotten, ripe for war and revolt. Mr. Ambler is a young man who knows his Europe, understands the politics and the finance of that Europe. His stories ring true: you read them and you say to yourself: "Why, this is the kind of thing that happens all the time."

> Alfred Hitchcock, "Introduction," *Intrigue: Four Great Spy Novels of Eric Ambler* (New York: Alfred A. Knopf, 1970), pp. vii–viii

---

**PAXTON DAVIS**     *The Intercom Conspiracy* is Ambler's *Tempest*—an autumnal work of extraordinary virtuosity that recapitulates, recombines, varies and inverts the principal themes of more than thirty years and adds to them a bleak yet human spirit of disenchantment and renunciation that reflects, like its predecessors, the spirit of its time.

Its twin Prosperos, Colonels Jost and Brand (both rogues in Ambler's most picaresque vein), prepare and execute a conspiracy of, even for Ambler, Byzantine intricacy. Bitter and bored with the Cold War, they surreptitiously, through a Swiss lawyer, Swiss bank accounts and a dummy office in Munich, purchase a rightwing newsletter—then, still covertly, leak military secrets (of little actual value) through its pages until the outraged CIA, KGB, British and West German intelligence, blackmailed but baffled as to how and by whom the thing has been done, drive up its price and buy it out of existence for an inordinate sum. In the end Jost and Brand find the retirement they seek—Brand, facing death, in the bosom of his family; Jost, chick in arm, on Majorca (appropriately, an island). The swindle has worked, and worked profitably.

Two innocents fall in the process, however. Theodore Carter, working editor of the newsletter, is driven nearly mad by the machinations of which he has no comprehension, and though in the outcome he suffers little more than a searing harassment at the hands of big-power agents, the scales have fallen from his eyes. The other victim, in one of Ambler's most elaborate inside jokes, is less lucky. Charles Latimer, who three decades before had tracked down the truth about Dimitrios, goes too far at last when, having ferreted out the way the "Intercom conspiracy" was worked, he falls into a trap set by Brand. He winds up buried in concrete on a highway near Versailles, his zeal for truth satisfied for good.

Ambler's wittiest and most sophisticated novel, *Intercom* is distinguished also by its antipathy to all power, left and right. In the 1930s a staunch anti-Fascist, in the 1950s suspicious in turn of Soviet policy, Ambler reveals himself in 1969 as purged of faith in the wisdom, good intentions or competence of either of the great post-war powers, and the conspiracy of Jost and Brand is his way, Prospero-like, of renouncing both. The hell with you all, he seems to say—surely echoing the antipathy to political action that has become so common, East and West, in these post-Hungary, post-Vietnam years.

Yet this is not to suggest that *Intercom* is in any way a swan song. Though the capstone of Ambler's career, the novel that—if he never wrote another— would add the ultimate touch to the continuous fable of international politics he has been writing since 1937, a fable that, as one critic has written, presents in microcosm "the century of uncertainty and fear, blundering and irresponsibility, through which all of us are groping our way," it also, by its technical daring and its high, dispassionate wit, hints at new and brighter things to come.

Paxton Davis, "The World We Live In: The Novels of Eric Ambler," Hollins Critic 8, No. 1 (February 1971): 10–11

---

**RONALD AMBROSETTI**       If Ambler's solution to the dilemma of whether the man of thought or the man of action shapes the progression of history is too obliquely stated in *A Coffin for Dimitrios*, the next novel, *Journey into Fear* (1940), makes that answer more explicit.

A *Journey into Fear* develops when a British ballistics engineer is dispatched to Turkey to provide the technical data to convert the British armaments for Turkish naval vessels. On the night before he is to return to England, a lone gunman attempts to murder him in his Istanbul hotel. It is late 1940, and Allied forces *must* arm the Turkish vessels before the imminent German Spring offensive. Colonel Haki enters the scene, and convinces Mr. Graham, the engineer, that the safest route back to England is an Italian steamer—and not the Orient Express (shades of Graham Greene). What follows is the "journey into fear."

The Italian steamer, *Sestri Levante*, is a "ship of fools" whereby modern man is displayed in the clinical showcase designed by Darwin and Freud. Ambler is extremely effective in bringing the age-old device of the shipboard community of diverse personalities to the espionage genre. Ambler does in fact outmaneuver the "Orient Express" in the element of suspense (and Anthony Burgess uses the ship community in his 1966 *Tremor of Intent*).

The reality of the Darwinian jungle is ubiquitous, just beneath the surface of appearances. The law of the jungle is also just beneath the surface of man's skin. Graham is forced to realize the existence of his own survival instincts when he is pressed to obtain a gun and is willing to kill in self-defense. He is also willing to entertain thought of a *liaison* with a Spanish dancer, and she forces him to recognize his sexual drives. Ambler indirectly resurrects Maugham's Ashenden formula of sex and violence: these two elements are never far removed from spy genre.

As in the previous Ambler novel, the thematic core of the work resides in the philosophy of history. In *Journey into Fear*, the philosophy of history is a hybrid form of combined Frazer and Spengler doctrines, ironically expounded by the chief German agent who is disguised as a German archaeologist. Ambler, writing in 1940, seems to indicate that it is the German nation which has learned the principal lesson of history: might makes right. The background for Ambler's novel is a Europe which is headed for self-destruction, and history is the cosmic working out of the death and resurrection ritual. Because of her power and will to exercise that power, Ambler warns, through the pronunciations of the German agent, that Germany may be the new phoenix to rise from the ashes of Europe's destruction. The German "archaeologist" preaches to the Englishman on the subject of historical identity.

> 'I used to spend hours standing in the shade by the Propylaea
> looking at it and trying to understand the men who built it. I was

young then and did not know how difficult it is for Western man
to understand the dream-heavy classical soul. They are so far
apart. The god of superlative shape has been replaced by the god
of superlative force and between the two conceptions there is all
space. The destiny idea symbolised by the Doric columns is
incomprehensible to the children of Faust. For us . . .' He broke
off.

At this point, the ventriloquism of Ambler breaks through the German
agent, and he momentarily loses his nationality. For the children of Faust
are toying with the ultimate Damoclean sword which perpetually hangs
above civilization itself.

But the arrayed forces of darkness are held back and, temporarily at
least, defeated in the novels of Eric Ambler. His fumbling, non-professional
"heroes" survive through some chance occurrence or providential event.
Latimer lives because of "a criminal's odd taste in interior decoration," and
Graham survives because of his final reliance on instinct and violence. The
quiet cognitive processes of deduction and reason singularly fail.

All this adds up to the *raison d'être* of the spy novel—the literature of
espionage. The major premise of Ambler's argument resides in the dangerously thin veneer of protection that civilization offers to modern man. The
ages of Medieval faith and Renaissance decorum are past: Darwin, Freud,
Frazer, and Spengler have triumphed. The world of the detective—the
interlocking, visible puzzle pieces of Newton, Dupin, and Holmes—is totally
inadequate in the face of technological warfare. The day of the spy had
dawned. The detective writer and the ballistics engineer had to doff the
velvet of the man, and temporarily assume the characteristics of Dimitrios
and Banat in order to survive. There is a little bit of Dimitrios in everyman—
every modern man, that is. Violence and betrayal in the global village—
this is the legacy of Dimitrios and the beginning for the spy to pick up the
pieces of the shattered Victorian closed-world of rationalism.

Ronald Ambrosetti, "The World of Eric Ambler: From Detective to Spy," *Dimensions
of Detective Fiction*, ed. Larry N. Landrum, Pat Browne, and Ray B. Browne (Bowling
Green, OH: Bowling Green State University Popular Press, 1976), pp. 106–8

**ERIC AMBLER**        I was staying at a bed-and-breakfast hotel on the
Canebière and the concierge had drawn my attention to a convenient bar

just round the corner. The bar was dark and cool, and so was the barman. At his suggestion I drank vermouth-cassis and let him teach me a game of pokerdice. I became interested, but it was only after he had totted up the score, when he smiled, that I understood the finer points. We had been playing for francs, not centimes as I had supposed. I knew that I had been cheated, but did not feel bold enough, or sure enough of my French, to tell him so. When I asked, a little coldly, how much I owed for my vermouth-cassis he said with a generous wave that the drinks were on him.

Back in the hotel room I assessed the disaster. It was Wednesday. The P & O boat for England would not dock until Friday morning and I could not board before midday. I would need enough French money to pay the hotel bill and to take a taxi to the docks. My steamer ticket was paid for, but my cabin steward would have to go without a tip. I would need English money for the fare home from Tilbury. The hotel daily rate included coffee and rolls for breakfast. If I spent nothing more on food I could just manage. If there were any real surprise extras on the hotel bill I would be in a real fix.

Before the expedition to the Château d'If I had bought a Tauchnitz edition of James Joyce's *Portrait of the Artist as a Young Man*. I spent most of Thursday reading that. There had been brioches for breakfast that day but by the afternoon I was feeling hungry. To take my mind off my stomach I planned an assassination.

I was in a corner room overlooking the intersection of the Canebière and the side street where the bar was. Outside my window there was a narrow balcony with a wrought-iron grille. Through the spaces in the grille I could see the roadway at the point where the barman would cross to the tram stop. With an imaginary rifle in my hands I lined up a space in the grille with a brass curlique on the base of the standard lamp. I waited and watched, with the intersecting curves of the tramlines in my sights, for nearly an hour. The barman never came and I returned to James Joyce.

It was quite a shock, a few weeks later, to see on the newsreels that same piece of the Canebière with the intersecting tramlines. The spot I had chosen for my sniper shot at the barman had also been chosen by the Croatian assassin of King Alexander of Yugoslavia. The King had come by sea to Marseilles on a state visit to France and had been met at the quay by the French foreign minister, Barthou. They had been driving slowly in the state procession up the Canebière when the Croat had run forward boldly firing his pistol into the back of the open car. He had mortally wounded both the King and Barthou before he was cut down by an officer of the escorting cavalry wielding a sabre. It was a messy death. If he had taken my room, I thought, and used a rifle he might have had a chance of getting away.

I saw the newsreel several times and cut out news pictures of the scene. I felt oddly guilty, but also pleased. In the Mediterranean sunshine there were strange and violent men with whom I could identify, and with whom, in a way, I was now in touch.

> Eric Ambler, *Here Lies: An Autobiography* (London: Weidenfeld & Nicolson, 1985), pp. 114–15

---

**DAVID LEHMAN**     Eric Ambler retained key elements of received thriller formulas but cut deeply against their grain. In his great prewar thrillers—*Journey into Fear, A Coffin for Dimitrios, Cause for Alarm*, and *Epitaph for a Spy*—Ambler intended a critique of the escapist mind, identifying it with the isolationist Briton who needed to be persuaded that neutrality in the age of Hitler was folly. It made literary sense to parody, though lightly, detective novel routines in *A Coffin for Dimitrios* (1939)—it distracted readers from noticing just how much energy Ambler was generating out of the very conventions he was sending up. As a portrait of the reader as an escapist, the hero of *A Coffin for Dimitrios* is triumphant in a key sense: He survives. Ambler waited until *The Intercom Conspiracy* in 1969 to kill him off on the grounds that the detective as a hero and the detective story as a form were through.

It could be said the Ambler did for the spy thriller what Hammett did for the detective novel. Before Ambler revolutionized the genre, espionage in fiction was largely a matter of drawing-room intrigue, madcap escapades in Monte Carlo casinos, and tuxedo-clad street agents on whose glamorous shoulders the fate of Western civilization depended. Ambler gave espionage back to the people who conspire for a cause, not just to provide the pretext for an international incident. The assassins in Ambler's prewar thrillers were deliberately prosaic thugs as opposed to the larger-than-life or uglier-than-sin villains who had previously populated the genre. Of the hired killer reeking of scent in *Journey into Fear*, for example, we're told that "his very insignificance was horrible. It lent a false air of normality to the situation." The menace in Ambler's novels was ever in inverse proportion to the apparent "normality" of the circumstances; the threat of violence, the logic of its inevitability, loomed greater than the actual violence depicted. Ambler always made sure his readers knew who was paying for the bullets. Espionage was business by other means: Behind the eponymous international criminal of *A Coffin for Dimitrios* stand the resources and prestige of the "Eurasian Credit Trust."

Unlike the spiffy, well-bred agents in E. Phillips Oppenheim's early espionage novels, Ambler favored rank amateurs, examples of "the wrong man." Unlike John Le Carré's professionals, Ambler's prewar protagonists are versions of his ideal reader, ordinary chaps thrust willy-nilly into extraordinary circumstances. The complacent ballistics engineer in *Journey into Fear* (1940) and the nervous production engineer in *Cause for Alarm* (1939) are alike in being middle-class innocents abroad who get disabused of their illusions despite wishing hard to cling to them. The education of these politically neutral English naïfs begins once they cross the channel and learn "that civilization was a word and that you still lived in the jungle." Then danger descends, the threat of imminent death, "waiting"—we're told in *Journey into Fear*—"to make nonsense of all your comfortable ideas about your relations with time and chance."

Ambler's reader is *you*. The aim of the exercise was, in part, to shatter "your" complacency. Paradoxically, Ambler used the escapist form of the thriller to dramatize the idea that danger was everywhere in the European thirties and that escape from its consequences was impossible. The European jungle lived by the application of Nietzschean principles. "What a man does depends on what he needs," says a character in *Journey into Fear*. "A man is an ape in velvet." Strip off the velvet and you get a man like Dimitrios, whose existence is proof that good and evil "were no more than baroque abstractions. Good Business and Bad Business were the elements of the new theology. Dimitrios was not evil. He was logical and consistent; as logical and consistent in the European jungle as the poison gas called Lewisite."

David Lehman, *The Perfect Murder: A Study in Detection* (New York: Free Press, 1989), pp. 191–93.

---

**PETER LEWIS**        The narrative style of Ambler's earlier novels written in the first person is neutral in that it focuses on the experiences undergone by the narrator rather than drawing attention to itself as a manifestation of his personality. In *The Light of Day*, however, the style is the man. The novel opens abruptly with one of Simpson's characteristic outbursts blaming everyone but himself for what has occurred, and ends with an angry, self-righteous warning to the British government to accede to his demands concerning his national status: "I give the government fair warning. I refuse to go on being an anomaly. Is that quite clear? I *refuse!*" As usual Simpson is full of sound and fury signifying very little. The effect of such rhetorical bluster is to put at least as much emphasis on the narrator himself as on events seen through his eyes. As a result the other characters, even the most important, are not developed at all fully. They take their places in the gospel according to Simpson.

Captain Lukey in *Passage of Arms*, whose pretensions to English gentility go hand in hand with his disreputable activities as an arms dealer, is a precursor of Simpson, but he pales in comparison. Ambler conceives Simpson on a more flamboyant, even Falstaffian scale, and a comparison with Shakespeare's un-knightly knight is illuminating, even though Simpson is a shabby, down-markey, twentieth-century version of the great original. Simpson is neither as old nor as fat as Sir John Falstaff, but he is over fifty and overweight. Both men have advanced in years without ever having grown up and retain childlike qualities well into middle age. This is part of their appeal but also their great weakness. Simpson frequently recalls his formative days at Coram's Grammar School in Lewisham (Southeast London), founded in 1781 "for the sons of Gentlemen," and often describes what is happening to him in terms of schoolboy experience. Coram's is partly modeled on Ambler's own school in Lewisham, Colfe's Grammar School, founded in 1652 "for the sons of Gentlemen." Simpson's abject conduct when discovered stealing Harper's traveler's checks is reminiscent of a cringing schoolboy interrupted while doing something naughty: "It's the first time I've ever been tempted, sir. I don't know what came over me." Simpson's obsequious employment of "sir," especially to men younger than himself, is a regression to the language for addressing his teachers.

As a knight Falstaff is not a lowlife character, but his associates include thieves and prostitutes, and his favorite haunts are common taverns. Because of his education at an elite school, Simpson attempts to sustain a dignified conception of himself that is totally at odds with the lowlife reality. Despite his insistence that he is a professional journalist, Simpson lives in Athens by his wits, mainly as a parasite on tourists—an amalgam of chauffeur, guide, con man, tout, pimp, and petty thief. ⟨. . .⟩

A character with such a background and life-style could be presented as thoroughly unpleasant or as a pathetic wreck, but Simpson, like the equally resilient Falstaff, achieves genuine comic status through the sheer energy and inventiveness with which he never fails to justify himself, however inconsistent he may appear. Simpson shares Falstaff's ability at bending words, as in his flattering euphemism for the gang of sophisticated criminals when asked by Harper what he knows about them: "You are all very sensible, tolerant persons, who are very broad-minded about things that the law doesn't approve of, but who don't like taking risks." Simpson's Falstaffian qualities make him an anarchic outsider capable of challenging conventional values by turning them upside down, even if he is not fully aware of this.

Peter Lewis, *Eric Ambler* (New York: Continuum, 1990), pp. 126–27, 129

# *Bibliography*

*The Dark Frontier*. 1936.

*Uncommon Danger* ⟨*Background to Danger*⟩. 1937.

*Epitaph for a Spy*. 1938.

*Cause for Alarm*. 1938.

*The Mask of Dimitrios* ⟨*A Coffin for Dimitrios*⟩. 1939.

*Journey into Fear*. 1940.

*Skytip*. 1950.

*Tender to Danger* ⟨*Tender to Moonlight*⟩. 1951.

*Judgment on Deltchev*. 1951.

*The Maras Affair*. 1953.

*The Schirmer Inheritance*. 1953.

*Charter to Danger*. 1954.

*The Night-Comers* ⟨*State of Siege*⟩. 1956.

*Passport to Panic*. 1958.

*Passage of Arms*. 1959.

*The Light of Day* ⟨*Topkapi*⟩. 1962.

*The Ability to Kill and Other Pieces*. 1963.

*A Kind of Anger*. 1964.

*To Catch a Spy: An Anthology of Favourite Spy Stories* (editor). 1964.

*Dirty Story*. 1967.
*The Intercom Conspiracy*. 1969.
*The Levanter*. 1972.
*Doctor Frigo*. 1974.
*Send No More Roses* ⟨*The Siege of the Villa Lipp*⟩. 1977.
*The Care of Time*. 1981.
*Here Lies: An Autobiography*. 1986.
*Waiting for Orders*. 1990.

✦ ✦ ✦

# John Buchan
## *1875–1940*

JOHN BUCHAN was born in Perth, Scotland, on August 26, 1875. He attended Hutcheson's Grammar School and the University of Glasgow, where he studied classics with the young Gilbert Murray. Buchan neglected to gain a degree, however (much later, in 1919, the university granted him an honorary degree), and went instead to Brasenose College, Oxford, on a scholarship in 1895. There he won the prestigious Stanhope Prize for his essay *Sir Walter Raleigh* (1897).

In 1901 Buchan passed the bar exam and became a barrister. Very shortly thereafter, however, he went to South Africa as private secretary to Lord Milner during the Boer War. Returning to England, Buchan settled into a law practice in which he was never entirely happy or comfortable, but in 1907 he joined the staff of the publisher Thomas Nelson in London. In that same year he married Susan Charlotte Grovesnor, with whom he had three sons and a daughter. During the early part of World War I he suffered ill health and while convalescing wrote *The Thirty-nine Steps* (1915), his first story about the adventurer Richard Hannay. Soon Buchan became a war correspondent and later worked as an intelligence officer for the Foreign Office.

After the war he settled down with his family at Elsfield Manor near Oxford, where he wrote the majority of his books. After having served as deputy chairman of Reuter's, he sought political office and won a seat in Parliament in 1927, representing the Scottish universities. From there his political stature grew. In 1932 Buchan became Lord High Commissioner to the General Assembly of the Church of Scotland. In 1935 he was appointed Governor-General of Canada by George V, and spent the remainder of his life there. His Canadian odyssey is recorded in the posthumously published autobiography *Canadian Occasions* (1940), a sequel to his account of his earlier years, *Memory Hold-the-Door* (1940; published in the U.S. as *Pilgrim's Way*). Buchan became a Companion of Honour in 1932, and was made

15

Baron Tweedsmuir in 1935. Some months before his death on February 11, 1940, he signed Canada's declaration of war against Germany.

Buchan was a hugely prolific author. He is known for his adventure novels involving Richard Hannay, which include *The Thirty-nine Steps*, *Greenmantle* (1916), *Mr. Standfast* (1918), and *The Three Hostages* (1924). Other adventure novels include *The Power-House* (1916), *Huntingtower* (1922), *John Macnab* (1925), *The Dancing Floor* (1926), *The Courts of the Morning* (1929), *Castle Gay* (1930), *The House of the Four Winds* (1935), and *Sick Heart River* (1941). Buchan also wrote a number of novels and tales of the supernatural, including *The Watcher by the Threshold and Other Tales* (1902), *Witch Wood* (1927), *The Runagates Club* (1928) (in which each story is narrated by a different character from Buchan's adventure novels), and *The Gap in the Curtain* (1932). He himself, however, felt that his most serious work was in history and biography, including *Augustus* (1937) and a history of World War I. His writings spanned virtually every branch of literature with the notable exception of poetry.

# ◈ *Critical Extracts*

**UNSIGNED**      But now for Mr. Buchan's story. Readers of *Prester John*, *The Moon Endureth*, and *The Watcher by the Threshold* need not be reminded that he is a first-rate hand at spinning a yarn, and though he is working here on a somewhat lower plane and appealing to a wider audience, his literary craftsmanship remains as sound as ever. He cannot suppress his love of landscape, even in the midst of the most thrilling and sensational incidents. There are no purple patches, and the tender passion does not enter into the scheme at all: indeed, no single female character is directly concerned in the plot. But still the presentation has just that quality of literary amenity which the average "shocker" conspicuously lacks; it lifts the book out of the ruck without being so pronounced as to repel the unlettered reader. To a certain extent the story may be regarded as an essay in literary discipleship; Mr. Buchan has learnt something, as he implies in his dedication, from the study of the American "dime novel," but he is influenced much more by the methods of Stevenson—the Stevenson of *The New Arabian Nights*, *The Wrecker*, and *The Wrong Box*. Yet it would be unfair to press the parallel;

the story ⟨*The Thirty-Nine Steps*⟩ is frankly eclectic, but not imitative, and so far as Stevenson is concerned, the resemblance is that of a family likeness, for, after all, Mr. Buchan is also a Scotsman, a romantic with a bent towards the fantastic, and a poet.

As for the plot, without revealing anything that might discount the joys of perusal, we may content ourselves with saying that it is an ingenious variation on the conditions that immediately preceded the outbreak of the war. The narrator-hero, who has just returned to England after many years of residence in South Africa, and finds himself unutterably bored by the futile feverishness of life at home, is suddenly confronted with a problem which exceeds his wildest dreams of adventure. In order to compass a patriotic end of vital importance, he incurs the suspicion of murder, and exposes himself to the double risk of capture by the police and assassination by the members of a powerful and relentless secret society. To carry out his plans he must disappear for a time. Hence the need of flight, and a constant change of disguises, accompanied by a policy of confiding—where advisable—in those who shelter him, and it is the alteration of the methods of elusion with those of audacity which lends the narrative much of its charm.

Unsigned, [Review of *The Thirty-nine Steps*], *Spectator*, 6 November 1915, p. 630

---

**GRAHAM GREENE**     More than a quarter of a century has passed since Richard Hannay found the dead man in his flat and started that long flight and pursuit—across the Yorkshire and the Scottish moors, down Mayfair streets, along the passages of government buildings, in and out of Cabinet rooms and country houses, towards the cold Essex jetty with the thirty-nine steps, that were to be a pattern for adventure-writers ever since. John Buchan was first to realize the enormous dramatic value of adventure in familiar surroundings happening to unadventurous men, members of Parliament and members of the Athenaeum, lawyers and barristers, business men and minor peers: murder in 'the atmosphere of breeding and simplicity and stability'. Richard Hannay, Sir Edward Leithen, Mr. Blenkiron, Archie Roylance and Lord Lamancha; these were his adventurers, not Dr. Nikola or the Master of Ballantrae, and who will forget that first thrill in 1916 as the hunted Leithen—the future Solicitor-General—ran 'like a thief in a London thoroughfare on a June afternoon'. ⟨. . .⟩

What is remarkable about these adventure-stories is the completeness of the world they describe. The backgrounds to many of us may not be sympathetic, but they are elaborately worked in: each character carries around with him his school, his regiment, his religious beliefs, often touched with Calvinism: memories of grouse-shooting and deer-stalking, of sport at Eton, debates in the House. For men who live so dangerously they are oddly conventional—or perhaps, remembering men like Scott and Oates, we can regard that, too, as a realistic touch. They judge men by their war record: even in *Sick Heart River*, fighting in the desolate northern waste for the Indians' salvation, is accepted by Leithen because 'he has served in a French battalion which had been on the right of the Guards at Loos'. Toc H and the British Legion lurk in the background.

> Graham Greene, "The Last Buchan" (1940), *The Lost Childhood and Other Essays* (New York: Viking Press, 1952), pp. 104–5

---

**SUSAN BUCHAN**       He must have had the idea of a story in his head before the war began, but if he had not had to go to bed at Broadstairs *The Thirty-Nine Steps* might never have been written. He was corresponding with the War Office about joining up in the Army, but was told that in his present state of health it was useless to think of it, and that he might be used in other ways later on. To distract his mind from the dull bedroom in our lodgings he started on the book. The Grenfells were also at Broadstairs. They had been lent a villa on the North Foreland: the tenancy carried with it the privilege of a key to what our Nannie called the "private beach," a small cove which was reached by a rickety wooden staircase. How many steps there were I do not know, but John hit on the number thirty-nine as one that would be easily remembered and would catch people's imagination. The staircase to the private beach has now disappeared and has been replaced by an imposing steel or iron erection. When this was done we received a small block of wood in the shape of a step bearing a minute brass plate with the words *The Thirty-Ninth Step*. But if the steps have disappeared the book maintains its early popularity. John used to read each chapter aloud to me and I waited breathlessly for the next one. In 1935 a film was made of it which has caused some controversy and a good deal of disappointment to those who love the book and who did not like the introduction of a woman into the story, and other drastic alterations to the plot. We went to the film *première* just before we sailed for Canada. John enjoyed it and did not mind the alterations in the least. My own opinion is, that it would have been a better film if the producer had stuck to the original story; but if one forgets about the book, *The Thirty-Nine Steps* as a film is a very good piece of entertainment.

Susan Buchan, *John Buchan by His Wife and Friends* (London: Hodder & Stoughton, 1947), pp. 73–74

**M. R. RIDLEY**     ⟨Buchan⟩ is often described as 'a mere writer of adventure stories'—this usually from would-be intellectuals, who would hardly recognize an adventure if they met one, and would move hurriedly in the opposite direction if they did. Anyway the statement is untrue. Much of Buchan's best work is not fiction at all, and even in fiction some of his best novels cannot, by any stretching of terms, be classed as thrillers. And again: 'He is so painfully obvious.' That is a comment characteristic and symptomatic of our time, when so many readers seem to prefer elaborate and often murky psychological analysis and a minimum of 'story' to any narrative of events. It is true that there is in Buchan very little avowed psychological analysis, and he makes clear his own position about this: 'The truth is, the pathological is too easy.' But there is plenty of acute psychological observation, and also at least one underlying theme which is not particularly 'obvious', though it is patently perceptible when one takes the trouble to perceive it.

But it is better to dismiss these, I think misguided, verdicts and examine what Buchan did in fact achieve in fiction and what his powers were. He is almost universally accepted as a master of the thriller, and as a kind of criterion, so that 'almost up to the Buchan standard' and the like are common-form critical phrases. But the odd thing is that his thrillers are by no means uniformly in the top class of that *genre*. As a 'simple' thriller *The Thirty-nine Steps* is hard to beat. It moves with extreme velocity and retains its momentum throughout; it does not strain credibility too far, and has some admirable episodes and an effective climax; and the characters, though there is no subtlety in the drawing of them, are reasonably human. It was at once accepted as a classic of its kind, and goes on being so accepted, even in spite of the distorting maltreatment of film adaptation. But *The*

*Power House*, which immediately followed, always seems to me a complete misfire. ⟨. . .⟩

After this 'misbegowk' he ran full into form again with *Greenmantle*. It has less sheer speed than *The Thirty-nine Steps*. This is partly because Buchan was experimenting with a technique which he developed, sometimes rather aggravatingly, later, by which different lines of plot are developed in parallel, till he can induce upon them an Einstein curve and get them to meet at a point. This involves periodically leaving one character or group of characters in a state of suspended animation while the adventures of others are described, or alternatively one character has to relate his past adventures to the rest. It is a method which Stevenson used twice in *Treasure Island*, and it is a very tricky one, though when the author is skilful enough it can be highly effective, since there is an element of excitement in watching the lines converge on the point. But even if the diminished speed is a defect—which is by no means certain—there are counterbalancing merits. The plot is more complex than that of either of the book's two predecessors, and a degree of complexity is a solid merit if it is not secured at the expense of coherence and clarity. In *Greenmantle* there is no episode which is not strictly related to the central action and does not advance the movement towards the climax. There are several characters more interesting than any in *The Thirty-nine Steps*, more fully drawn and more in the round. There is even a touch of the subtlety with which Buchan is usually not credited in the picture of the reactions of Sandy Arbuthnot to the diableries of Hilda von Einem. The climax is skilfully contrived and superbly handled. The tension slowly rises as the sands run out for the apparently doomed party on the castrol, relieved only by the occasional dry comments of Blenkiron; there is a sudden moment of relaxation of tension; and then both key and tempo change to the furious exaltation of the ride with the victorious Cossacks to the gates of Erzerum. Even if the book is 'just a thriller', it is at least a masterpiece of vivid and controlled narration, and the verdict of those many readers who put it top of Buchan's thrillers may well be the right one.

> M. R. Ridley, "A Misrated Author?," *Second Thoughts: More Studies in Literature* (London: J. M. Dent & Sons, 1965), pp. 3–5

---

**JANET ADAM SMITH**        Surveying his own work near the end of his life, Buchan took little credit for the thrillers, which 'I never consciously invented with a pen in my hand; I waited until the story had told itself and then wrote it down, and since it was already a finished thing, I wrote it fast'. More conscious creation had gone into the historical romances, which he rated more highly. 'Being equally sensitive to the spells of time and of space, to a tract of years and a tract of landscape, I tried to discover the historical moment which best interpreted the *ethos* of a particular countryside, and to devise the appropriate legend.' His biographies had been 'laborious affairs compared to my facile novels', but had given him the greatest satisfaction of all. Two certainly are likely to endure, those where he enters imaginatively into the lives of the two Scots whom he had loved since boyhood—Scott and Montrose.

Yet it is the thrillers which have appealed most to the modern readers, appearing and reappearing in paperback, often with luridly inappropriate pictures on the cover. It is from them that phrases like 'a Buchan hero' and 'a Buchan adventure' derive. What gives them their continuing vitality is something over and above Buchan's mastery of the standard thriller ingredients—suspense, surprise, speed of narrative, well-observed background. It is his ability to touch deeper concerns than the triumph of hero or the fall of villain. He can convey a sense of the real possibility of evil and irrational forces breaking through the façade of civilized life. Many of the social attitudes of his thrillers are outdated; not so their intimations of destruction and disorder, their warning that civilization cannot be taken for granted. In 1940 Graham Greene found that 'Buchan prepared us in his thrillers better than he knew for the death that may come to any of us, as it nearly came to Leithen, by the railings of the park or the doorway of the mews. For certainly we can all see now "how thin is the protection of civilization".' The kidnapping of children of the rich and powerful is not as unthinkable in the later part of the twentieth century as it was to the original readers of *The Three Hostages*.

Janet Adam Smith, *John Buchan and His World* (New York: Charles Scribner's Sons, 1979), pp. 77–79

---

**DAVID DANIELL**     John Buchan wrote over a hundred books, and very many of them are still read, with delight, by a countless host of people across the world. He was a biographer of distinction: his lives of Scott and Montrose remain standard works. He wrote lucid history, notably of the First World War, which he regarded with horror but explained with insight even while it was being fought, often writing from the Front. He was a fine editor, effectively of the *Spectator* for a spell, for which journal alone he wrote nearly a thousand articles, as well as so far uncounted regular columns for the daily, weekly and monthly press on both sides of the Atlantic. He was a pleasing poet, and a great contributor to considered collections of discussion and commentary. He was by formal training a classicist, principally at home in pastoral Greece and Augustan Rome. He wrote a technical book about the law relating to the taxation of foreign income.

In his official life, after Oxford, one of Lord Milner's Young Men in South Africa at the end of the Boer War, and then barrister, publisher, wartime Director of Information, a director of Reuters, MP for the Scottish Universities, and Governor-General of Canada as Lord Tweedsmuir. He was a profoundly happy family man with a great wealth of friendships, a fine fisherman, a clever climber and a prodigious walker. He was a man much loved and much admired. Several generations of young people owe to his friendship and interest the confidence to begin their own special endeavours. He died in Canada in February 1940 at the age of sixty-four, and he is still much missed.

And of course he wrote fiction: nearly thirty novels and seven collections of short stories. Some of the novels, like *Witch Wood*, set in seventeenth-century Scotland, or *Salute to Adventurers*, in eighteenth-century Virginia, or *The Blanket of the Dark*, in Tudor England, continue to surprise the unwary modern reader who does not quite expect such clarity, atmosphere, characterization and grasp of large affairs. Other novels, such as those in which the lawyer Sir Edwin Leithen plays a major part, like *John Macnab*, *The Dancing Floor* or *Sick Heart River*, treat, with unusual organization, far profounder matters than their ease of reading might suggest. Buchan is most widely known, of course, for the adventure stories containing the South African ex-mining engineer Richard Hannay. The first, *The Thirty-Nine Steps*, his twenty-seventh book, written at great speed while he was confined to a bed in the second year of the War, has become a record-breaking best-seller, and is his single best-known book. This has been not altogether to his advantage, as early in the book a terrified young American spy makes to the South African engineer Hanny an anti-semitic remark which has, absurdly, been taken to represent the considered judgements of the author. Buchan has not been helped here either by the three curious films of the book, little recognisable as having any connection.

David Daniell, "Introduction," *The Best Short Stories of John Buchan* (London: Michael Joseph, 1980), pp. 7–8

**WILLIAM BUCHAN**        From 1921 to 1937 JB produced a book a
year in his popular style—distinct, that is, from histories or biographies—
several of which came into the category which he insisted on calling 'shockers'. This was a real misnomer since, in the terms with which we are now
familiar, there was nothing shocking about those books, nothing to insult,
distress or revolt the reader. Shocker, as a description, was a survival from
the days pre-1914 when detective stories, full of murders, were sold on
bookstalls for one shilling, and known as 'shilling shockers'. JB's use of it
represents the kind of meiosis of which he was rather fond.

Reading other references to John Buchan by other writers, I can see that
what might be taken for modesty—as I believe it genuinely was—about his
popular books can be a source of irritation to those who have not found
success to come easily. When he spoke of himself as 'a copious romancer',
and implied that writing fiction came so fluently, so pleasantly to him, that
he scarcely deserved credit for producing it, I have no reason to doubt that
he meant what he said. Writing novels was truly, for him, relaxation. He
worked them out in his head, almost down to the last detail of the dialogue,
before he ever took up his pen. To examine his manuscripts is to be astonished
by the rarity of corrections, of scratchings-out, of any of the stops and starts,
false trails and confusions which mark most writers' work. What sticks in
some throats, I fancy, is that JB not only enjoyed writing his novels, easily,
professionally and punctually, but that he also made a good deal of money
out of them. Even that might be forgiven, were it not that he acquired a
vast and devoted public which did not desert him at his death. The books,
therefore, cannot seriously be dismissed as popular trash, dug out of a lucky
vein at some remove from the true mines of literature. They are too consistently good in their own terms and they continue to be read.

William Buchan, *John Buchan: A Memoir* (London: Buchan & Enright, 1982), pp.
183–84

**ROBIN W. WINKS**        John Buchan is the father of the modern spy
thriller. This is so even though the Hannay books are not, strictly speaking,
about spies at all in the professional sense of the word. They are about
penetration of the enemy, about lonely escape and wild journeys, about the
thin veneer that stands between civilization and barbarism even in the most
elegant drawing-room in London. Buchan wrote the formula, and from the

appearance of *The Thirty-Nine Steps* until the rise of the disillusioned spy, of the man who has discovered that there is no difference between "us" and "them"—that is, until John le Carré's third book, in 1963, *The Spy Who Came In from the Cold*—the formula remained tied to Buchan. The formula was not well understood, certainly, for most books that appeared under the confident declaration that they were "in the Buchan mold" bore only surface resemblance to that mold, but it was there, a goal to be attained by the few.

Because Buchan's shockers were seen as formulaic, they tended to be dismissed by "serious" critics, who also dismissed western, detective, mystery, and later science fiction because, it was said, they were written to a formula. Most were and are, it is true, and most are dismissable, unless one is a student of popular culture. But just as a precedent does not truly exist until it is followed—one cannot know that a precedent is a precedent until a second occurrence—the person who invents a formula is not to be blamed when his invention becomes formulaic. It is not, after all, a formula until it is followed by others. One would not charge Whitman with the tawdry on the ground that many a tawdry poet tried to imitate his "barbaric yawp." Buchan wrote the words and set them to his own music.

What is the Buchan formula? *The Thirty-Nine Steps* shows the formula at its most pure, for the subsequent Hannay novels depart in some measure from it. Take an attractive man, not too young—Hannay is thirty-seven in *Steps*, two years younger than Buchan when he began to write the book— and not too old, since he must have the knowledge of maturity and substantial experience on which he will draw while being able to respond to the physical rigors of chase and pursuit. Let the hero, who appears at first to be relatively ordinary, and who thinks of himself as commonplace, be drawn against his best judgment into a mystery he only vaguely comprehends, so that he and the reader may share the growing tension together. Set him a task to perform: to get the secret plans, let us say, from point A to point B, or to bring the news from Ghent to Aix. Place obstacles in his path—the enemy, best left as ill-defined as possible, so that our hero cannot be certain who he might trust. See to it that he cannot turn to established authority for help, indeed that the police, the military, the establishment will be actively working against him.

Then set a clock ticking: the hero must get from point A to point B in a sharply defined time, a time-frame known to both pursuer and pursued. In *Steps* we are informed at the outset that it is May 19; on May 24 the clock starts: Hannay reckons that he must stay on the move for three weeks, the first twenty days in hiding if possible, with a single day then left to complete his task. Be certain that pursuit takes place across a marginally familiar ground, so that the reader may identify with it, though be equally certain that the ground is sufficiently exotic to test the mettle of both sides in the Great Game. The winner will be the person with the resourcefulness to use the environment to his advantage, to go to ground *with* rather than against the landscape. Thus the locale is of the greatest importance, not simply because it may be exotic, or vaguely threatening, but because it is in reality the third player in the game, a great, neutral (and therefore, to the harried, apparently malevolent) landscape. The hero may possess some esoteric knowledge from what proves to be a more unconventional past than we had at first suspected—he will know how to throw a Mashona hunting-knife into the air and catch it between his lips, just so! or how to render an opponent unconscious by pressing precisely here, behind the ear. At stake will be the salvation of the world, or the future of Britain, which for the purposes of fiction is to be seen as much the same thing. The device is then wound up and set in motion.

> Robin W. Winks, "John Buchan: Stalking the Wilder Game," *The Four Adventures of Richard Hannay* (Boston: David R. Godine, 1988), pp. xi–xii

# ▩ *Bibliography*

*Essays and Apothegms* by Sir Francis Bacon (editor). 1894.

*Sir Quixote of the Moors: Being Some Account of an Episode in the Life of the Sieur de Rohaine.* 1895.

*Musa Piscatrix* (editor). 1896.

*Scholar Gipsies.* 1896.

*Sir Walter Raleigh.* 1897.

*John Burnet of Barns: A Romance.* 1898.

*The Pilgrim Fathers: The Newdigate Prize Poem, 1898.* 1898.

*Brasenose College.* 1898.

*Grey Weather: Moorland Tales of My Own People.* 1899.

*A Lost Lady of Old Years: A Romance.* 1899.

*The Half-Hearted.* 1900.

*The Compleat Angler* by Izaak Walton (editor). 1901.

*The Watcher by the Threshold and Other Tales.* 1902.

*The African Colony: Studies in the Reconstruction.* 1903.

*The Law Relating to the Taxation of Foreign Income.* 1905.

*A Lodge in the Wilderness.* 1906.

*Some Eighteenth-Century Byways and Other Essays.* 1908.

*Prester John.* 1910.

*Buchan's Diagrammatic Chart of the Evolution of Parties within the Arena of Political Action Since the Year 1845.* 1911.

*Sir Walter Raleigh.* 1911.

*The Moon Endureth: Tales and Fancies.* 1912.

*What the Home Rule Bill Means.* 1912.

*The Marquis of Montrose.* 1913.

*Andrew Jameson, Lord Ardwall.* 1913.

*Britain's War by Land.* 1915.

*Nelson's History of the War.* 1915–19. 24 vols.

*The Achievement of France.* 1915.

*The Thirty-nine Steps.* 1915.

*Salute to Adventurers.* 1915.

*Ordeal by Marriage: An Eclogue.* 1915.

*The Future of the War.* 1916.

*The Power-House.* 1916.

*The Battle of Jutland.* 1916.

*Greenmantle.* 1916.

*The Battle of the Somme: First Phase.* 1916.

*The British Front on the West.* 1916.

*The Purpose of War.* 1916.

*Poems, Scots and English.* 1917.

*The Battle of the Somme: Second Phase.* 1917.

*Mr. Standfast.* 1918.

*These for Remembrance.* 1919.

*The Island of Sheep* (with Susan Buchan). 1919.

*The Battle-Honours of Scotland 1914–1918.* 1919.

*The History of the South African Forces in France.* 1920.

*Francis and Riversdale Grenfell: A Memoir.* 1920.

*The Long Road to Victory* (editor). 1920.

*Miscellanies, Literary and Historical* by Archibald Primrose, Earl of Rosebery (editor). 1921.

*Great Hours in Sport* (editor). 1921.

*The Path of the King.* 1921.

*Huntingtower.* 1922.

*A Book of Escapes and Hurried Journeys.* 1922.

*The Thirty-nine Steps and The Power-House.* 1922.

*"The 51st Highland Division."* 1922.

*The Last Secrets: The Final Mysteries of Exploration.* 1923.

*A History of English Literature* (editor). 1923.

*The Nations of Today: A New History of the World* (editor). 1923–24. 12 vols.

*Midwinter: Certain Travellers in Old England.* 1923.

*The Memory of Sir Walter Scott.* 1923.

*Days to Remember: The British Empire in the Great War* (with Henry Newbolt). 1923.

*Some Notes on Sir Walter Scott.* 1924.

*The Three Hostages.* 1924.

*Lord Minto: A Memoir.* 1924.

*The Northern Muse: An Anthology of Scots Vernacular Poetry* (editor). 1924.

*The History of the Royal Scots Fusiliers (1678–1918).* 1925.

*John Macnab.* 1925.

*The Man and the Book: Sir Walter Scott.* 1925.

*Two Ordeals of Democracy.* 1925.

*The Dancing Floor.* 1926.

*The Fifteenth—Scottish—Division 1914–1919* (with John Stewart). 1926.

*Modern Short Stories* (editor). 1926.

*Homilies and Recreations.* 1926.

*To the Electors of the Scottish Universities.* 1927.

*Witch Wood.* 1927.

*Empire Builders.* 1927.

*South Africa* (editor). 1928.

*The Runagates Club.* 1928.

*The Teaching of History* (editor). 1928–30. 11 vols.

*Montrose.* 1928.

*A Protestant and the Prayer Book.* 1928.

*The Courts of the Morning.* 1929.

*To the Electors of the Scottish Universities* (with George A. Berry). 1929.

*Medical Education of Women in London.* 1929.

*The Causal and the Casual in History.* 1929.

*What the Union of the Churches Means to Scotland.* 1929.

*The Four Adventures of Richard Hannay.* 1930.

*The Kirk in Scotland 1560–1929* (with George Adam Smith). 1930.

*Montrose and Leadership.* 1930.

*The Revision of Dogmas.* 1930.

*Castle Gay.* 1930.

*Lord Rosebery 1847–1930.* 1930.

*The Battlefield of Bannockburn Appeal.* 1930.

*The Blanket of the Dark.* 1931.

*The Novel and the Fairy Tale.* 1931.

*The Poetry of Neil Monro* (editor). 1931.

*Sir Walter Scott.* 1932.

*The Gap in the Curtain.* 1932.

*Julius Caesar.* 1932.

*The Magic Walking-Stick.* 1932.

*Sir Walter Scott 1832–1932: A Centenary Address* (with William C. Van-
     Antwerp). 1932.

*The Massacre of Glencoe.* 1933.

*A Prince of the Captivity.* 1933.

*Andrew Lang and the Border.* 1933.

*The Margins of Life.* 1933.

*The Free Fishers.* 1934.

*Gordon at Khartoum.* 1934.

*Oliver Cromwell.* 1934.

*The Scottish Church and the Empire.* 1934.

*The Principles of Social Service.* c. 1934.

*The King's Grace.* 1935.

*The Adventures of Sir Edward Leithen.* 1935.

*Men and Deeds.* 1935.

*The House of the Four Winds.* 1935.

*An Address.* 1935.

*Four Tales.* 1936.

*Address.* 1936.

*The Adventures of Dickson M'Cunn.* 1937.

*Augustus.* 1937.

*The Interpreter's House.* 1938.

*Presbyterianism Yesterday, Today, and Tomorrow.* 1938.

*Five Fold Salute to Adventure.* 1939.

*Adventures of Richard Hannay.* 1939.

*Memory Hold-the-Door* ⟨*Pilgrim's Way: An Essay in Recollection*⟩. 1940.

*Comments and Characters*. Ed. W. Forbes Gray. 1940.

*Canadian Occasions*. 1940.

*Sick Heart River*. 1941.

*The Long Traverse*. 1941.

*Adventurers All*. 1942.

*The Clearing House: A Survey of One Man's Mind*. Ed. Lady Tweedsmuir. 1946.

*Life's Adventure: Extracts from the Works of John Buchan*. Ed. Lady Tweedsmuir. 1947.

*Best Short Stories*. Ed. David Daniell. 1980–82. 2 vols.

⬥ ⬥ ⬥

# James M. Cain
## *1892–1977*

JAMES MALLAHAN CAIN was born on July 1, 1892, in Annapolis, Maryland, the first of five children of James William and Rose Mallahan Cain. His father was a professor at St. John's College in Annapolis and later president of Washington College in Chestertown, Maryland, where Cain earned a B.A. in 1910 and an M.A. in 1917. In 1918–19 he served in France during World War I, where he edited (and largely wrote) his division's newspaper, the *Lorraine Cross*, and coedited the history of his troop (1919). Cain was a reporter for Baltimore newspapers from 1918 to 1923, then—after a year teaching journalism at St. John's College in Annapolis—wrote editorials for the *New York World* from 1924 to 1931. In each city he gained a mentor who encouraged him to write: H. L. Mencken in Baltimore and Walter Lippmann in New York. He married Mary Rebekah Clough in 1920; they divorced in 1923. In 1927 he married a Finnish woman, Elina Sjösted Tyszecka, but they divorced in 1942.

Although he wrote a few short and unsuccessful plays in the 1920s, Cain's first true book was *Our Government* (1930), a collection of satirical dialogues first published in the *World*. After serving as managing editor of the *New Yorker* for ten months in 1931, he moved to Los Angeles, where he wrote screenplays (including *Algiers*, 1938) and, in 1934, *The Postman Always Rings Twice*. This terrifically popular "hard-boiled" novel introduced what were to be Cain's trademarks: terse first-person narration and a tightly knit plot involving sex, money, and violence. The story has been filmed four times, was adapted for the stage by Cain in 1936, and most recently has become an opera. Albert Camus credited it as an important influence on his work, notably *The Stranger*.

Once Cain had found his voice, he became a prolific novelist. Books such as *Serenade* (1937), *Mildred Pierce* (1941), *Double Indemnity* (serialized in 1936; published in book form in 1943), and *The Butterfly* (1947) managed to please both readers and critics. The screen adaptations of Cain's books were the vanguard of a new film genre, *film noir*—a cinematic equivalent to hard-boiled fiction. In the mid-1940s, at the height of his popularity, Cain attempted to organize a writers' union, to be called the American Authors Authority, but the project eventually failed.

In 1944 Cain married Aileen Pringle, although they divorced the next year. He moved back to Maryland in 1947 after marrying his fourth wife, the opera singer Florence Macbeth, who would die in 1966. He continued to write, varying his formula to include historical novels such as *Past All Dishonor* (1946), but his fame gradually slipped away. Although the Mystery Writers of America honored him with their Grand Master Award, many of his books went out of print. Cain was plagued with ill health for much of his life, and suffered alternately from tuberculosis, ulcers, and high cholesterol; heavy alcohol consumption over many years did not help his condition. He wrote little in the last three decades of his life. A revival of interest in Cain's work followed his death in University Park, Maryland, on October 27, 1977.

# ▒ *Critical Extracts*

**WILLIAM ROSE BENÉT**     Mr. Cain is to be congratulated upon making his exciting and disagreeable novel ⟨*The Postman Always Rings Twice*⟩ carry conviction. His style is like the metal of an automatic. You can't lay his story down, for all its brutality and ugliness. He is good at dialogue, too. In the hard-boiled school of today here is a new student of considerable promise.

> William Rose Benét, "Hard-Boiled Jellyfish," *Saturday Review*, 24 February 1934, p. 503

**EDMUND WILSON**     The hero of the typical Cain novel is a good-looking down-and-outer, who leads the life of a vagrant and a rogue. He invariably falls under the domination—usually to his ruin—of a vulgar and determined woman from whom he finds it impossible to escape. In the novels of ⟨Horace⟩ McCoy and ⟨Richard⟩ Hallas, he holds our sympathy through his essential innocence; but in the novels of Cain himself, the situation is not so simple. Cain's heroes are capable of extraordinary exploits, but they are always treading the edge of a precipice; and they are doomed, like the heroes of Hemingway, for they will eventually fall off the precipice. But whereas in Hemingway's stories, it is simply that these brave and decent men have had a dirty deal from life, the hero of a novel by Cain is an individual of mixed unstable character, who carries his precipice with him like Pascal.

His fate is thus forecast from the beginning; but in the meantime he has fabulous adventures—samples, as it were, from a *Thousand and One Nights* of the screwy Pacific Coast: you have jungle lust in roadside lunchrooms, family motor-trips that end in murder, careers catastrophically broken by the vagaries of bisexual personality, the fracas created by a Mexican Indian introduced among the phonies of Hollywood.

All these writers are also preeminently the poets of the tabloid murder. Cain himself is particularly ingenious in tracing from their first beginnings the tangles that gradually tighten around the necks of the people involved in those bizarre and brutal crimes that figure in the American papers; and is capable even of tackling—in *Serenade*, at any rate—the larger tangles of social interest from which these deadly little knots derive. Such a subject might provide a great novel: in *An American Tragedy*, such a subject did. But as we follow, in a novel by Mr. Cain, the development of one of his plots, we find ourselves more and more disconcerted at knocking up—to the destruction of illusion—against the blank and hard planes and angles of something we know all too well: the wooden old conventions of Hollywood. Here is the Hollywood gag: the echo of the murdered man's voice reverberating from the mountains when the man himself is dead, and the party in *Serenade*, in which the heroine stabs the villain under cover of acting out a bullfight; the punctual Hollywood coincidence: the popping-up of the music-loving sea-captain, who is the *deus ex machina* of *Serenade*; the Hollywood reversal of fortune: the singer who loses his voice and then gets it back again, becoming famous and rich in a sequence that lasts about three minutes.

Mr. Cain is actually a writer for the studios (as are also, or have also been, Mr. Hallas and Mr. McCoy). These novels are produced in his off-time; and they are a kind of Devil's parody of the movies. Mr. Cain is the *âme damnée* of Hollywood. All the things that have been excluded by the Catholic censorship: sex, debauchery, unpunished crime, sacrilege against the Church—Mr. Cain has let them loose in these stories with a gusto as of pent-up ferocity that the reader cannot but share. What a pity that it is impossible for such a writer to create and produce his own pictures!

In the meantime, *Serenade* is a definite improvement on *The Postman*. It, too, has its trashy aspect, its movie foreshortenings and its too-well oiled action; but it establishes a surer illusion. *The Postman* was always in danger of becoming unintentionally funny. Yet even there brilliant moments of insight redeemed the unconscious burlesque; and there is enough of the real poet in Cain—both in writing and in imagination—to make one hope for something better than either.

Edmund Wilson, "The Boys in the Backroom" (1940), *Classics and Commercials: A Literary Chronicle of the Forties* (New York: Farrar, Straus, 1950), pp. 20–22

---

**JAMES T. FARRELL**      Cain's stories are swift moving, punctuated by shocks and violence. His novels are written as a kind of literary movie. But since greater latitude is permitted the novelist than the scenarist, novels like *Mildred Pierce* have the appearance of greater reality than do most films. Unrestrained by a production code, a Cain story can follow the patterns of real life more closely than can a motion picture. In *Mildred Pierce*, Cain began with a real problem, one relatively untouched in contemporary writing. *Mildred Pierce* could have been a poignant account of the middle-class housewife. The fictional character, Mildred, could have been representative of hundreds of thousands of such women. At times there are suggestions of this. The opening portions of the book are promising. But then we see where James M. Cain has learned his literary lessons. Story values take the place of Mildred's problems. Plot involvements, relationships based on plot and story, falsify what was begun as a story about people.

In the first part of the book we see how things, objects, commodities have become the basis for the spiritual content of Mildred's life, and how Bert, having lost all his things, has become a good-natured but ineffectual person. We see further Mildred's development from a cook into a business-woman. Things and money creep out of every page of this book. They are fetishes which have been pressed into Mildred's very soul. She has affairs. There are scenes of anger and reconciliation with her daughter. She knows success and wins prestige. But one of her high moments is when she gives Bert a few drinks, steals the key to the automobile, which he had taken when they separated, and thus gets possession of the car. After taking Bert home, she drives rather wildly. She feels elated, almost ecstatic. At the wheel of the car she forgets herself even more than in sexual affairs with Wally or Monty. Much has been written about the standardization of human beings in modern American society. But here was the promise of a vivid, empirically grasped, and well-presented fictional account of the structure of American standardization. Here, in Bert and Mildred, were the beginnings of two characterizations which would reveal how things take the place of human relationships. This was what made the novel so promising, and why I winced when I saw that this fine beginning was wrapped up in a package of cheap glamour and cynical melodrama.

Cain writes of people who are cruel, violent, self-centered, and who have a minimum of awareness. In his world there is neither good nor bad, and there is little love. The values of these people are very crude, and they are described in such a way that no concept of experience worthy of the name can be implied to the author. People commit adultery and the wicked are not always punished. If the wicked are punished it is purely fortuitous: punishment is the result of the needs of the story and not of the stern hand of Providence or of the pitiless forging of a chain of necessities. This, plus the element of violence, frequently unmotivated, deceives careless readers: they consider Cain to be a serious writer.

James T. Farrell, "Cain's Movietone Realism" (1946), *Literature and Morality* (New York: Vanguard, 1947), pp. 83–84

---

**W. M. FROHOCK**     Two things may be said about James M. Cain with the greatest assurance. One is that nothing he has ever written has been entirely out of the trash category. The other is that in spite of the cheapness which sooner or later finds its way into his novels, an inordinate number of intelligent and fully literate people have read him. He has been translated in many parts of the world, and writers whose stature makes him look stunted have paid him the compliment of imitating him—as Albert Camus did, for example, in *The Stranger*. Even in America Cain enjoys a special status. We have plenty of trash written in the off moments of first-class men: Hemingway committed *To Have and Have Not*; Faulkner did a thing like *Mosquitoes*; Caldwell regaled us with *Tragic Ground* and *Georgia Boy*. And to these may be added, if you like, a good part though by no means all of the bibliography of John Steinbeck. But these are the same men who have also written *The Sun Also Rises, Trouble in July, Light in August,* and *In Dubious Battle.* With Cain there is no choice—you take the trash or you don't get Cain.

Moreover, you get what Cain intends you to get. The preface to *Three of a Kind* makes it clear that he has schooled himself grimly to produce the kind of effect he wants, with every sentence supercharged and a new jolt for the reader on every page. He is one of the few writers now practicing in America who are really sure-handed in the manipulation of their materials. And if he writes what he does, it is because he has had ample proof that it is what the public wants.

There is a character in one of Cain's novels who gets so far down on his luck that he sets out to be the "Professor" in a cathouse, making the kind of music the customers want. Somehow I can never get it out of my head that this man is a symbol—quite an unintentional one, of course, but a symbol nonetheless—standing for the artist who has decided to get a living from his art, no matter what.

This knowledge of what the public wants makes Cain both a literary and a sociological phenomenon, of a kind remarkably useful to our understanding of what has gone on in America in our lifetime. For a pertinent comment on *The Postman Always Rings Twice* cannot help but be a pertinent comment on the time which took Cain and his best-known book to its bosom. *The Postman* is a distinguished book, certainly not for what is in it, but for the number and kind of people who read it. An analysis of it is bound to teach us a lot about the literary climate in America *circa* 1934.

*The Postman* is Cain's book, almost in the same sense in which *Don Quixote* is Cervantes' book: nothing he ever writes will break down the association—he can neither live it down nor live up to it. The obvious ingredients of its success have been enumerated many times before this, but every time we run down the list we discover something new about Cain and about ourselves. The list must always include a large item of just plain trickery. By this I mean things like the strange device at the end of *The Postman,* where we suddenly find that what we have just read has been written down by a man in his death cell. The first-person narrative has carried us along with it because we have been listening to the man talk. The sentences and even the mistakes in grammar are the sentences and the mistakes of a living human voice, and catch the rhythms of vernacular speech with an authenticity which can be achieved only by the special

talents of an O'Hara, a Lardner, or of Cain himself—talents close to a kind
of genius. And during the course of our becoming acquainted with Frank
Chambers, the one fact of which we have been the most thoroughly convinced is that he is anything but a creature of superior perception. Discovering that this story which has so long enthralled us is composed of the
deathbed jottings of a man who could have made his living any time writing
for M-G-M is like being caught by the rising house-lights wiping our eyes
at an especially corny movie.

> W. M. Frohock, "James M. Cain: Tabloid Tragedy," *The Novel of Violence in America*
> (Dallas: Southern Methodist University Press, 1950), pp. 87–89

---

**JOYCE CAROL OATES**      ⟨. . .⟩ it is not Cain's writing so much as
the success of that writing which is interesting. His works may be discussed
as mirrors of the society that gave birth to them and rewarded their creator
handsomely for them, but the ambiguities and paradoxes of the works bear
analysis. Money is important, but it is important secondarily. Of first importance is the doomed straining toward a permanent relationship—an emotional unit which the male both desires and fears. Whether love or sex, it
is certainly dominated by unconscious motives, a complex of impulses which
shuttle between violence and tenderness. Thus the innocent victim of *The
Butterfly* becomes a moonshiner and, rather abruptly, a brutal murderer
because of his confused feelings toward his "daughter"; and once his power
is relinquished to her, his doom is certain. To love and therefore to relinquish
one's power are tantamount to being destroyed. One must remain solitary
and invulnerable, yet one cannot—and so the death sentence is earned.
Mildred Pierce, masculine in her determination for economic success and
possession of her daughter, survives only because in her novel, Cain attempts
to write a realistic story, without the structural contrivance of murder and
retribution. Mildred is "destroyed" in a thematic sense, but in the suspense-
novel genre she would have been killed.

Cain's parable, which is perhaps America's parable, may be something
like this: the passion that rises in us is both an inescapable part of our lives and
an enemy to our lives, to our egoistic control of ourselves. Once unleashed it
cannot be quieted. Giving oneself to anyone, even temporarily, will result
in entrapment and death; the violence lovers do to one another is no more
than a reflection of the proposed violence society holds back to keep the

individual passions in check. Freud speaks in many of his works of the strange relationship between the impulse of love and the impulse of destruction, how the sadistic impulse (see *Civilization and Its Discontents*) may be an expression of Eros—but an Eros concerned with the self and its survival. The self cannot fulfill its destiny without the alter-ego or anima, but, in relinquishing its power to external agents, it becomes vulnerable to destruction from without. The highest expression of Eros, which is spiritual, is of course beyond Cain's infantile characters. Just as the soap operas and the American movies not only of the thirties and forties but of the present have played back again and again certain infantile obsessions to the great American public, so Cain's novels serve up, in the guise of moral tracts, the lesson of the child who dares too much and must be punished. And there is satisfaction in knowing he will be punished—if not for one crime, then for another; if not by the law, then by himself or by an accomplice. In any case the "postman," whatever symbol or fate or death or order in the form of a uniformed and familiar person, will "ring twice"; there is no escape.

There is perhaps no writer more faithful to the mythologies of America than Cain, for he writes of its ideals and hatreds without obscuring them in the difficulties of art.

> Joyce Carol Oates, "Man under Sentence of Death: The Novels of James M. Cain," *Tough Guy Writers of the Thirties*, ed. David Madden (Carbondale: Southern Illinois University Press, 1968), pp. 127–28

---

## JAMES M. CAIN and DAVID ZINSSER    INTERVIEWER:
Which of your own books would you say stand up best?

CAIN: The book that stands up for me is the one that sold the most copies; that's the only test for me and that one was *The Postman Always Rings Twice*. It didn't sell as many in the first edition as *The Butterfly* did. But there's the silver kangaroo over there on the shelf that Pocket Books gave me when *The Postman* passed the million copy mark. That must have been thirty years ago. The thing still goes on, and how many editions, how many copies it's sold, I haven't the faintest idea. Certainly it's done the best in English, but it's been translated into eighteen languages.

INTERVIEWER: How did you react to Albert Camus' praise of your writing?

CAIN: He wrote something about me—more or less admitting that he had patterned one of his books on mine, and that he revered me as a great American writer. But I never read Camus. In some ways I'm ignorant. In other ways I'm not. At fiction I'm not. But I read very little of it. I'm afraid to because I might like some guy's book too well! Another thing: when you write fiction, the other guy's book just tortures you—you're always re-writing it for him. You don't read it just as a reader; you read it as a guy in the business. Better not read it at all. ⟨. . .⟩

INTERVIEWER: How related is style to your objectives? You are so well-known for your "hard-boiled" manner of writing . . .

CAIN: Let's talk about this so-called style. I don't know what they're talking about—"tough," "hard-boiled." I tried to write as people talk. That was one of the first arguments I ever had with my father—my father was all hell for people talking as they *should* talk. I, the incipient novelist, even as a boy, was fascinated by the way people *do* talk. The first man I ever sat at the feet of who enchanted me not only by what he told me but by *how* he talked, was Ike Newton, who put in the brick wall over at Washington College, right after my father became President. ⟨. . .⟩ Well, Ike Newton put the bricks in, gauging them with his eye, and doing a beautiful thing, and as he worked he talked. The way he'd use language! I'd go home and talk about it, to my mother's utter horror, and to my father's horror too because he was such a shot on the way people *should* talk. My childhood was nothing but one long lesson: not "preventative" but "preventive"; not "sort of a" but "a sort of"; not "those kind," but "that kind" or "those kinds." Jesus Christ, on and on and on.

INTERVIEWER: Since language is obviously such an important part of your own writing, do you feel the motion pictures were able to transplant and communicate the Cain story and style?

CAIN: When they were making *Double Indemnity* in Hollywood, Billy Wilder complained that Raymond Chandler was throwing away my nice, terse dialogue; he got some student actors in from the Paramount school, coached them up, to let Chandler hear what it would be like if he would only put exactly what was in the book in his screenplay. To Wilder's utter astonishment, it sounded like holy hell. Chandler explained to Wilder what the trouble was—that Cain's dialogue is written to the eye. That ragged right-hand margin that is so exciting and wonderful to look at can't be recited by actors. Chandler said, now that we've got that out of the way, let's dialogue it with the same spirit Cain has in the book but not the identical words. Wilder still didn't believe him. They got me over there, purportedly to discuss something else, but the real reason was that Wilder hoped I would contradict Chandler, and somehow explain what had evaporated when the kids tried to do my lines. But, of course, I bore Chandler out, reminding Wilder I could write spoken stuff well enough, but on the page there just wasn't any room for talkie climaxes.

James M. Cain and David Zinsser, "James M. Cain: The Art of Fiction LXIX," *Paris Review* No. 73 (Spring 1978): 135–38

---

**ROY HOOPES**      As I read over the reviews of Cain's books and the appraisals and comments on his writing, one fact struck me as consistently significant: As a rule, the conventional literary critics put him down while *writers* praised him, sometimes almost in reverence. James M. Cain, I decided, was clearly a writer's writer. And this, it seems to me, is why he is studied in colleges today primarily in writing courses and workshops rather than literary classes . . . as Cain himself would have preferred.

Whether or not James M. Cain will eventually become established as a major American author will be left to the only critic Cain himself felt was competent to judge—Posterity. But there is little doubt that he is the perfect subject for a biography. He enjoyed three careers—as a journalist, novelist, and screenwriter—wrote seventeen books, and had four wives and a long life that spanned the first seven decades of the twentieth century. As far as "golden ages" go, he was invariably in the right place at the right time: New York in 1920s, Hollywood in the 1930s and 1940s, and Washington in the 1950s. It was a life dedicated to and supported solely by writing, from that memorable day in 1914 when, sitting across from the White House on a bench in Lafayette Park, he arbitrarily decided to become a writer. ⟨. . .⟩

During my interviews with Cain, I was struck by a curious paradox. Despite his remarkable career and his seventeen books, several of them highly acclaimed worldwide best sellers, he said he did not have a sense of accomplishment in his life; it was, he maintained, one of the reasons he had no inclination to write an autobiography. When I told him I thought he had led a fascinating life, he replied: "It may be to you, but it's never been interesting to me. There's something very peculiar about me that I don't understand. I cannot write in the third person—and it seems to have something to do with this sense of a lack of accomplishment. I have written three books in the third person, and they came off all right, but did not have the bite of the others. And the reason is that I simply can't imagine why I know what the character is thinking of. What am I, God or something? Now, when I write in the first person, that's different. But to write anything, I have to pretend to be somebody else."

Roy Hoopes, *Cain* (New York: Holt, Rinehart & Winston, 1982), pp. xiv–xvi

---

**STODDARD MARTIN**     Of his own characteristic adaptation of the *Tristan* myth to the thriller, Cain concludes,

> Murder, I said, had always been written from its least interesting angle, which was whether the police could catch the murderer. I was considering, I said, a story in which the murder was the *love-rack,* as it must be to any man and woman who conspire to commit. But, I said, they would commit the perfect murder. It wouldn't go, of course, quite as they planned it. But in the end they wouldn't get away with it, and then what? They would find, I said, that the earth is not big enough for two persons who share such a dreadful secret, and eventually turn on each other. . . . The whole thing corresponded to a definition of tragedy I found later in some of my father's writings: that it was the 'force of circumstances driving the protagonist to the commission of the dreadful act'.

The purest realisations of this formula are *The Postman* and *Double Indemnity.* Few novels have been written in a more direct, obsessive manner. 'As a result of my first fiasco at novel-writing, I had acquired such a morbid fear of boring the reader that I got the habit of needling the story at the least hint of a let-down.' Dialogue constitutes more than 50 per cent of *The Postman,* and it is a sharp telegraphic dialogue uncluttered by 'he said'–'she replied'. 'Sometimes Cain's dialogue, typographically, has the impact of a graph,' ⟨David⟩ Madden writes; indeed, there is a visual clarity to it that reminds one that it belongs to the era of the hard lines of Art Deco and the high polish of chrome hubcaps against white-sidewall tyres. Aurally the dialogue suggests the chromatic progressions of late Romantic opera, which had already been adapted to the incremental progression of movie-scenes: 'Key words regarding future attitude and action at the end of one scene are picked up and developed in the next with almost mathematical precision'

⟨David Madden⟩. Cain uses, moreover, the Modernist technique of omission to achieve compression and concentration of effect. Foreshadowing, echo-pattern and recapitulation are employed to provide context. What is actually given are the bare bones of the story: an Expressionistic grid against which the reader must flesh in the details: a less obscure and lofty version of the style Eliot used in *The Waste Land*. The reader, Madden says, finds his greatest satisfaction in a Cain novel from observing the authorial control: 'He observes Cain manipulating his concept of the popular reader, and in the process, he becomes a captive himself.' The confessional first-person generally has the result of implicating the reader in the narrator's behaviour; this effort is deepened considerably in Cain through the use of dramatic irony. The reader of *The Postman*, for instance, is considerably more knowledgeable than the District Attorney, who invents several scenarios for how Cora's husband might have been murdered. Aware of Cora's and Frank's guilt from the first, the reader's concern is not with 'who dun it' but whether and when they will be caught. Cain is quite different from conventional detective writers such as Hammett and Chandler: anticipation is the hook here, not suspense.

Stoddard Martin, "The Tough Guys," *California Writers: Jack London, John Steinbeck, the Tough Guys* (New York: St. Martin's Press, 1983), pp. 154–56

---

**DAVID FINE**     Architectural structures, often linked with the high-way, are another source of Cain's symbolism. The improvised highway stop, obsolete now in an age of Holiday Inns and Travelodges, was a conspicuous part of the 1930s landscape. That this meeting ground of high-speed mobility and domesticity becomes a battleground for Frank and Cora is thematically central to Cain's first novel. A significant part of the lure of Southern California in the boom of the twenties was the promise of the detached house. Houses in every conceivable historic design found a place in the instant townscape of the twenties and thirties. Novelists found an inexhaustible supply of images of disparity and dislocation in the eclectic building styles of Southern California. ⟨. . .⟩

Cain avoided this kind of exaggerated architectural imagery. Instead, he set his characters typically in the "Spanish" style houses of white stucco with red tile roofs favored by many of the subdividers as "authentic" evocations of the region's past. These ordinary houses served Cain both as ironic contrasts to the extraordinary actions and behavior of their inhabitants—common-place domestic facades behind which adultery, murder, and extortion were played out—and, in their banality, expressions of the frustrations, failures, and betrayed dreams of his people. Houses externalized the mental states of their owners.

Consistently, he underscored the monotony of architecture. The Twin Oaks Tavern is "like millions of others in California." The first description of the "House of Death" in *Double Indemnity*—located in Hollywoodland, a 1920s subdivision along Beechwood Avenue above Hollywood Boulevard and beneath the famous sign—combines a flat ordinariness with a sense of the grotesque in its incongruous details:

> It didn't look like a House of Death when I saw it. It was just a Spanish house, like all the rest of them in California, with white walls, red tile roof, and a patio out to one side. It was built cock-eyed. The garage was under the house, the first floor was over that, and the rest of it was spilled up the hill any way they could get it in.

Inside, he piles on more symbolic details. Although the house has a living room "like every other living room in California," the most conspicuous features in it are "blood-red drapes" run on iron spears, red velvet tapestries, and a "Mexican" rug made in Oakland, California. The insisted-on conventionality, set against its "cock-eyed" floor plan, the blood-red domination of its interior, and the rug carry elements of deception which run through the novel.

David Fine, "Beginning in the Thirties: The Los Angeles Fiction of James M. Cain and Horace McCoy," *Los Angeles in Fiction*, ed. David Fine (Albuquerque: University of New Mexico Press, 1984), pp. 53–54

---

**RICHARD BRADBURY**      James M. Cain's contribution to the writing of crime fiction was to recognise the potential afforded by the writing from within the 'criminal's' perspective. This is the formal coup of *The Postman Always Rings Twice*, *Double Indemnity*, and *The Butterfly*: at the end of these three texts the reader 'discovers' that what he or she has been reading is the transcription of a confession. The possibilities that this opened up were recognised, most famously, by Albert Camus when he acknowledged his debt to *The Postman Always Rings Twice* in the writing of *L'Etranger*. Cain's writing makes possible an examination of motivation more convinc-ing, precisely because it is internalised, than the revelation necessary to bring to a conclusion a work written from the investigator's point of view. The reader, then, can discard the more or less interesting question, 'who dunnit?' and replace this with an attention directed towards a demonstration of the reasons behind the act. At the same time, the first-person narrative eliminates the possibility of a return to normality because all three of these novels conclude, explicitly or implicitly, with the death of the author. There is no informing intelligence within the text which returns the reader to the realm of external and rational explanation. It is, clearly, this absence of any sense of a privileged normality which attracted Camus to Cain's work. And Robbe-Grillet's comment on the mechanisms whereby Camus achieves this could equally well be applied to Cain's writing: 'Just change the tenses of the verbs very slightly, replace the first person . . . by the ordinary third person of the past definite, and Camus's universe immediately disappears, together with the whole interest of his book.' For Cain's world in the Depression-year novels is a world of essentially 'homely' characters plunged into a material deprivation which enforces the need for extreme action in order to survive in a fashion anything like that to which they are accustomed. It is a world in which the quintessentially American posture of individual effort being rewarded with security has been shattered by the economic collapse. And thus it is as a world in which the restitution of normality at the end of any single text can only appear as a bad joke.

And, although he shows no direct interest in the political consequences of the Wall Street crash, dismissing as he does the thirties novels of social protest as based on a theme which is 'a dead seed for a novelist', the spectres of the crisis stalk around the edges of his fiction. Herbert Pierce is ruined by Black Thursday, and the opening description of Frank Chambers makes him a close relative of Tom Joad. The urge for financial gain, for access to the means of acquiring material fulfilment, is welded to the urge for sexual fulfilment. Even in *Mildred Pierce*, the least interesting of the 'five great novels' for the purposes of this essay, Cain has a clear understanding of the interaction between money and sexuality as he charts Mildred's use of both to gain power and success—those two chimeras of the Depression years. This historical period, then, is much more than simply a backdrop to his writing; it is an external fact which shapes the broad contours of the internal action of the text. In this era of material deprivation, the possibility of acquiring money and property acts as a force to drive the characters to extremes of behaviour. Although Freud claimed that money was not a great source of psychological motivation, much American crime fiction of the thirties seems to argue against him. The source of this, in all probability, lies in the naturalist writers of the earlier part of the century—in their identification of the search for financial security and success as an almost sexual desire.

> Richard Bradbury, "Sexuality, Guilt and Detection: Tension between History and Suspense," *American Crime Fiction: Studies in the Genre,* ed. Brian Docherty (London: Macmillan Press, 1988), pp. 89–90

# Bibliography

*79th Division Headquarters Troop: A Record* (editor; with Malcolm Gilbert). 1919.

*Our Government.* 1930.

*The Postman Always Rings Twice.* 1934.

*Serenade.* 1937.

*Mildred Pierce.* 1941.

*Love's Lovely Counterfeit.* 1942.

*Cain Omnibus* ⟨*The Postman Always Rings Twice, Serenade, Mildred Pierce*⟩. 1943.

*Career in C Major and Other Stories.* 1943.

*Double Indemnity.* 1943.

*Three of a Kind* ⟨*Career in C Major, The Embezzler, Double Indemnity*⟩. 1943.

*The Embezzler.* 1944.

*For Men Only: A Collection of Short Stories* (editor). 1944.

*Past All Dishonor.* 1946.

*The Butterfly.* 1947.

*Sinful Woman.* 1947.

*The Moth.* 1948.

*Three of Hearts* ⟨*Love's Lovely Counterfeit, Past All Dishonor, The Butterfly*⟩. 1949.

*Jealous Woman.* 1950, 1955 (with *Sinful Woman*).

*The Root of His Evil.* 1952.

*Galatea.* 1953.

*Mignon.* 1962.

*The Magician's Wife.* 1965.

*Rainbow's End.* 1975.

*The Institute.* 1976.

*Hard Cain* ⟨*Sinful Woman, Jealous Woman, The Root of His Evil*⟩. 1980.

*The Baby in the Icebox and Other Short Fiction.* Ed. Roy Hoopes. 1981.

*Cloud Nine.* 1984.

*The Enchanted Isle.* 1985.

*60 Years of Journalism.* Ed. Roy Hoopes. 1985.

*Career in C Major and Other Fiction.* Ed. Roy Hoopes. 1986.

*The James M. Cain Cookbook: Guide to Home Cooking, Physical Fitness, and Animals (Especially Cats).* Ed. Roy Hoopes and Lynne Barrett. 1988.

# Raymond Chandler
## *1888–1959*

RAYMOND CHANDLER was born in Chicago on July 23, 1888. When he was seven years old his parents divorced; his mother took him home to England, where he attended public school. Although Chandler wanted to become a writer, his mother and grandmother insisted he join the civil service. He acceded, but quit after six months. After trying his hand unsuccessfully at freelance writing, Chandler emigrated to the United States in 1912. He held a number of odd jobs in Los Angeles before enlisting in the Canadian Army in 1917. He distinguished himself fighting in France and returned to the U.S. in 1919. Back in California, Chandler moved from city to city and job to job; he married Cissy Pascal in 1924, then settled into an executive position with an oil company. He was fired in 1932 for drunkenness and irresponsibility.

In 1933 Chandler sold his first stories to *Black Mask*, the magazine that published "hard-boiled" writers such as Dashiell Hammett, Horace McCoy, and Erle Stanley Gardner. Later he became a member of the Fictioneers, a group comprised mostly of pulp fiction writers. Most of the twenty-one stories Chandler wrote between 1933 and 1939 featured detectives named Mallory, Carmady, or Johnny Dalmas. Eventually, they evolved into Philip Marlowe, a tough but idealistic private investigator in a corrupt Los Angeles. Chandler's first Marlowe novel, *The Big Sleep* (1939), an expansion of several of his stories, was an immediate success, despite its confusing plot (Chandler later admitted he did not know who committed one of the murders). More novels followed, each extending the range of mystery writing into new literary terrain: *Farewell, My Lovely* (1940), *The High Window* (1942), *The Lady in the Lake* (1943), *The Little Sister* (1949), and *The Long Goodbye* (1953), which has been called Chandler's masterpiece. Each of Chandler's novels was adapted to the screen, some more than once. Chandler was himself a screenwriter; his screenplays for *Double Indemnity* (1944) and *The Blue Dahlia* (1946) were nominated for Academy Awards, and he shared writing credits on Alfred Hitchcock's adaptation of Patricia Highsmith's novel, *Strangers on a Train* (1950).

Although he returned repeatedly to Marlowe, Chandler longed to be recognized as more than just a writer of detective fiction and tried his hand at a variety of forms, including fantasy and mainstream fiction. He earned renown as an essayist, and in 1944 wrote the controversial "The Simple Art of Murder," which defined the characteristics of the hard-boiled detective story and contrasted its realism with the artificiality of much classic detective fiction. Chandler was the recipient of two Edgar Awards from the Mystery Writers of America and served briefly as president of the association in 1959.

Cissy Chandler died in 1954 and Chandler attempted suicide shortly thereafter. His drinking grew heavier, and he wrote only one more novel, *Playback* (1958), before his death in La Jolla, California, on March 26, 1959. "The Poodle Springs Story," a Marlowe story left unfinished at his death, was completed by Robert B. Parker as the novel *Poodle Springs* in 1989.

# ▧ *Critical Extracts*

**RALPH PARTRIDGE**    I have reserved *The Big Sleep* and ⟨George Harmon Coxe's⟩ *The Frightened Women* to the last, as my judgment on the merits of American tough thrillers is by now hopelessly impaired by addiction. The only question you can ask a dope fiend about the composition of his dope is whether it gives him an authentic kick. As there are adulterated products in circulation I can guarantee these two are full strength blends of sadism, eroticism and alcoholism. If you like to pretend you read the stuff for any reason but sordid mental intoxication, these ingredients are crystallised around a central thread of detection. But if you take your medicine straight, you'll never notice it.

> Ralph Partridge, "Death with a Difference," *New Statesman and Nation*, 10 June 1939, p. 910

**RAYMOND CHANDLER**    In everything that can be called art there is a quality of redemption. It may be pure tragedy, if it is high tragedy, and it may be pity and irony, and it may be the raucous laughter of the strong man. But down these mean streets a man must go who is not himself mean, who is neither tarnished nor afraid. The detective in this kind of story must be such a man. He is the hero; he is everything. He must be a complete man and a common man yet an unusual man. He must be, to use a rather weathered phrase, a man of honor—by instinct, by inevitability, without thought of it, and certainly without saying it. He must be the best man in his world and a good enough man for any world. I do not care much about his private life; he is neither a eunuch nor a satyr; I think he might seduce a duchess and I am quite sure he would not spoil a virgin; if he is a man of honor in one thing, he is that in all things.

He is a relatively poor man, or he would not be a detective at all. He is a common man or he could not go among common people; he has a sense of character, or he would not know his job. He will take no man's money dishonestly and no man's insolence without a due and dispassionate revenge; he is a lonely man and his pride is that you will treat him as a proud man or be very sorry you ever saw him. He talks as the man of his age talks— that is, with rude wit, a lively sense of the grotesque, a disgust for sham, and a contempt for pettiness.

The story is this man's adventure in search of a hidden truth, and it would be no adventure if it did not happen to a man fit for adventure. He has a range of awareness that startles you, but it belongs to him by right, because it belongs to the world he lives in. If there were enough like him, the world would be a safe place to live in, without becoming too dull to be worth living in. Such is my faith.

Raymond Chandler, "The Simple Art of Murder," *Atlantic Monthly* 174, No. 6 (December 1944): 59

---

**W. H. AUDEN**      In the detective story, as in its mirror image, the Quest for the Grail, maps (the ritual of space) and timetables (the ritual of time) are desirable. Nature should reflect its human inhabitants, *i.e.*, it should be the Great Good Place; for the more Eden-like it is, the greater the contradiction of murder. The country is preferable to the town, a well-to-do neighborhood (but not too well-to-do—or there will be a suspicion of ill-gotten gains) better than a slum. The corpse must shock not only because it is a corpse but also because, even for a corpse, it is shockingly out of place, as when a dog makes a mess on a drawing room carpet.

Mr. Raymond Chandler has written that he intends to take the body out of the vicarage garden and give murder back to those who are good at it. If he wishes to write detective stories, *i.e.*, stories where the reader's principal interest is to learn who did it, he could not be more mistaken; for in a society of professional criminals, the only possible motives for desiring to identify the murderer are blackmail or revenge, which both apply to individuals, not to the group as a whole, and can equally well inspire murder. Actually, whatever he may say, I think Mr. Chandler is interested in writing, not detective stories, but serious studies of a criminal milieu, the Great Wrong Place, and his powerful but extremely depressing books should be read and judged, not as escape literature, but as works of art.

    W. H. Auden, "The Guilty Vicarage: Notes on the Detective Story, by an Addict," *Harper's Magazine* 196, No. 5 (May 1948): 408

**JOHN DICKSON CARR**    Mr. Chandler is a serious minded man, and it would be unjust not to take him seriously. Few writers have been more mannered (I do not say ill-mannered) or more uneven. His similes either succeed brilliantly or fall flat. He can write a scene with an almost suffocating vividness and sense of danger—if he does not add three words too many and make it funny. His virtues are all there. If, to some restraint, he could add the fatigue of construction and clues (the writer he most admires, Mr. Hammett, never disdained clues and has always given them fairly)—then one day he may write a good novel.

I say nothing of new ideas or plot-twists, because Mr. Chandler does not have them. He will never disturb the laurels of Mr. Queen or Mr. Gardner or Mr. Stout. Perhaps it is best to let him alone, and offer no suggestions. In his new book, *The Simple Art of Murder*, few of the novelettes are new. Yet many are good and two are first-class. When he forgets he cannot write a true detective story, when he forgets to torture words, the muddle resolves and the action whips along like a numbered racing car.

    John Dickson Carr, "With Colt and Luger," *New York Times Book Review*, 24 September 1950, p. 36

**LUKE PARSONS**       Mr. Chandler is interesting to anyone studying
the American literary scene because he comes half-way between the prolific
time-killers like Erle Stanley Gardner and serious novelists such as John
Steinbeck and Ernest Hemingway. His writing is more ambitious and imaginative than the former; has less 'message', in modern jargon, than the latter.
When we find serious implications in his novels and draw serious conclusions
from them, we must remember not to be too long-haired and solemn about
it all. As craftsman and professional writer, Mr. Chandler's first object is
to thrill, baffle and entertain us—and in this he succeeds very well. His
books, after all, are detective stories. His most obvious forebear is Dashiell
Hammett and one of his literary ancestors was Sir Arthur Conan Doyle.
Indeed, chess problems and drink are to Marlowe what the violin and
hypodermic were to Sherlock Holmes. Just because Mr. Chandler writes so
well, we must take care not to apply to him inappropriate literary standards.
When all has been said about the violence and viciousness in his books,
we must recognize that there is an escapist element in them too. Mr.
Chandler's California is to some extent a country of the mind and we need
not, after reading about it, feel too disturbed about the state of the Union.
The elements common to the tough school of American novels—their
violence, alcoholism, promiscuity and moral nihilism—are curious and ugly
conventions; disturbing literary phenomena even for a young, raw civilization. Mr. Chandler, while accepting these conventions, infuses a small glow
of humanity into this cold world. If, like our own 'saint in the gutter'
novelists, he finds it easier to love his less fortunate neighbours, this is only
human. Such inverted snobbery in a writer, however, diminishes his stature.
Great novelists are able to view all their characters without envy.

> Luke Parsons, "On the Novels of Raymond Chandler," *Fortnightly* 181, No. 5 (May
> 1954): 351

---

**IAN FLEMING**       I pulled his leg about his plots, which always seemed
to me to go wildly astray. What holds the books together and makes them
so compulsively readable, even to alpha minds who would normally not
think of reading a thriller, is the dialogue. There is a throw-away, down-
beat quality about Chandler's dialogue, whether wise-cracking or not, that
takes one happily through chapter after chapter in which there is no more
action than Philip Marlowe driving his car and talking to his girl, or a rich

old woman consulting her lawyer on the sun porch. His aphorisms were always his own. 'Lust ages men but keeps women young' has stuck in my mind.

Ian Fleming, "Raymond Chandler," *London Magazine* 6, No. 12 (December 1959): 50

---

**JULIAN SYMONS**     Chandler's passionate concern with the sound and value of words is vividly illustrated in letters which express indignation about proof readers who were ready to improve his style, about novelists who used clichés by force of habit, about "the assumption on the part of some editorial hireling that he can write better than the man who sent the stuff in, that he knows more about phrase and cadence and the placing of words". He wished always to be judged by the standards of art, and was aware how often he fell short of them. Two years before his death he wrote, modestly enough, to his literary agent, Mrs. Helga Greene, that: "To accept a mediocre form and make something like literature out of it is in itself rather an accomplishment . . . We [artists] are not always nice people, but essentially we have an ideal that transcends ourselves."

Chandler's distinctive marks as a writer were the depth and sharpness of his observation, his power to create atmosphere, and the crackling wisecracks which, either in dialogue or in the first person comments of his detective Philip Marlowe, enliven almost every page of his novels. "Did I hurt your head much?" Marlowe asks the blonde with silver fingernails in *The Big Sleep*, after he has hit her with his gun. Her reply has the exact tone and timing that mark Chandler's jokes: "You and every other man I ever met." It is impossible to convey in a single quotation Chandler's ear for dialogue, but no reader of *The Second Chandler Omnibus*, which contains his last three books, can fail to hear, in the conversations of film stars and publicity agents, rich men and gangsters, and policemen both honest and corrupt, an ear for the form of speech such as few writers are lucky enough to possess.

Julian Symons, "Marlowe's Victim," *Times Literary Supplement*, 23 March 1962, p. 200

---

**PHILIP DURHAM**     In "Blackmailers Don't Shoot" Chandler created his hero, the hero—somewhat weathered and weaker—he was still writing about when he died twenty-six years later. Although the Chandler hero, frequently called the hard-boiled hero, became distinctive, he was by no means an original creation. Rather he was a part of a continuous tradition that had begun in American literature on the frontier in the 1830's. The American literary hard-boiled hero (suggested by Washington Irving's Brom Bones, the "burly, roaring, roystering blade" who had "a mingled air of fun and arrogance" and "was always ready for either a fight or a frolic") originated in the tales of August Longstreet, Charles Webber, and Joseph Baldwin, and he continued in *The Desperadoes of the South-West* by Alfred Arrington where he was one who "dares danger, laughs at pain, and challenges death." In 1860 the hero was taken over by the Beadle and Adams dime-novel writers and utilized by them until the 1890's. At the beginning of the twentieth century he was ready made for such early "western" writers as Owen Wister and Zane Grey, and in the westerns he is still active. As a detective hero he first appeared in the pages of the *Black Mask* in the early 1920's where his creator was Carroll John Daly. Daly's private eye, Race Williams, arrived only a few months before Dashiell Hammett's Continental Op appeared in the same magazine. Thereafter the *Black Mask* became known, especially during the regime of Editor Joseph Shaw from 1926 through 1936, as the leader of the Hard-Boiled School of Detective Fiction. In this group and into this tradition Raymond Chandler contributed his own version of the hard-boiled hero, the man who was to become Philip Marlowe. When Chandler began publishing detective stories, the characteristics of the hero were already clearly evident: courage, physical strength, indestructibility, indifference to danger and death, a knightly attitude, celibacy, a measure of violence, and a sense of justice were the things that mattered. Chandler accepted these characteristics, and they became a part of Philip Marlowe.

When Editor Shaw received "Blackmailers Don't Shoot," from a man he had never heard of, he could not decide whether it was remarkably good or cleverly fraudulent, so he sent it to one of his established writers, W. T. Ballard, for an opinion. The answer was a vote for "remarkably good." Although the hero of the story, Mallory (or ten other names before he became Philip Marlowe), was at the outset rather sparsely drawn, he was gradually to evolve into a well-rounded character. Physically in the beginning he was a stock character, "tall, with wide-set gray eyes, a thin nose, a jaw of stone." His black hair was "ever so faintly touched with gray, as by an almost diffident hand." His distinction, that which set him apart from the stereotype detective, was that while he was a man of the people he wore clothes that "fitted him as though they had a soul of their own, not just a doubtful past." He was tough enough to handle a hood, strong enough to bounce back from the inevitable sapping, determined to take nothing from a couple of crooked cops, and sufficiently hard-boiled to kill when it came his turn. Mallory, essentially the same as a dozen or more pulp detectives, had found his destiny in the West.

Philip Durham, *Down These Mean Streets a Man Must Go: Raymond Chandler's Knight* (Chapel Hill: University of North Carolina Press, 1963), pp. 80–82

---

**R. W. LID**    Chandler was a master at portraying the schizoid aspects of American culture and the ways in which the base and ideal and their manifestations are so closely intertwined as to be inseparable if not indistinguishable. The lives of his characters reveal this split in motive and intention and conduct, just as the patterns of his novels reveal the cohesiveness of American life which underlies and makes a whole of this self-perpetuating opposition.

Marlowe crosses and crisscrosses the landscape of great Los Angeles, which provides almost infinite variety of background, moving from terrain to terrain, locale to locale, setting to setting. Chandler bears down so heavily on landscape in his novels that physical property almost takes on a value and meaning of its own; one is reminded of the motion picture and the way in which the camera invests physical props with significance by panning back and forth over them, by lingering with them. But, while the vastly different places Chandler's Marlowe visits, and the people he encounters, are seemingly held together by a thread of meaning solely of Marlowe's making, a pattern gradually emerges, a meaningful arrangement and sequence of events; and behind this pattern lies, broadly speaking, the pattern of American society as Chandler sees it: mobile, fluid, a reticulated crisscrossing of people through time and circumstance. One begins to see why, in Chandler's fiction, the world of Los Angeles' Bunker Hill, with its decayed buildings and decaying people, is just a stone's throw away from the deep lawns and private driveways and stately mansions of Santa Monica; why, in other words, all segments of society are inextricably linked in Chandler's sun-filled but nightmarish landscape.

R. W. Lid, "Philip Marlowe Speaking," *Kenyon Review* 31, No. 2 (1969): 156–57

**G. A. FINCH**     Chandler's conception of the duties of a writer were fairly simple. (He was old fashioned enough to think of the obligations of a writer to himself and to his profession as duties.) Like Henry James, he believed that the first duty of a novel was to be well written. He also felt that the prime consideration of the novelist was clear attention to and perception of the immediate experience. Chandler's special gift was an uncanny ease in blending into Marlowe's account of his experiences graphic notations on people and places. Marlowe makes people visible and certain to us through his observation alone and he never requires the support of reflective pauses for character guess-work nor the psychological stereotyping which so many writers of his time in and out of the mystery genre fell back upon.

His private detective Philip Marlowe appears as a normally even-tempered man, unmarked by the eccentricities of mind or habit that many detective characters acquire as part of an endowment of unique abilities. He has qualities of person and mind that attract people to him, and if his occupation leads him into a rather unsocial way of life, it does not diminish his interest in people though it does nothing to raise his estimate of human nature. He knows well the terrain of his investigations; his knowledge of the city of Los Angeles and the areas around it is exact and exceptional: his sense of the people who inhabit the canyons and the ugly back streets is sharpened by his whole experience of the area and his awareness of the changes that are constantly taking effect in it. He does not have a 'cop mentality', he does not identify his persona with his occupation; as a private eye he is expressing his character as a man.

By the time Chandler wrote his first novel he fully perceived the private eye who had been evolving in his pulp novelettes as a good man in a dirty business. What started as a peculiarity of Philip Marlowe finally emerged as his distinction. Chandler was able to demonstrate why it was dirty business; also that it was one about which Marlowe had no illusions.

G. A. Finch, "Marlowe's Long Goodbye," *Armchair Detective* 6, No. 1 (October 1972): 7

---

**E. M. BEEKMAN**     Chandler made metropolitan California into a metaphor of America in a manner which has the same harsh clarity as the paintings of Edward Hopper. His fictional world has an unremitting gloom:

injustice and the seven deadly sins are paramount and decency is something of a vice.

But, like Faulkner, Chandler fostered a negative heroism. This bleak world is illuminated by the stubborn endurance of his hero, Philip Marlowe, a man who insists on a private code which is not so much one of justice as one of *humanitas*. Marlowe is not a bright shiny volunteer for a superlative of good. He is an angry and bitter man, tainted by the world he invades in his violence, his gallows humor and his melancholy—a melancholy which is at times close to despair since he knows that his efforts are so futile. But he is a man who must endure and who must persist in his defiance against the forces of coercion—a sad man since he realizes the futility; and a noble man because he will not be vanquished.

Marlowe, who was described by Marshall McLuhan as "Chandler's echo of Christopher Marlowe's supermen Tamburlaine and Dr. Faustus," is in a long line of Romantic heroes. He is an outsider, a loner, a man who will not fit the pattern, a character who must not toe the line. If Marlowe were an archetype he would be a somber knight on a never finished quest, recharging his faith by adversity. A Romantic Hero, to be sure, but one who has been mired in reality. As an outsider, in his preference for solitude, in his stubborn defiance and power to endure, Marlowe is very much the archetypal hero of American fiction, from Melville's Ishmael and Bartleby to Hemingway's Frederic Henry and Robert Jordan. In Chandler's novels Marlowe is the only figure with warmth and compassion, but there is a constant infiltration of the autumnal mood, of weariness and futility. This is why these novels are not simply crime fiction: at their close little has been resolved despite the fact that the murderer has been found. All of them end on a note of dissatisfaction.

Marlowe is thus not a simplistic creation. In fact, he is quite subtle and ambiguous. In this character there is a fierce grief which has little oportunity to be assuaged—a grief for a loss, perhaps a primeval Eden, perhaps a community of decent men. Not a grief, however, simply for a loss of inno-cence, but a bitter frustration about the fact that things *are* as they are though they shouldn't be that way. There is a revulsion for this world yet also a distaste for his own defiant nobility, a nobility very much like a pawned code of honor. In all these particulars Marlowe is a reflection of the most typical American fictional hero, and I think that not enough emphasis has been put on his furious grief which can only escape through a tenuously controlled pathos, or through the painfully blasphemous fury of, for example, Frederick Henry at the end of Hemingway's A *Farewell to Arms*. Exiles ever, these characters are not destined to join their fellow men.

E. M. Beekman, "Raymond Chandler and an American Genre," *Massachusetts Review* 14, No. 1 (Winter 1973): 166–67

---

**BERNARD A. SCHOPEN**     While he admired Hammett's pithily terse use of the underworld argot and vernacular rhythms, Chandler developed these into a prose capable of more and subtler effects. Most of the colloquial similes for which he is noted Chandler devised himself; and, fusing this pseudo-argot with the language of literature, he produced a prose through which he could paint the garish hues of the Southern California landscape and society and render the texture of the psychological and moral lives of the people who lived there. Through this style, the private detective who articulated it, and the vision which informed both, Chandler liberated the American detective novel from the rigidly Naturalistic world in which it had been born. After Philip Marlowe, the American private detective would still walk the shadowy alleys of the city, but he would also move down tree-lined suburban streets and the winding drives of the affluent. The whole of American society became his haunt.

Philip Marlowe's voice, unique as it is to the detective, merely reflects his character. As his language is stylized, so is Marlowe a figure from literature rather than from life. The Continental Op was a detective as Hammett knew him to exist; and as he remarked, Sam Spade was idealized only "in the sense that he is what most of the private detectives I've worked with would *like* to have been." But Marlowe bears the same relationship to a private detective as did Natty Bumppo to an early American woodsman. Behind his "hardboiled" exterior there lies an educated, romantic, and rigorously moralistic sensibility which, in the mean streets Marlowe often walks, stands out like spats at an Iowa picnic.

Chandler's re-creation of the character of the detective led to a radical shift in narrative perspective. In the first-person Continental Op novels, the reader listened to the Op describe his experiences and watched him act; in Chandler's novels, he listened to Marlowe evaluate his experiences and watch himself. As Chandler developed his art, his novels came to contain as much rumination as action. Plot, character, and action serve as occasion for Marlowe's introspective disquisitions on the nature of society and aperçus of the failing of humanity. Thus the conflict of the novels he narrates centers not so much in his confrontation with the world as in his encounters with himself.

Bernard A. Schopen, "From Puzzles to People: The Development of the American Detective Novel," *Studies in American Fiction* 7, No. 2 (Autumn 1979): 182

---

**PAUL SKENAZY**     Chandler had the express motive of creating a contemporary version of the medieval romance tradition. When Hammett began writing, his first hero was nameless. Even his own alias, "Peter Collinson," signified "nobody's son" in street jargon. The voice of the stories came from the crowd. Chandler, on the other hand, experimented with "Mallory" as his hero's name in the early stories, and settled finally on Philip Marlowe, referring to Philip Sidney and Christopher Marlowe, a reference at once literary, historic, and chivalric. The name is natural and affected, realistic and symbolic. The detective partakes of the everyday yet is guided by the imperative "must" of Chandler's remarks.

Chandler writes of actual Los Angeles streets, and he gives his characters allusive names such as Quest, Grayle, Kingsley. He entitles his books *The Big Sleep, Farewell, My Lovely, The Long Goodbye, The Lady in the Lake*. He invests the sordid environment with romantic longing, with tradition, with an added grace note of sentiment. He also willingly mocks his own pretensions: the "sleep" is death; the "lovely" is a killer and the "farewell" a killing; the "goodbye" is long because a man betrays Marlowe and preys upon his friendship; the "lady" is a murder victim and a dangerous killer, the "lake" a discarded Hollywood set, a military base, a vacation resort.

These poetic evocations and Arthurian echoes function as irony and emphasis. They remind us how romance and idealism have been corrupted by seduction and deceit, and how, even within the inverted and immortal patterns of experience the contemporary world offers, a kind of epic meaning remains, as well as a need for a "hero," a man "in search of hidden truth."

Paul Skenazy, *The New Wild West: The Urban Mysteries of Dashiell Hammett and Raymond Chandler* (Boise: Boise State University, 1982), pp. 32–33

---

**SCOTT R. CHRISTIANSON**     By the end of Chandler's novels, Philip Marlowe has come to the end of a series of episodic experiences; he has also realized—and proceeds to offer—some explanation of the mysteries and problems he has encountered. He details "whodunit." But the image of modern chaos and corruption revealed in the course of his "case" overwhelms any mere solution to "whodunit," because the world is in such disorder, and the reasons for that are so very complex. Moreover, in the evolution of Chandler's fiction from *The Big Sleep* (1939) to *Playback* (1958), Marlowe's attitude toward the civilization of modern California and the city-scape of Los Angeles changes from one of savvy-if-critical comfort in the milieu to unmitigated disgust and disillusionment. As Geoffrey O'Brien remarks about "the extended arias of *The Little Sister* [1949] and *The Long Goodbye* [1953]," Marlowe "collides with an ultimate sense of the void."

Consider the basic structure of Chandler's novels: Marlowe proceeds almost blindly, at the mercy of disparate and unconnected experiences, now hitting upon something which might be a clue to some part of the mysteries he has encountered, then getting beaten up, shot full of "dope," kidnapped and imprisoned, at once helped and hindered by the nefarious characters he encounters. *Farewell, My Lovely* (1940) is paradigmatic in this respect, with Marlowe's sojourn in the cultish asylum and his various violent encounters with Moose Malloy and others of his ilk. Like Hamlet, the only thing Marlowe knows is that there is something rotten in the state of Denmark—or rather, California. Like Prufrock, however, Marlowe knows he is "not Prince Hamlet, nor was meant to be"; while he is the protagonist in his own story, he's just a bit player in the social drama of the L.A. Underworld. The "denouement" in Chandler's novels offers only the return of the detective to the same place he began. As in *The Big Sleep,* he is always Doghouse Reilly living Eliot's dictum that "in my end is my beginning"; in that novel, the reader will recall, one of the first characters Marlowe encounters—Carmen Sternwood—is revealed at the end to be the murderer. In a pattern repeated throughout the novels, Marlowe is no richer and has no fuller understanding of the world except for a wider experience of its discontinuity and futility.

All Marlowe can do is wait for the next case—and attempt to convey his experiences through language. And he can only convey; he cannot order that experience, except in a series of fragments or episodes. But more importantly, he can only attempt to "set his own lands in order"—which, as the course of his text reveals, has been an attempt at least to achieve some self-control, and control over his perceptions of the world, through tough talk, wisecracks, and hardboiled conceits that convey his complex sensibility.

> Scott R. Christianson, "A Heap of Broken Images: Hardboiled Detective Fiction and the Discourse(s) of Modernity," *The Cunning Craft: Original Essays on Detective Fiction and Contemporary Literary Theory*, ed. Ronald G. Walker and June M. Frazer (Macomb: Western Illinois University, 1990), p. 143

**MARTIN AMIS**     Raymond Chandler created a figure who hovered somewhere between cult and myth: he is both hot and cool, both virile and sterile. He pays a price for his freedom from veniality: he is untouchable in all senses; he cannot be corrupted, not by women, not by money, not by America.

> Martin Amis, "Sin Has Come a Long Way Since 1939," *New York Times Book Review*, 27 January 1991, p. 9

# ▨ *Bibliography*

*The Big Sleep.* 1939.

*Farewell, My Lovely.* 1940.

*The High Window.* 1942.

*The Lady in the Lake.* 1943.

*Five Murderers.* 1944.

*Raymond Chandler's Mystery Omnibus.* 1944.

*Five Sinister Characters.* 1945.

*Red Wind: A Collection of Short Stories.* 1946.

*Spanish Blood: A Collection of Short Stories.* 1946.

*Finger Man and Other Stories.* 1947.

*The Little Sister.* 1949.

*The Simple Art of Murder.* 1950.

*Trouble Is My Business and Other Stories.* 1950.

*Pick-Up on Noon Street: Five Stories from* The Simple Art of Murder. 1950.

*The Long Goodbye.* 1953.

*The Raymond Chandler Omnibus.* 1953.

*Smart-Aleck Kill.* 1953.

*Playback*. 1958.

*Pearls Are a Nuisance*. 1958.

*Raymond Chandler Speaking*. Ed. Dorothy Gardiner and Kathrine Sorley Walker. 1962.

*The Second Chandler Omnibus*. 1962.

*Chandler on Proof Reading*. 1963.

*Killer in the Rain*. 1964.

*Chandler Before Marlowe: Raymond Chandler's Early Prose and Poetry 1908–1912*. Ed. Matthew J. Bruccoli. 1973.

*The Blue Dahlia: A Screenplay*. Ed. Matthew J. Bruccoli. 1976.

*The Notebooks of Raymond Chandler and English Summer: A Gothic Romance*. Ed. Frank MacShane. 1976.

*Letters: Raymond Chandler and James M. Fox*. Ed. James Pepper. 1978.

*Selected Letters*. Ed. Frank MacShane. 1981.

*Backfire*. 1984.

*Raymond Chandler's Unknown Thriller: The Screenplay of Playback*. 1985.

*Raymond Chandler's Los Angeles*. Ed. Elizabeth Ward and Alain Silver. 1987.

*Poodle Springs* (with Robert B. Parker). 1989.

⊞ ⊞ ⊞

# Daphne du Maurier
## *1907–1989*

DAPHNE DU MAURIER was born on May 13, 1907, in London, the second daughter of the actor and manager Gerald du Maurier and the granddaughter of George du Maurier, author of *Trilby* and other popular novels of the late nineteenth century. Du Maurier was very reluctant to release biographical information about herself, and we know little beyond what she herself tells us in her autobiography, *Growing Pains* (1977; published in the U.S. as *Myself When Young*), which carries her life down to 1932. It is clear from that memoir that du Maurier is obsessed with her own family history: she has written an account of her family, *The du Mauriers* (1937); a biography of her father, *Gerald: A Portrait* (1934); and a novel based on her ancestors, *The Glass-Blowers* (1963).

Gerald raised his three daughters as boys, teaching them cricket and boxing. In *Growing Pains* du Maurier writes: "Why wasn't I born a boy? They do all the brave things." In 1916 the family moved to Hampstead, where du Maurier attended a day school in Oak Hill Park and later took private lessons. In 1923 she was sent to a finishing school at Camposena, near Paris. By the time she had graduated, her family had purchased an estate in Cornwall, named Ferryside. For most of the rest of her life du Maurier would live in this region, drawing inspiration from it and writing two descriptive accounts of it, *Vanishing Cornwall* (1967) and *Enchanted Cornwall* (1989).

Du Maurier had attempted short stories and plays in the early 1920s, but in 1929 she worked on her first novel, *The Loving Spirit*, which was published in 1931. The novel so captivated Frederick A. M. Browning, a major in the Grenadier Guards, that he wished to visit the region in Cornwall in which it was set; he and du Maurier met the next year, and they married on July 19, 1932. They would eventually have three children.

In 1936 du Maurier published *Jamaica Inn*, about an actual hostelry in Cornwall. The next year, while stationed with her husband in Alexandria,

Egypt, she wrote *Rebecca* (1938), which became a best-seller; Alfred Hitchcock's film version of it won Best Picture at the Academy Awards. Du Maurier also wrote a play version of it. Over the next several years she had to fend off two accusations that the novel had been plagiarized, but on both occasions she was exonerated. A notebook she had kept while writing the novel was published in 1980.

In 1943 du Maurier purchased a nearby estate in Cornwall, Menabilly, where she lived until 1969. It was here that she wrote most of her novels, many of which became best-sellers: *Frenchman's Creek* (1941), *Hungry Hill* (1943), *The King's General* (1946), *My Cousin Rachel* (1951), and others. Du Maurier's formula of mixing the genres of mystery, suspense, melodrama, and historical fiction attracted many readers; in some of her short stories she even ventured into the supernatural, notably in "The Birds" (in *The Apple Tree*, 1952), also filmed by Hitchcock. Du Maurier was made a Fellow of the Royal Society of Literature in 1952 and a Dame Commander of the Order of the British Empire in 1969, but mainstream critics still failed to take her seriously.

In 1965 du Maurier's husband died, leaving her devastated. Four years later she moved out of Menabilly and into Par, a neighboring town in Cornwall. Although continuing to write novels and stories, she turned her attention more to nonfiction, writing two books about Sir Francis Bacon and her autobiography. Daphne du Maurier died on April 19, 1989.

# ▓ *Critical Extracts*

**J. D. BERESFORD**      *Rebecca* is a book temptingly easy to criticise or to praise. It will unquestionably be popular, a book to be read on holiday or at any other time. After the rather too highly coloured first chapter, which with the beginning of the second might more fitly have come at the end instead of the beginning, the story is one that will abstract the attention from the most insistent surroundings, a crowded beach or an hotel lounge. I am not ashamed to say that it held me so powerfully that I grudged all interruptions until it was finished.

Nevertheless, if I am to be honest in criticism, I must not let my enthusiasm forbid any reference to the faults of which I was actually conscious in reading.

Of the other faults I recognise now, nearly a week later, I will say nothing. They represent the chilly business of purely literary criticism. But even at the moments of deepest absorption I was a little irritated by my consciousness that two of the characters were overdrawn. The first of them is Mrs. Danvers, the housekeeper of the lovely house in the West Country, known tout court as Manderley, in which the greater part of the action is played out. All I have to say of Mrs. Danvers is that she is like a character out of one of Le Fanu's most bizarre novels, a creature of the novelist's imagination. The other is Jack Favell, who is consistently more caddish than any man ought to be, even in fiction. These two people momentarily disturbed my sense of reality in reading, as did also the "cold dank fog" that came up from the sea on the wrong kind of day at the wrong time of year and endured just long enough to serve the author's rather too evident purpose.

But, having entered a note of these reactions, I can now praise *Rebecca* without stint. ⟨. . .⟩

I have no intention of spoiling the reader's pleasure in the book by revealing the plot. It is sufficient to suggest that our girlish heroine, so deeply in love with her middle-aged husband, so painfully conscious of her own gaucherie and ignorance in that world still overpoweringly redolent of the beauty and efficiency of the dead Rebecca, emerges at a stroke from her oppression by that powerful ghost not by any forcing of the circumstances or action but by a sudden revelation of what is, in effect, the inevitable truth, which explains, as truth must, without any distortion of the facts. And, as a last word, I must add that the actual writing of the book has the compelling quality that holds the attention in thrall, keeping our interest unintermittently rapt in the story.

J. D. Beresford, "Two Novels for Holiday," *Manchester Guardian*, 5 August 1938, p. 5

---

**JOHN RAYMOND**     In the 'thirties Miss du Maurier was a kind of poor woman's Charlotte Brontë. Her *Rebecca*, whatever one's opinions of its ultimate merits, was a *tour de force*. In its own way and century, it has achieved a position in English Literature comparable to "Monk" Lewis's *The Bleeding Nun* or Mrs. Radcliffe's *Mysteries of Udolpho*. To-day Miss du Maurier the novelist is Miss Blurb's favourite Old Girl whose published appearances are heralded with the brouhaha of a privileged ex-hockey captain come down to give the home team a few hints about attack. This, one imagines her telling newcomers to St. Gollancz's, is how it should be done. Frankly, I cannot help feeling that Miss du Maurier's books have been successfully filmed so often that by now she may be said not so much to write a novel as shoot it. The present scenario ⟨My Cousin Rachel⟩ is a honey for any Hollywood or Wardour Street tycoon. Slick, effective, utterly mechanical, the book is a triumphant and uncanny example of the way in which a piece of writing can be emasculated by unconsciously "having it arranged" for another medium. Close-ups, fade-ins, sequences by candlelight or long shots from the terrace—it has all been taken care of in the script and there is little call for anything in the way of imagination on the part of the director. One can hear the Technicolor cameras turning happily on page 59:

> The waggonettes were silhouetted on the further hill, and the waiting horses and the moving figures black dots on the skyline. The shocks of corn were golden in the last rays of the sun. The sea was very blue, almost purple where it covered the rocks, and had that deep full look about it that always comes with the flood tide. The fishing fleet had put out and were standing eastward to catch the shore breeze. Back at home the house was in shadow now, only the weather-vane on the top of the clock-tower catching a loose shaft of light.

The recipe is a simple but golden one. Time (vaguely Regency), place (Cornish Riviera) and Theme (the Wicked Lady) have all been unerringly chosen. The cast—Siren, Siren's lover, Hero-narrator, Hero-narrator's cousin, Nice Girl, Nice Girl's Father, Family Butler, Family Butler's Stooge— loom up appealingly at us out of Spotlight. Producers, admiring the general effect, will forgive such occasional anachronisms, as "forget it," "slapped my bottom with a hair-brush," and "Why not tell these gossips I'm a recluse and spend all my spare time scribbling Latin verses? That might shake them." Boyish sulks, mares in a lather, and a lot of old lace at the throat and wrist, eked out with constant cups of poisoned tisane, complete the formula. A rare and irresistible bit of kitsch, whose clichés will soon be jostling and clashing in merry carillons up and down the premier cinema circuits of the English-speaking world.

John Raymond, "New Novels," New Statesman and Nation, 11 August 1951, p. 163

**SYLVIA BERKMAN**     Daphne du Maurier is a specialist in horror. Her creative intelligence is resourceful, her command of eerie atmosphere persuasive and precise, her sense of shock-timing exceptionally skilled. In this collection of eight stories ⟨Kiss Me Again, Stranger⟩ (of which all but two are very long) she explores horror in a variety of forms; in the macabre, in the psychologically deranged, in the supernatural, in the fantastic, most painfully of all, in the sheer cruelty of human beings in interrelationship. Yet on the whole the volume offers absorbing rather than oppressive reading because chiefly one's intellect is engaged: the emotional content remains subordinate. Broadly speaking, for the most part these are stories of detection as well, with the contributing elements of excitation, suspense, and climax manipulated with a seasoned hand.

Miss du Maurier is most successful, I believe (as most of us are), when her intentions are unmixed. "Kiss Me Again, Stranger," the title story, adeptly marshals the ingredients best suited to her abilities. Here in a trim, fluently moving narrative she developed an incident in war-torn London, with no purpose beyond the immediate recounting of a sad and grisly tale. A young mechanic, a simple, sensitive, likable good chap, attracted by a pretty usherette at a cinema palace, joins her on her bus ride home, to be led, bewildered, into a cemetery, where her conduct baffles him, to say the least. The girl, so gentle, wistful, languorous, and sleepy, turns out to be psychopathically obsessed, with a vindictive animus against members of the R.A.F. The summary is unjust, for Miss du Maurier forcibly anchors her story in a strange lonely graveyard atmosphere, with night rain falling cold and dreary on the flat tombs, which both reflects and reinforces the mortal impairment of the young girl's nature and the destruction of the young man's hopes, in a charnel world dislocated by the larger horror of war.

In "Kiss Me Again, Stranger," all separate aspects of the narrative fuse. "The Birds," however, essentially a far more powerful story, is marred by unresolved duality of intent. Slowly, with intensifying accurate detail, Miss du Maurier builds up her account of the massed attack of the starving winter birds on humankind, the familiar little land birds, the battalions of gulls bearing in rank upon rank from the sea, the murderous predatory birds of prey descending with ferocious beaks and talons to rip, rend, batter, and kill. The struggle involved is the ancient struggle of man against the forces of nature, Robinson Crusoe's struggle to overcome an elemental diversity through cunning, logic, and wit. The turning of this material also into a political fable, with overt references to control from Russia and aid from

America, to my mind dissipates the full impact of a stark and terrifying tale. ⟨. . .⟩

Miss du Maurier is not primarily concerned with character. Her figures are presented with swift unhesitating strokes; through them a fairly complicated history unfolds. Yet every account of human action contains its residue of human experience; and Miss du Maurier's main themes, if seriously regarded, are neither haphazard nor trivial: again and again she returns to the consideration of our human predicament, to frustration, destruction, loss, betrayal, and needless suffering, Joyce's themes of the *Dubliners,* conveyed through the obverse method of a decided emphasis on plot. In general in this volume complexities of plot disinfect horror to a pungent and provocative spice.

Sylvia Berkman, "A Skilled Hand Weaves a Net of Horror," *New York Herald Tribune Book Review,* 15 March 1953, p. 4

---

**LaTOURETTE STOCKWELL**     Daphne Du Maurier is one of the most widely read of contemporary novelists, but rarely, and then only in reviews, have her writings been responsibly considered by serious critics.

How does it happen that an author who labors so diligently and well as to be irresistible to millions of readers in at least seven countries is ignored by the literary critics? What do her readers find so satisfying? Why do the critics turn away? If these questions are explored and answered it may be possible not only to assess fairly Miss Du Maurier's considerable literary effort but also to arrive at some conclusions about contemporary taste and the difference between a popular novel and an important one. ⟨. . .⟩

E. M. Forster, some years ago, characterized one type of novel reader (*not* the kind he admires) as saying, "What does a novel do? Why tell a story of course, and I've no use for it if it didn't. Very bad taste on my part no doubt, but I like a story. You can take your art, you can take your literature, you can take your music, but give me a good story. And I like the story to be a story, mind, and my wife's the same."

Liking a good story has been a characteristic of the human race for some time, and Mr. Forster's man epitomizes the attitude of the "common reader," of whom there are many more today than there have ever been. Miss Du Maurier is a masterly teller of stories, and, in all fairness, it must be said that it is unlikely that her main purpose has even been anything more than to entertain. At her best, she entertains superbly. Her facility as a raconteuse, her skill in building up dramatic suspense, the fertility of her invention in creating characters who live adventurously and love unconventionally (but never with shoddy eroticism), all these appeal overwhelmingly to the average reader looking for a temporary escape from the perils of this mortal life.

But art goes beyond the immediate interest and satisfaction of the uncritical reader. Virtuosity and literary technique alone cannot produce a work of art. If a novel is to possess even the intimations of immortality, there must be a relationship between literature and ideas, between literature and society. Convictions must be shaken, emotions disturbed. It is here that Miss Du Maurier fails, and the critics walk out. In indulging her predilection for creating an escape world for her readers, she has set a serious limitation upon her talents, and it is positively exasperating to have to conclude that an author who writes as well as Miss Du Maurier does has yet to produce an important novel.

> LaTourette Stockwell, "Best Sellers and the Critics: A Case History," *College English* 16, No. 4 (January 1955): 214, 221

**BEVERLEY NICHOLS**        Daphne du Maurier's almost passionate delight in long periods of solitude has sometimes been diagnosed as a "neurosis." The label is an ugly reflection on contemporary values. If it is neurotic to crave for silence in which to think and to create, then all the saints were neurotics and all the poets and the musicians—though not, perhaps, all the contemporary novelists, whose works so often give the impression of having been composed during a rush hour in one of the more popular public conveniences of the larger railway stations or bus terminals.

Neurosis or no neurosis, she draws silence round her like a cloak. You would think that Menabilly was quiet enough, with its great rooms that are so often empty, and its vast kitchens in which—if she can possibly prevent it—no domestic servants are in evidence. ⟨. . .⟩

But Menabilly is not quiet enough for her. Hence the hut. It is a little wooden affair which reminds one of Bernard Shaw's hut at Ayot St. Lawrence. It stands on the edge of the woods, looking out to sea. Here every morning soon after ten she sits down at a typewriter and creates. It is an exhausting business. She said to me, "Every book is like a purge; at the end of it one is empty . . . like a dry shell on the beach, waiting for the tide to come in again." ⟨. . .⟩

She said also, "I am not so much interested in people as in types—types who represent great forces of good or evil. I don't care very much whether John Smith jilts Mary Robinson, goes to bed with Jane Brown and then refuses to pay the hotel bill. But I *am* passionately interested in human cruelty, human lust and human avarice—and, of course, their counterparts in the scale of virtue."

Thus, one might say, she creates in reverse. An abstract vice or virtue moves her—and it moves her so strongly that it becomes personified. It comes to life in her mind as a cardboard symbol. And then, little by little, the cardboard becomes saturated by her own concern for the forces which evoked it—and thereby comes to life. 〈. . .〉

All of which makes one feel that there may perhaps be some truth in her remark that writers must be difficult to live with. A sadistic, drunken innkeeper, with a side line in wrecking and murder, must sometimes have been an embarrassing guest at Menabilly, even if his spirit was temporarily housed in the slight figure of a lady in a faded blue suit.

> Beverley Nichols, "Daphne du Maurier," *Ladies' Home Journal*, November 1956, pp. 29, 32

---

**MARGARET MILLAR**     This 〈*Don't Look Now*〉 is a collection of five uneasy pieces. In each one the reader is given an intriguing situation, a series of neatly planted clues and a generous number of plot twists, the kind of thing that Bennett Cerf has lovingly referred to as shenanigans. His taste for shenanigans must be shared by a great many readers: Miss du Maurier has been a household word for more than 30 years, and the most famous Rebecca in the world today is not from Sunnybrook Farm or the Book of Genesis but from a lonely old English mansion called Manderley.

> Margaret Millar, [Review of *Don't Look Now*], *New York Times Book Review*, 17 October 1971, p. 56

---

**ROGER BROMLEY**     First published in 1938, at a time that is when capitalist society was experiencing one of the deepest crises in its history, Daphne du Maurier's *Rebecca* at first sight seems remarkable for its total lack of reference to anything that might even hint of the existence of that crisis. The simplest way of accounting for this lack of reference would be to consign the text to the category of 'escapist fiction', a means of relief for people whose everyday experience was dominated by the reality of the depression. Another response would be to describe the text as likely to be read by those upon whom the realities of unemployment and deprivation would be likely to have had little impact. It is very difficult, at this distance in time, to reconstruct a map of the possible readership of the novel, but that it was an immediate bestseller indicates that it is improbable that a simple pattern of readership along class lines could be produced. This would certainly be even more improbable for an analysis of the cinema audiences that saw the film version in 1941. ⟨. . .⟩

As surface explanations these accounts might seem adequate, but a cultural analysis of *Rebecca* ⟨. . .⟩ argues for a reading of the text that sees its apparent absences as determining presences at the level of its deep structures. In other words, *Rebecca* can be read as a response to the crisis of the 1930s, if it is seen in the broader context of the various means sought to resolve what was not only an economic crisis but also a crisis in hegemony. ⟨. . .⟩

In bourgeois ideology, woman's sexuality and reproduction have to be incorporated in the sphere of the family which, in turn, becomes the repository of emotions, of sexuality, physical well-being, and the space for situating the free choice of a unique beloved. ⟨. . .⟩ In *Rebecca*'s extensive crisis of self and family, Maxim's emotional distress, physical ill-health, absence of affection, and his 'possession' by Rebecca all thwart the fulfilment of the bourgeois ideals. The terror and neurosis experienced by the heroine at Manderley reproduce his experience crisis, which can only be resolved in mutuality and exile from Manderley. Their original return to Manderley could be structurally related to a desire in the thirties for a return along the road back to 1913, the gold standard, free trade, laissez-faire, etc. This was an economically nostalgic solution to 1931 and the crisis, as was their attempt to return to a pre-bourgeois Manderley in which the heroine sought to reproduce the image and style of Rebecca. Both actions were doomed, and could only persist at a distance and in retrospect as a cultural memory and image of an *idea* of a golden age: socially marked by grace, beauty, and an edenic landscape; economically, by free trade, a non-interventionist stage, the gold standard, etc.

The heroine grows as Rebecca recedes, as she expels her shadow self, the image within. The text ritually sheds the 'perverted' woman, Eve incarnate, the spoiler of the paradisal estate, to which there is no going back. It is important that Rebecca's body is recovered from the sea, because until that time her spirit cannot be laid. Her significantly decomposed *body* (vessel of life for woman and, in this instance, the agency of carnality) is buried in the family vault. This burial marks not just her displacement by the heroine (the truly spiritual woman, though materially poor and of 'humble' origin) but it denotes the burying of a model of family also. The seemingly spiritual woman is revealed as grossly carnal, and the recovery of her body prefigures the guarantee of the real aristocratic legacy, its persistence as an *idea*, or a codification of a set of ideas, which have no practical function but serve the ruling bloc as a series of fundamental principles, general truths, and rules of conduct (maxims, in other words!) manifested above all in style—'gestures which reveal quintessences'—and, at a local level, in the private co-existence of an exclusive, bourgeois-styled relationship enjoyed in exile by Mr. and Mrs. de Winter, sustained by a cultural memory. ⟨. . .⟩

Maxim loses his country house (a reference to a specific historical reality recognised by the text) and gives up many of the functions, political and social, consequent upon its ownership, for a personal life relatively confined and austere, and in some ways rootless. What he recovers and retains, through the fusion and assimilation of his 'lowly' second wife, is a transfusion of ideals and values, and a *style* with an important ideological function, that of the gentleman, signed by a morality of fair play, selflessness, courage, moderation and self-control, independence and responsibility. All of which can be summed up by the word *authority*, commanding deference. This authority is something which, incidentally, is bestowed upon the narrative by the nature of its being a personal testament (the ultimate reference in a liberal ideology): an 'I' for the truth, commanding acquiescence in its veracity. The text, therefore, has an authoritative structure as well as being about authority.

> Roger Bromley, "The Gentry, Bourgeois Hegemony and Popular Fiction," *Literature and History* 7, No. 2 (Autumn 1981): 166, 172–3, 176

---

**RICHARD KELLY**     Du Maurier's literary style seems inextricably related to her insulated life-style. There is a vast body of knowledge and a large segment of society she never really knew or understood. *Hungry Hill*, for example, is a notable failure because she knows little about Ireland and even less about the Irish poor. She is not interested in ideas, in science, technology, religion, politics, economics, or philosophy. She exhibits little

curiosity about or knowledge of cultures other than her own. Her circum-
scribed world is a fantasy built upon Cornish history, family life, sailing,
nineteenth-century poetry, gardens, love affairs, upper-middle-class sensibili-
ties, and supernatural happenings. Her fiction reflects the psychology of a
reclusive woman accustomed to success who, in her youth, was desirous of
burning with a hard gemlike flame, aspiring towards freedom and heightened
emotion, and who, later in life, was content to stoke the home fires of
family and patriotism.

The literary establishment clearly wants nothing to do with Daphne du
Maurier. There are no critical essays or books about her. Her only critics
to date have been the many book reviewers who, for the most part, heralded
each novel as a gift of genius, though most agree that she never surpassed
the level of excellence she achieved in *Rebecca*. The fact that millions of
people read her novels certainly works against her approval by literary critics,
who are not inclined to prize what the popular audience does. By the
standards of contemporary literary criticism, most of du Maurier's works do
not hold up well. Her prose, while straightforward and clear, is not especially
interesting. There is little imagery, symbolism, or ambiguity in her writing.
Her characters are often undeveloped, and her plots become all-important.
Her style is conventional, her sentences unmemorable, and her story lines
contrived. Compared with authors like Graham Greene or John Steinbeck
she seems shallow and commercial.

Why, then, have her novels been so successful? Why is it that she has
so many closet readers, sophisticated people who enjoy her works but who
are reluctant to proclaim their enjoyment? Despite her failure as a thinker
and as a stylist, du Maurier is a master storyteller who knows how to
manipulate female fantasies. She creates a world that is simple, romantic,
usually unambiguous, adventuresome, mysterious, dangerous, erotic, pictur-
esque, and satisfying. It is a world that contrasts sharply with the mundane
realities of ordinary existence, and it is a world that does not require the
reader to suffer the pains of introspection and analysis. It is, in short, a
world that brings considerable pleasure to millions of readers, especially
women.

Richard Kelly, *Daphne du Maurier* (Boston: Twayne, 1987), pp. 141–42

---

**MARGARET FORSTER**     Her writing career, properly beginning
in 1931 with the publication of *The Loving Spirit*, and effectively ending in

1977, spanned a time of great change in literary fashions and tastes and in the growth and importance of women's fiction. For a while, Daphne was flowing with the tide, but after the publication of *The Scapegoat* in 1957 her kind of novel, as she herself realized, was no longer in sympathy with the trend towards the realistic fiction she hated. She had it in her to change and produce something different but not the desire: she wanted to stay true to an older tradition. Her writing self, that 'No. 2' which caused her so much trouble, demanded escapism, not reality, and it was only obliquely, and especially in her short stories, that she was able to give expression to it. This distinction—between her living self and her writing self, between the person she was on the outside and the quite different person she knew herself to be on the inside—was one she herself made repeatedly. When she was able to balance the two selves, she was happy, as she was in the thirties, but when the two separated, as they began to do towards the end of the fifties, she was miserable, and the strain of juggling these two different personae brought her near to breakdown. In the mid-seventies, when her writing ability left her, it became tragically clear that her 'living' self could not be content, or even survive, on its own. Never was there a clearer case of a writer who 'lived to write', or of a writer for whom life came to have no meaning and little joy without writing.

Daphne du Maurier, Dame of the British Empire, a world-wide and enduring bestselling author for nearly fifty years, had a loving family, devoted friends, and everything, it would seem, a woman could possibly have wanted, but if she could not write all this seemed worthless. Her novels and stories gave pleasure to millions, and among them were at least three worthy of a place in any literary canon—*Rebecca*, *The Scapegoat* and *The House on the Strand*—but what they gave to *her* was more important. Through writing she lived more truly than she did in her daily life—it gave her satisfaction, release and a curious sense of elation. Norman Collins so astutely said, 'No one ever imagined more than Daphne.' And it was the fire of her imagination which warmed and excited her millions of readers, and still does.

Margaret Forster, *Daphne du Maurier* (London: Chatto & Windus, 1993), pp. 415–16

# ⬛ *Bibliography*

*The Loving Spirit.* 1931.

*I'll Never Be Young Again.* 1932.

*The Progress of Julius.* 1933.

*Gerald: A Portrait.* 1934.

*Jamaica Inn.* 1936.

*The du Mauriers.* 1937.

*Rebecca.* 1938.

*Rebecca* (drama). 1940.

*Happy Christmas.* 1940.

*Come Wind, Come Weather.* 1940.

*Frenchman's Creek.* 1941.

*Escort.* 1943.

*Hungry Hill.* 1943.

*Nothing Hurts for Long and Escort.* 1943.

*Consider the Lilies.* 1943.

*Spring Picture.* 1944.

*Leading Lady.* 1945.

*The Years Between.* 1945.

*London and Paris.* 1945.

*The King's General.* 1946.

*September Tide.* 1949.

*The Parasites.* 1949.

*My Cousin Rachel.* 1951.

*The Young George du Maurier: A Selection of His Letters 1860–67* (editor). 1951.

*The Apple Tree: A Short Novel and Some Stories (Kiss Me Again, Stranger: A Collection of Eight Stories, Long and Short).* 1952.

*Mary Anne.* 1954.

*Early Stories.* 1954.

*The Scapegoat.* 1957.

*The Breaking Point: Eight Stories.* 1959.

*The Infernal World of Branwell Brontë.* 1960.

*The Treasury of du Maurier Short Stories.* 1960.

*The Lover and Other Stories.* 1961.

*Castle Dor* (with Sir Arthur Quiller-Couch). 1962.

*The Glass-Blowers.* 1963.

*Best Stories* by Phyllis Bottome (editor). 1963.

*The Flight of the Falcon.* 1965.

*Vanishing Cornwall.* 1967.

*The House on the Strand.* 1969.

*Not After Midnight and Other Stories* ⟨*Don't Look Now*⟩. 1971.

*Rule Britannia.* 1972.

*The Birds.* 1972.

*Golden Lads: Sir Francis Bacon, Anthony Bacon, and Their Friends.* 1975.

*The Winding Stair: Francis Bacon, His Rise and Fall.* 1976.

*Echoes from the Macabre: Selected Stories.* 1976.

*Growing Pains: The Shaping of a Writer* ⟨*Myself When Young: The Shaping of a Writer*⟩. 1977.

*The Rendezvous and Other Stories.* 1980.

*The Birds and Other Stories.* Ed. Richard Adams. 1980.

*The Rebecca Notebook and Other Memories.* 1980.

*Daphne du Maurier's Classics of the Macabre.* 1987.

*Enchanted Cornwall: Her Pictorial Memoir.* Ed. Piers Dudgeon. 1989.

*Selections from Menabilly: Portrait of a Friendship.* Ed. Oriel Malet. 1992.

# Ian Fleming
## 1908–1964

IAN LANCASTER FLEMING was born in London on May 28, 1908. His father, a Conservative Member of Parliament, was killed in World War I. Fleming's early history runs almost parallel to that of his creation James Bond. A wealthy and reckless adolescent, he was educated at—and expelled from—Eton, Sandhurst, the University of Munich, and the University of Geneva. Instead of entering the Secret Service, however, Fleming became Moscow correspondent for Reuters news service, a post he held from 1929 to 1933. He worked in London as a banker and stockbroker before returning to Moscow in 1939 as a reporter for the London *Times* and spy for British Naval Intelligence, acquiring knowledge he would later use in his Bond stories.

Fleming returned to journalism after the war as foreign manager of Kemsley (later Thomson) Newspapers, remaining there until 1959. In 1949 he began to publish the *Book Collector*, a periodical he maintained for the rest of his life. The year 1952 proved a turning point for Fleming: he married Anne Charteris, Lady Rothemere, with whom he would have one child; built Goldeneye, his beloved house in Jamaica; and there wrote *Casino Royale*, the first James Bond novel, published the next year. Like Fleming, Bond was an avid gambler, gourmet, sportsman (he particularly liked golf, as detailed in *Goldfinger* [1959]), and driver of fast cars. Both were meticulous about their appearance and idiosyncratic in their taste in women. Unlike Fleming, Bond was a secret agent, licensed to kill, pursued by beautiful women and grotesque villains.

The Bond books—which Fleming produced annually from 1953 on—were successful from the first, but sales exploded in 1961 when the film version of *Dr. No* was released. It was the first of an apparently endless series. Fleming began to experiment with the Bond formula at about the same time, writing a story collection, *For Your Eyes Only* (1960), a first-person account by a damsel in distress, *The Spy Who Loved Me* (1962), and a concluding trilogy that took Bond through marriage, a nervous breakdown, and brainwashing: *On Her Majesty's Secret Service* (1963), *You Only Live Twice* (1964), and *The Man with the Golden Gun* (1965). Two additional stories were collected in the posthumous *Octopussy and The Living Daylights* (1966).

In addition to the Bond books, Fleming wrote a *Times* column in the 1950s as "Atticus"; two nonfiction books, *The Diamond Smugglers* (1957) and *Thrilling Cities* (1963); and the children's adventure *Chitty-Chitty-Bang-Bang* (1964), which was filmed four years later. Ian Fleming died on August 12, 1964. Kingsley Amis attempted in 1968 to continue the Bond series; the American suspense writer John Gardner has done so since 1981.

# ▓ *Critical Extracts*

**PAUL JOHNSON**      I have just finished what is, without doubt, the nastiest book I have ever read. It is a new novel entitled *Dr No* and the author is Mr Ian Fleming. Echoes of Mr Fleming's fame had reached me before, and I had been repeatedly urged to read his books by literary friends whose judgment I normally respect. When this new novel appeared, therefore, I obtained a copy and started to read. By the time I was a third of the way through, I had to suppress a strong impulse to throw the thing away, and only continued reading because I realised that here was a social phenomenon of some importance.

There are three basic ingredients in *Dr No*, all unhealthy, all thoroughly English: the sadism of a schoolboy bully, the mechanical, two-dimensional sex-longings of a frustrated adolescent, and the crude, snob-cravings of a suburban adult. Mr Fleming has no literary skill, the construction of the book is chaotic, and entire incidents and situations are inserted, and then forgotten, in a haphazard manner. But the three ingredients are manufactured and blended with deliberate, professional precision; Mr Fleming dishes up his recipe with all the calculated accountancy of a Lyons Corner House.

Paul Johnson, "Sex, Snobbery and Sadism," *New Statesman*, 5 April 1958, p. 430

**IAN FLEMING**      When I wrote the first one, in 1953, I wanted Bond to be an extremely dull, uninteresting man to whom things happened; I wanted him to be the blunt instrument. One of the bibles of my youth was Birds of the West Indies, by James Bond, a well-known ornithologist, and when I was casting about for a name for my protagonist I thought, My God, that's the dullest name I've ever heard, so I appropriated it. Now the dullest name in the world has become an exciting one. Mrs. Bond once wrote me a letter thanking me for using it. ⟨. . .⟩

⟨. . .⟩ I think the reason for his success is that people are lacking in heroes in real life today ⟨. . .⟩ Heroes are always getting knocked—Philip and Mountbatten are examples of this—and I think people absolutely long for heroes. The thing that's wrong with the new anticolonialism is that no one has yet found a Negro hero. They're scratching around with Tshombe, but . . . Well, I don't regard James Bond precisely as a hero, but at least he does get on and do his duty, in an extremely corny way, and in the end, after giant despair, he wins the girl or the jackpot or whatever it may be. My books have no social significance, except a deleterious one; they're considered to have too much violence and too much sex. But all history has that. I finished the last one, my tenth James Bond story, in Jamaica the other day; it's long and tremendously dull. It's called The Spy Who Loved Me, and it's written, supposedly, by a girl. I think it's an absolute miracle that an elderly person like me can go on turning out these books with such zest. It's really a terrible indictment of my own character—they're so adolescent. But they're fun. I think people like them because they're fun. A couple of years ago, when I was in Washington, and was driving to lunch with a friend of mine, Margaret Leiter, she spotted a young couple coming out of church, and she stopped our cab. "You must meet them," she said. "They're great fans of yours." And she introduced me to Jack and Jackie Kennedy. "Not the Ian Fleming!" they said. What could be more gratifying than that? They asked me to dinner that night, with Joe Alsop and some other characters. I think the President likes my books because he enjoys the combination of physical violence, effort, and winning in the end—like his PT-boat experience. I think James Bond may be good for him after the dry pack of the day.

Ian Fleming, cited in "Bond's Creator," New Yorker, 21 April 1962, pp. 32–34

**KINGSLEY AMIS**    These days any book in which one character inflicts physical pain on another risks being given the *sadism* label, just as any scene in which two unmarried persons embrace courts that of *compensation-*

*fantasy.* Mr. Fleming was known to be sensitive to adverse criticism of the moralizing sort, far more so than might have been expected of a writer so popular and, in his detractors' view, so painstakingly vicious. This sensitivity was probably responsible for the marked alleviation of Bond's sufferings in the last few years. In the first seven novels, ending with *Goldfinger,* he only once escaped captivity-plus-ill-usage. Since 1959, however, he has gotten away with it every time except in *You Only Live Twice,* and even there he takes a mere ten hand-blows to the head.

However, Bond's tendency to find himself tied to a chair under scientific torment is an important feature of his total character. *Sadism,* even so, comes in here oddly, I feel, since it's Bond and not any of his opponents whom the reader is invited to identify with, and Bond suffers pain, never wantonly inflicts it. *Masochism* is a more appropriate label at first sight, but is impaired by the difficulty that the masochist enjoys being knocked about. Bond gives no sign of pleasure when, for instance, he gets his little finger broken by Mr. Big's lieutenant. But I suppose he might really be enjoying himself all the time, almost without knowing it. I look forward to being told by some learned puritan that since there are "really" no accidents in life, Bond is "secretly" a glutton for punishment in some sense approaching the literal, and seeks capture "deliberately" in order to land himself a treat. "The man's very name is an indispensable implement of the perversion—*desmophilic algolagnia*—that has enslaved him"—I'll get in first if you don't look out.

All talk about a sexual component in Bond's sufferings mistakes the author's intention and misrepresents the reader's response. When Le Chiffre goes to work on Bond's testicles with a carpet beater, to take the most conspicuous case, a very well-established and basic element of the thriller story is at work. The incident has two closely related effects. It makes us feel admiration and sympathy for the hero and fear and hatred for the villain. All these feelings are heightened by the particularly dreadful and cruel method of torture used by Le Chiffre. To have pulled Bond's hair and given him a lot of lip would have been ineffective, upon both Bond and the reader. ⟨. . .⟩

The effect of this ground base of violence is partly to entertain the reader by showing him glimpses of a semi-fantasy world he might like to inhabit, but dare not. In addition, however, he is also the more likely to admire Bond as one who not only inhabits such a world by choice, but survives the worst it can do to him and comes out on top. Further, against a background so variously lethal, Bond can be seen as relatively responsible—never killing wantonly; never, or hardly ever, in cold blood; hesitating (almost fatally) to dispatch Scaramanga, probably the most efficient one-man death-dealer in the world. Now and then he even struggles with his conscience over the morality of the whole thing.

Kingsley Amis, "Sit Down, 007," *The James Bond Dossier* (New York: New American Library, 1965), pp. 12–15

---

**HENRY A. ZEIGER**     Another weak point of Fleming's is logic. There is often no good reason for people in Fleming's books to do the things they do. In *Live and Let Die,* why does Bond come to New York in the first place, since the illicit coins are coming from the Caribbean and the assignment takes him directly to Florida after he has not accomplished anything in New York? The real reason is, of course, that Fleming wants to have a scene in Harlem, mainly to throw in some New York atmosphere, but this is far too apparent. Then, why does Bond leave for Florida on a train? Mr. Big is after him and it is clear that a train ride will give him a much better crack at Bond than a plane will, yet Bond takes the train. This kind of thing, while it creates incidents that are exciting, actually diminishes suspense, for if the hero keeps making wrong moves solely to create situations in which he is in danger, we do not believe that the danger is real; if it were, he would need all his resources in order to stay alive. ⟨. . .⟩

The typical Fleming novel ⟨. . .⟩ has a beginning and an end but there is nothing much in the middle that necessarily takes us from one to the other. There is often excitement to the episodes in this middle part of the book, but these episodes rarely strengthen the tension implicit in the opposition of Bond and the villain. We never seem to feel in the course of one of these books that we are witnessing the operation of a well-adjusted machine or watching the growth of an increasingly fascinating organism from the few seeds present at the beginning. There is no sense of continuity to these books, no sense in which we feel that since X has happened, then Y must happen, which will in turn inevitably lead to Z. Without this kind of feeling, there can be no sense of urgency to the narrative and no suspense.

Still, Fleming must be doing something right, or can twenty million Englishmen be wrong? Fleming *is* doing something, something that people enjoy intensely. If a Fleming book lacks suspense, it has other qualities that make it unique. Fleming's books all unquestionably have an identity. If they are put together somewhat at random, still they are always put together in a certain way, so that the books, while very similar to each other in important respects, are rather different from those of other thriller writers.

It is my opinion that Fleming creates a consistent self-contained world which his readers can enter joyfully. ⟨. . .⟩ This world has an identifiable landscape and a unique morality, and because of this, it is not important that the books lack suspense. People who like Fleming like becoming involved in the world of these books and are not after anything so superficial as the momentary tingles of suspense.

Henry A. Zeiger, "The World of James Bond," *Ian Fleming: The Spy Who Came In with the Gold* (New York: Duell, Sloan & Pearce, 1965), pp. 129–30, 137–38

---

**DAVID HOLBROOK**        What is it in Ian Fleming's work that causes so many millions of people to be engrossed by it so that the actor who plays '007' becomes the favourite film star of the year? What enables the films to be made the biggest box-office ever? Some of this can no doubt be attributed to enormous promotion investment. But even promotion must have something to work on, and the film industry obviously saw potentialities in Fleming. Allowing for the differences between the books and the films— what were these? What causes intellectuals to write books on the 'James Bond dossier' and to take up space in weekly journals and radio programmes applauding his achievement? What brings the monarchy to the première of a Bond film? What makes for that awed adulation in the Press?

It cannot, certainly, be the quality of the writing. It is interesting to hear from teachers of slow adolescent readers that despite the lure of the cult these pupils find Fleming's prose boring. When I first read *Goldfinger* myself I found it tedious. The action is at the level of a boy's adventure paper: the same melodramatic gestures by the same paper supermen. There are the same clichés of action writing one finds in a 'Biggles' book. The crises are essentially those of the ancient staple of 'adventure' stories with the heroine tied to the rails or the hero sewn up in a sack, albeit in a new guise. The poise of the hero, with his 'equable' voice in danger, his 'quick' 'penetrating glances', and his perpetual readiness, have a long, lame ancestry. And as for 'realism'—even the dullest and most insensitive war book or 'escape' story seldom sinks to the level of such a series of stereotype phrases as Fleming's 'action' prose. ⟨. . .⟩

Considered as novels, or even as entertainment, the books are so poor in the writing that even by the standards of detective or adventure stories their quality cannot explain their world-wide appeal. When Fleming turns from adventure and action to the novelist's sphere and seeks to convey a manly 'knowingness' about human affairs in this cliché-ridden prose, this writer must surely hardly convince the kind of pupil, of average academic ability, who can yet write with clarity and sincerity in school.

> Bond said thoughtfully, 'I wouldn't get anywhere sucking up to him, asking him for a job or something of that sort, sir. I should say he's the sort of man who only respects people who are tougher or smarter than he is. I've given him one beating and the only message I got from him was that he'd like me to play golf with him. Perhaps I'd better do just that.'
> 'Fine way for one of my top men to spend his time.' The sarcasm in M.'s voice was weary, resigned.

The morality would hardly serve for an adventure story in the Biggles mode, while the language it is couched in would hardly pass in a boy's story when he reads it aloud to his class. 'Fine way for one of my top men to spend his time,' is dilute *Boy's Own Paper*. 'Weary, resigned' is an old boy's adventure story tag, too. The adventure books I read as a boy, and the stories in *The Gem* and *The Wizard* were full of this kind of heavy-handed opening: 'James Bond booked in at the Hotel des Bergues, took a bath and shower and changed his clothes. He weighed the Walther PPK in his hand and wondered whether he should take it or leave it behind. He decided to leave it.' And how often did one find this kind of chapter ending: 'Goldfinger, lit with glory by the setting sun, but with a long black shadow tied to his heels, followed Bond slowly, his eyes fixed thoughtfully on Bond's back'.

David Holbrook, "Unconscious Meaning in the 'Spy' Story," *The Masks of Hate: The Problem of False Solutions in the Culture of an Acquisitive Society* (Oxford: Oxford University Press, 1972), pp. 67–69

---

**PHILIP LARKIN**     Looking at the original canon after some twenty years confirms their almost mesmeric readability. "I ask weekly at the library for another Ian Fleming", wrote George Lyttelton to Rupert Hart-Davis in 1957, "but they are always out":

> How bad, and at the same time compellingly readable, [his] thrillers are! The pattern of all four that I have read is identical. Bond does not attract me, and that man with brains on ice and pitiless eye who organises the secret service in London seems to be a monument of ineptitude. Everything about Bond and his plans is known long before he arrives anywhere. But I cannot help reading on and there are rich satisfactions . . .

Indeed there are: the first sixty pages of *Moonraker*, culminating in the bafflement of grand-slammed Drax; the giant centipede in the bed in *Dr No*; the meeting with "Captain Nash" on the train in *From Russia with Love*; all these and many more are vibrant triumphs of excitement. And the villains seem as grotesquely menacing as they ever did; *Dr No* with his metal hands, Le Chiffre with his "obscene" Benzedrine inhaler, Mr Big and his great grey football of a head. Fleming was, in short, a natural writer with a vividly bizarre imagination and a mastery of tension. But what strikes one today is their unambiguous archaic decency. So far from being orgies of sex and sadism, as some outraged academics protested at the time, the books are nostalgic excursions into pre-Carnaby Street values, Gilbert and Sullivan as opposed to the Beatles. England is always right, foreigners are always wrong (Fleming's best villains are all foreign). Nobody, at least on our side, is a double agent, or has the remotest connection with Philby and Co. Girls are treated with kindness and consideration, lust coming a decorous third. Life's virtues are courage and loyalty, and its good things a traditional aristocracy of powerful cars, vintage wines, exclusive clubs, the old Times, the old five-pound note, the old Player's packet.

Philip Larkin, "The Batman from Blades," *Times Literary Supplement*, 9 June 1981, p. 625

---

**MEIR STERNBERG**     First, from the normative viewpoint the Bond tales project an "unrealistic" world view in that the two sides in the dramatic conflict are wholly identified with two sides in a black-and-white conflict of values, and the final dramatic result corresponds to the ideal demands of poetic justice. This structuring of values must not be dismissed as an automatic or even obligatory convention of the thriller. True, one of the most massive inter-generic developments in the history of fiction is the shift of the Renaissance and neoclassical requirement of poetic justice, with its various implications for plot (notably the happy or morally proportionate ending), from canonical to popular literature. But at the time Fleming began to write, in the early fifties, he was already free to resort to other normative options—with which he indeed flirts in his first novel, *Casino Royale* (1953), but significantly in it alone. In Maugham, for instance, Ashenden discovers to his surprise that the traitor he has been sent to trap is personably likable ⟨. . .⟩; the moral lines of demarcation intersect rather than overlap with the political lines dividing the Germans from the Allies; and dramatic probability does not necessarily coincide with any ideal moral order. Fleming, however, tends to avoid such "realistic" mixtures and complications. The conflict is patterned so as to produce in the reader a basic emotional and moral polarization (the representative of the powers of light, Western democracy with Britain at its head, confronting the powers of darkness, the Russians and their hatchet men or private archterrorists), and finally to satisfy his normatively-conditioned expectations. The plot takes the form of our desires. Fleming's (and Bond's) normative framework thus corresponds not to Ashenden's but rather to that of Ashenden's jingoistic superior, who regards any moral and psychological exploration as wasteful, un-English, and unpatriotic.

Second, from the viewpoint of the primary selection of materials, many of the characters and events populating Bond's world seem implausible (or what once used to be called "marvellous") in themselves, even to one who does not narrowly identify realism with the concentration on the ordinary and the common. Fleming's basic repertoire includes: (1) the monumental figure of the villain, driven to subdue the world by monomaniacal ambition (like Ernst Stavro Blofeld) or typical Russian imperialism (like Rosa Klebb in *From Russia, with Love*); (2) the villain's gigantic plot, whether the spoliation of Fort Knox (*Goldfinger*) or the hijacking of NATO nuclear bombs with a view to extorting a ransom of £100,000,000 (*Thunderball*); (3) the head of the British Secret Service—retired admiral, member of aristocratic clubs, known by the initial M—who inspires his agents to amazing feats of self-sacrifice; (4) the tough (and necessarily beautiful) girl who, after a token resistance, is charmed by the hero to the point of cheerfully risking her life for his sake; and of course (5) the hero himself, vanquishing single-handed the formidable enemy who has reduced the whole might of the West to a state of helplessness. ⟨. . .⟩

Third, the combinational principles generating and propelling ("dynamizing") the sequence of events also raises a big realistic question mark. Again, what I have in mind are problems of probability underlying Fleming's art as a whole rather than locally arising in this or that work, owing to such variable factors as the obtrusive series of coincidences in *On Her Majesty's Secret Service*. In this respect, the Bond stories are characterized by a formulaic patterning of events: starting from the disclosure of the assignment in M's office; passing through the stages of exploratory action and clash, which usually result in Bond's being captured by his adversary; and ending in miraculous escape and sexual reward. Indeed, one can say of Fleming—what is true of most writers, including popular writers, only at a higher level of abstraction—that he produced a single story in about a dozen variations.

Meir Sternberg, "Knight Meets Dragon in the James Bond Saga: Realism and Reality-Models," *Style* 17, No. 2 (Spring 1983): 143–45

---

**JOHN G. CAWELTI and BRUCE A. ROSENBERG**      Fleming revitalized the heroic version of the spy story, creating a new formula that would be widely imitated in novels, on film, and in television. His work combined traditional narrative patterns with a tone of irony and cynicism which made the patterns of heroic adventure more acceptable to the public in an age of skepticism and doubt. In addition, Fleming found ways of building into his stories the elaboration and resolution of certain key conflicts of value which were of central concern to English and American publics in the mid-twentieth century: the tradition of individual action versus modern bureaucracy and technology, the tradition of worldly asceticism versus contemporary hedonism, affluence, and abundance, and the traditions of romantic love and monogamous relations versus contemporary sexual liberation. By making the spy story into a fantasy structure in which heroic action overcomes these conflicts, Fleming enables us to temporarily enter a fictional world in which we are freed from the ambiguous feelings that characterize our ordinary lives. For so long as the fantasy holds, we share the hero's triumph over the restrictions of organizations, the dangers of technology, the ambiguities of affluence, and the uncertainties of sexual liberation. Because real frustrations and tensions are eliminated by Fleming's rhetoric and fantasy, the reader can experience the fundamental satisfaction of simultaneously affirming and escaping from his sense of reality. ⟨. . .⟩

⟨. . .⟩ James Bond, like Sherlock Holmes, is a striking compendium of conflicting cultural themes. Holmes unified in one person the contending cultural forces of poetry and science, the "two cultures," which since the mid-nineteenth century have been so ambivalently hostile to each other. Bond's character and activities bring together a number of the conflicting cultural values of the mid-twentieth century: he is an organization man who remains a determined individualist; he is cool and detached, yet committed to his country; he is a man of technology yet capable of exercising the brute physical force of a primitive savage; he is a bureaucrat and a killer; he is sexually liberated but capable of romantic love; he is an affluent consumer, yet alienated from a corrupt and decadently materialistic society; he is something of a racist, yet he loves the exotic and is always involved with men and women of other races and cultures. While these may be superficial conflicts which reflect the limited ideologies and attitudes of a specific culture, they are nonetheless a source of frustration and anxiety for mid-twentieth-century Americans and Europeans. Fleming's 007 saga enables us to participate vicariously in the adventures of a character who contains and transcends these conflicts. This yoking together of conflicting characteristics and values is one major reason why James Bond has become such an archetypal character for the contemporary public imagination.

⟨. . .⟩ Fleming understood, or was at least able to project, the emotional and cultural concerns which give the spy story its peculiar power. Because of this, he became the king of the secret agent adventure. The unique integration between his imaginative powers and the patterns of the formula make his work last, even after the general popularity of the secret agent thriller has given way to other forumulas, just as Conan Doyle's Sherlock Holmes stories have far outlasted the age of their broad general popularity and even show signs of surviving the decline of the classical detective story. While Ian Fleming cannot be compared to the serious novelists of his era, there will probably always be a significant place for him in the history of literature and culture.

John G. Cawelti and Bruce A. Rosenberg, "Bonded Excitement," *The Spy Story* (Chicago: University of Chicago Press, 1987), pp. 150–51, 153–55

## BRUCE A. ROSENBERG and ANN HARLEMAN STEWART

For several reasons, Bond is hard to take seriously. Because Fleming was not interested in life in the shadows, in the life of the spy as it is really lived today, but instead wanted to write heroic adventures, realism went out the window. Unlike the world of other contemporary spies, the world of James Bond is nearly entirely fantastic. Although other secret agents of our acquaintance—Samson, Smiley, Quiller, Leamas, Scylla—are fictional, their lives are set ostensibly in the real world, a world we know something about, where the CIA and MI6 are in the trenches against the KGB and its Warsaw Pact subordinates. Their experiences could have happened: their authors make us believe in them to that extent. But Fleming forgoes that verisimilitude. We can hardly believe in the reality of Dr. No, Hugo Drax, Mr. Big, Goldfinger, Blofeld. We cannot believe that the world is in danger from the likes of such mythical organizations as SMERSH or SPECTRE. While Fleming has had some success in drawing readers into this far-side-of-the-moon passed off as reality, this is fantasyland stuff. ⟨. . .⟩

Ian Fleming had great appeal for Englishmen of the 1950s and 1960s; he gave them an upbeat message at a time when his contemporaries pictured the world as a place full of treachery, deceit, and dark shadows where hidden dangers from unknown sources are constant threats. The further reaches of Bond's world—the British Empire, the power of Great Britain—may be somewhat ragged on the fringes. For some it seems more important than ever to cling to the beliefs of the old Empire. During the first few decades of this century the racism and the smug imperialism of Hannay and Drummond were not as offensive as they are to us today. Bond, because of Fleming's biases, shares their attitudes toward the "inferior races," but the worldwide might of England is a wistful memory. A certain defensive quality tints all of Bond's attitudes toward his country. He is as patriotic as anyone, unquestionably, but the object of that patriotic faith must not strike English readers as being as solid or as indestructable as it once had been.

Because Bond did little bona fide spying—he was not a secret agent in the manner of such real spies as Fuchs, Burgess, MacLean, and Philby—Fleming never exploited the potential of the genre. The themes, ideas, concerns packed into the novels of Le Carré, or Deighton, or fifty other contemporary writers for that matter—ideas that Greene and Ambler exploited in the late thirties—pass by Fleming in the night. Questions of loyalty and betrayal, trust and suspicion, faith and doubt, hypocrisy and obligation, the moral ontology of a clandestine agency within an ostensibly open and free society—all of these issues are unavailable to the readers of Fleming because they were never dreamed of in the philosophy of Fleming himself.

In this deeper sense Fleming was not a spy novelist. He did not know what the spy novel was about, what its possibilities were. He called his adventurer a "spy," and placed him within a bureaucracy that he labeled an espionage apparatus. But the association of James Bond with spying was only skin-deep; it did not go down to the bone.

> Bruce A. Rosenberg and Ann Harleman Stewart, "James Bond and the Modern Spy Novel," *Ian Fleming* (Boston: Twayne, 1989), pp. 80–82

# ◈ *Bibliography*

*Casino Royale.* 1953.

*Live and Let Die.* 1954.

*Moonraker.* 1955.

*Diamonds Are Forever.* 1956.

*The Diamond Smugglers.* 1957.

*From Russia, with Love.* 1957.

*Dr. No.* 1958.

*Goldfinger.* 1959.

*For Your Eyes Only.* 1960.

*Thunderball.* 1961.

*The Spy Who Loved Me.* 1962.

*On Her Majesty's Secret Service.* 1963.

*Thrilling Cities.* 1963.

*You Only Live Twice.* 1964.

*Chitty-Chitty-Bang-Bang.* 1964.

*The Man with the Golden Gun.* 1965.

*Ian Fleming Introduces Jamaica.* Ed. Morris Cargill. 1965.

*Octopussy and The Living Daylights.* 1966.

# Graham Greene
## 1904–1991

GRAHAM GREENE was born on October 2, 1904, in Berkhamsted, Hertford-
shire, the son of Marion Raymond Greene and Charles Henry Greene, the
headmaster of Berkhampsted school. He attended Balliol College, Oxford,
from 1922 to 1925, when he published his only book of verse, *Babbling April*
(1925). In 1926 he joined the staff of the London *Times*, and converted
to Catholicism; the following year, he married Vivien Dayrell-Browning,
with whom he had two children. *The Man Within* in 1929 was the first of
more than thirty novels by Greene, who for three decades would label them
either "novels" or "entertainments." The former include *England Made Me*
(1935); Greene's own favorite, *The Power and the Glory* (1940), which won
the Hawthornden Prize; *The Heart of the Matter* (1948), winner of the James
Tait Black Memorial Prize; *The End of the Affair* (1951), which won the
Catholic Literary Award; and *The Quiet American* (1955), the first major
novel to address the Vietnam conflict.

Greene's "entertainments" share many characteristics with his "novels":
the search for God and the pervasiveness of evil; a seedy setting, called
"Greeneland" by some of his critics; and a fascination with social outcasts,
irony, and anarchy. They include *Stamboul Train* (1932), his first popular
success; *A Gun for Sale* (1936; titled *This Gun for Hire* in the U.S.); *Brighton
Rock* (1938); *The Confidential Agent* (1939); and *Our Man in Havana* (1958).
This last book displays the wry humor that characterizes such later Greene
novels as *Travels with My Aunt* (1969) and *Monsignor Quixote* (1982).

Besides his novels, Greene wrote short stories, several plays, travel books,
essays, criticism, biographies, and books for children, including one in the
form of a thriller, *The Little Steamroller: A Story of Adventure, Mystery and
Detection* (1953). His screenplays include *The Fallen Idol* (1948), *The Third
Man* (1950), and *Saint Joan* (1957); more than a dozen of his novels have
been adapted to the screen. He was also active as a publisher, directing the
houses of Eyre & Spottiswoode in the 1940s and The Bodley Head in the

1960s. Greene was made a Companion of Honour in 1965 and a Chevalier of the Legion of Honour in 1969; his other awards include the Pretzak Award in 1960, the Shakespeare Prize in 1969, the Thomas Moore Medal in 1973, and the Mystery Writers of America Grand Master Award in 1975. He died on April 3, 1991, at Vevey, Switzerland.

# Critical Extracts

**RICHARD J. VOORHEES**        His detectives are scarcely nearer to the normal than the criminals whom they hunt. In *This Gun for Hire* (1936) Mather, the Scotland Yard man, gets along fairly well in the world only because the contours of his neurosis fit, as it were, those of his environment. If he had not found in the police force an organization suitable to his temperament, he might, like his brother who found no such organization, have drowned himself. And the detective in *The Ministry of Fear*, although he exhibits nothing so extreme as a tendency to suicide, nevertheless carries eccentricity to the point of the grotesque. The best of Greene's men and women move through life with a minimum of nobility; their gestures are those of people furtively scratching at some dermatitis or trying to conceal a faulty dental plate.

If the people in Greene have any dignity, they derive it from their capacity to endure suffering, and their lives provide them with plenty of opportunity to test this capacity. Children do not know what lies in wait for them, and even adolescents may mistake their progress toward misery for one toward happiness; but men who have arrived at maturity cannot possibly misunderstand the nature of the universe in which they must live. To be a human being, one must, sooner or later (in Scobie's words), "drink the cup." But then a strange thing happens. One gradually develops a taste for the bitter drink. He not only accepts his unhappiness but even comes to prefer it to happiness. In *The Heart of the Matter* there is a subordinate character named Harris who has all the makings of a comic figure of Evelyn Waugh. When he finds that his quarters are infested with cockroaches, he turns the hunting of them into an elaborate game between himself and a fellow civil servant. But in Greene he is not so funny. He feels for the school where he has spent the most miserable years of his life "the total loyalty we all feel to unhappiness—the sense that that is where we really belong." And Scobie is appalled at the idea of retiring to a neat little place and getting away from his stinking office and his grisly routine. His insurance pays off only after death. Similarly, "D," the hero of *The Confidential Agent* (1939), who has come from civil war on the Continent, almost prefers "the prison cells, the law of flight" to the kind of comfort, luxury, and prosperity he finds in peaceful England. Greene seems to share his characters' perverse preference. In *This Gun for Hire* there is a sequence in which a group of pathetic stammerers gathers at a Masonic hall to hear a lecture on speech correction. The hall is hung with the portraits of Masonic dignitaries, and Greene makes the prosperity and success of the men in the paintings seem even less enviable than the frustration and failure of the stammerers.

Richard J. Voorhees, "The World of Graham Greene," *South Atlantic Quarterly* 50, No. 3 (July 1951): 390–91

---

**FRANCIS L. KUNKEL**      In an essay on James, an essay on Dickens, and an essay on Fielding, in *The Lost Childhood*, Greene indicates his attitude towards villains. He approves of James' villains—"Mme Merle, Gilbert Osmond, Kate Croy, Merton Densher, Charlotte Stant"—and Dickens' villains—"Fagin, Monks and Sykes"—because they possess the sense of supernatural evil. He disapproves of Fielding's villains because "they completely lack the sense of supernatural evil. . . . Evil is always a purely sexual matter: the struggle seems invariably to take the form of whether or not the 'noble lord' or Colonel James will succeed in raping or seducing Amelia." Greene regards intense moral struggle as a *sine qua non* for supernatural evil, "and it is the intensity of the struggle which is lacking in Fielding." But Greene's entertainments do present an intense moral struggle, and the evil that enmeshes his villains is never a purely sexual matter. Willi Hilfe in *The Ministry of Fear* and Harry Lime in *The Third Man*, Greene's two most outstanding villains, illustrate this perfectly. Greene's practice in this matter conforms to his theory.

Willi Hilfe and Harry Lime are the kind of villain Greene specializes in, utterly selfish amoralists who have lost the sense of the worth of human life. Lime organizes a vicious black market operation that culminates in mass murder in post-war Vienna during the occupation; Hilfe organizes espionage, terrorism, and murder in wartime London. Lime steals penicillin from military hospitals, dilutes it, and sells it for a very high sum to the children's hospital, for use against meningitis. Apprised that many children have been killed by his fake drugs, he merely shrugs the information off and boasts how he clears thirty thousand pounds a year, tax free.

Harry Lime and Willi Hilfe have about them the same diabolical quality as Mrs. Baines in "The Basement Room," Greene's most memorable short story. Mrs. Baines "was darkness when the night light went out in a draught; she was the frozen blocks of earth he had seen one winter in a graveyard when someone said, 'They need an electric drill'; she was the flowers gone bad and smelling in the little closet room at Penstanley. There was nothing to laugh about." Nor do Lime and Hilfe afford anyone anything to laugh about. Not ordinary criminals, they are ambitious, clever, educated, warped, and completely unscrupulous. They never think in terms of human beings; they can endure pain—other people's pain—endlessly, and they treat murder as a joke. Not old-fashioned murderers, killing from fear, from hate—least of all from love—they murder for position, for substantial profit—even to become respectable. They meet appropriately violent deaths: Hilfe in a public lavatory; Lime in a public sewer.

Francis L. Kunkel, *The Labyrinthine Ways of Graham Greene* (New York: Sheed & Ward, 1959; rev. ed. Mamaroneck, NY: Paul P. Appel, 1973), pp. 76–77

---

**GRAHAM GREENE**     I married, and I was happy. In the evenings I worked at *The Times,* in the mornings I worked on my third novel. Now when I write I put down on the page a mere skeleton of a novel—nearly all my revisions are in the nature of additions, of second thoughts to make the bare bones live—but in those days to revise was to prune and prune. I was much tempted, perhaps because of my admiration for the Metaphysical poets, by exaggerated similes and my wife became an adept at shooting them down. There was one, I remember, comparing something or someone in the quiet landscape of Sussex to a leopard crouching in a tree, which gave a name to the whole species. Leopards would be marked daily on the manuscript, but it took a great many years for me to get the beasts under control, and they growl at me sometimes yet.

One day in the winter of 1928 I lay in bed with a bad attack of flu, listening to my wife in the kitchen washing up the breakfast things. I had posted copies of the typescript to Heinemann and The Bodley Head about

ten days before, and I was now resigned to a long delay. Hadn't I waited
last time nine months for a refusal? Anyway, uncertainty was more agreeable
to live with then the confirmation of failure. The telephone rang in the
sitting room and my wife came in and told me, "There's a Mr. Evans wants
to speak to you."

"I don't know anyone called Evans," I said. "Tell him I'm in bed. Tell
him I'm ill." Suddenly a memory came back to me: Evans was the chairman
of Heinemann's, and I ran to snatch the telephone.

"I've read your novel," he said. "We'd like to publish it. Would it be
possible for you to look in here at eleven?" My flu was gone in that moment
and never returned.

Nothing in a novelist's life later can equal that moment—the acceptance
of his first book. Triumph is unalloyed by any doubt of the future. Mounting
the wide staircase in the elegant eighteenth-century house in Great Russell
Street I could have no foreboding of the failures and frustrations of the next
ten years.

Graham Greene, *A Sort of Life* (New York: Simon & Schuster, 1971), pp. 194–95

---

**PETER WOLFE**     *Our Man in Havana* has a fine reputation. Except
for Harvey Curtis Webster, who, dismissing the three entertainments of the
1950s in a paragraph, calls it "barely consequential," everyone who has
written about it has praised it. Most of the praise, furthermore, is intelligent.
De Vitis calls it "a delightful satire with a serious edge, one of the funniest
books to appear in many a day." Kunkel pays tribute to its range and
flexibility when he speaks of its witchlike brew of "mirth and murder,
pomposity and poison, satire and suspense." Atkins praises it as "one of the
most professional pieces of writing Greene has given us; it moves with . . .
speed and precision . . . and it manages to pass comments on life which are
central to Greene's thinking." The salute ends with Atkins's calling the
book "the best of the entertainments."

These tributes are hard to gainsay. *Our Man in Havana* is freshly conceived
and brilliantly executed. A warm, colorful work, it has all the absurd delicious
trimmings of our technocratic age. It also maintains the difficult balance
between comedy and terror. Greene builds to terrifying, even tragic,
moments, but he always leaves a banana peel on the scene of the tragedy.
This mixture of knockabout and terror cushions the suspense. But it restrains

our laughter, too, lest we discover that the supports have gone out from under us and that we are laughing at ourselves. ⟨. . .⟩

*Our Man in Havana* uses the right modes and forms to develop its ideas. It issues a serious warning without losing cheer. One of Greene's best books, it balances vision, timeliness, and control. Here is no snobbery of pessimism: humanity has not worn thin, love is worth working for, and gadgets do not matter more than people. Nor is life futile. That existence is unreasonable does not cancel out its values. Greene always insists on a reality beyond causality. One of his outstanding gifts has been the ability to make this reality a force even when not in view. This ability—which accounts for much of the greatness of great art—is best summarized by Flannery O'Connor:

> The fiction writer presents mystery through manners, grace
> through nature, but when he finishes there always has to be left
> over that sense of Mystery which cannot be accounted for by any
> human formula.

The mystery both energizes and transcends human activity. Greene's entertainments merit special praise for conveying it in everyday human terms and for affirming the importance of human acts because of its presence. The blend of journalism and metaphysics in the entertainment is unique. The affirmation ringing through them shows in another way their masterful use of the right forms and ideas to convey their ideas.

Any artist who generates serious, compelling ideas dramatically gives a new outlook on reality. What more can we ask of him? Graham Greene deserves to be viewed as one of the century's great writers in English.

Peter Wolfe, *Graham Greene: The Entertainer* (Carbondale: Southern Illinois University Press, 1972), pp. 146–47, 164–65

---

**GEORG M. A. GASTON**    Three years after *The Quiet American*, Greene brought forth *Our Man in Havana* (1958), a book which was both typical and new for him. Like so many of his previous works, it refers to such large issues as personal responsibility, commitment, imagination, faith, and love. Moreover, it is cast in the framework of a thriller, and stylistic similarities between it and Greene's previous fiction abound. However, it represents something of a departure, too. This resides in its aggressively comic nature. Greene's previous work may often have had some comic elements or undertones. Now, however, comedy, or more precisely farce, comes to the fore not only as a method but also as a theme.

The situation which Greene sets up begins earnestly enough. Wormold, the protagonist of the story, is pictured as a dull, worried middle-aged man who sells vacuum cleaners to make a living and, rather desperately, tries to raise the daughter who was left him by an abandoning wife. Then he is unexpectedly engaged as an agent for the British Secret Service, and the story quickly develops into a hilariously sharp-edged burlesque which, if one didn't know better, might have been written by a writer such as Kingsley Amis. Once Wormold takes the job, which he does for extra money he needs to support his daughter's expensive desires, he reluctantly faces up to the fact that the Service requires intelligence reports of him. In a fit of desperation, or more properly inspiration, he begins to invent an organization of personal recruits and sends in reports which detail an ominous new military build-up in a remote area of Cuba, but which actually consists of sketches of the Atomic Pile vacuum cleaners he has been unsuccessfully trying to sell at his shop. For a time, things go amazingly well for Wormold. But eventually there are some unforeseen, painful consequences; and in the end events simply catch up with his masquerade. Before that happens, though, Wormold manages to fall in love (with a beautiful agent sent to help him), to make provisions for the future of his daughter, and, most important, to discover a creative new way of life.

The framework of the story itself indicates that Wormold resembles those protagonists in Greene's previous novels who are rejuvenated by acts of imagination, responsibility, and love. However, the very last paragraph of the novel underlines the fact that Greene wants us to understand that Wormold's salvation depends even more on the factor of "madness." In those final lines, Wormold is made to express his fear that in the future "he would never be quite mad enough." This is, obviously, a way of saying that this quality has become so essential to him he doesn't wish to imagine life without it.

Precisely what kind of "madness" is under consideration? In the context of this story, it refers on one level to risk taking. On another, more important, level it refers to those qualities inherent in the traditional kind of clown the story alludes to on more than one occasion. This clown, because of his permanent act of comedy, goes through life unchanged by the various political waves of the age's great catastrophes or discoveries. In other words, the clown endures because of his ageless and somewhat anarchic farcical behavior; and all this applies to Wormold's final disposition. Even if he may not yet fully realize it himself, Wormold has finally reached the point where he has acquired a permanent strength to face the pressures of the contemporary world because of the comic vision he has learned to adopt.

Georg M. A. Gaston, *The Pursuit of Salvation: A Critical Guide to the Novels of Graham Greene* (Troy, NY: Whitston Publishing Co., 1984), pp. 72–73

---

**NEIL McEWAN**      John Buchan invented the simplified story of crime, espionage and pursuit involving ordinary people, although his people were gentlemen: Richard Hannay, Sandy Arbuthnot, Edward Leithen. Greene's view of Buchan's last novel observes that *The Thirty-nine Steps* (1915) has been 'a pattern for adventure-writers ever since' and asks 'who will forget the thrill in 1916 . . . as the hunted Leithen [in *The Power-House*] "ran like a thief in a London thoroughfare on a June afternoon"?' Greene's plot devices are Buchan's: how to get out of London without money; how to evade the police when they will not believe your story; how to prevent, in the next few hours of hide-and-seek, a world war. But when he mentions Buchan's influence on *A Gun for Sale*, he qualifies it: by the 1930s, 'it was no longer a Buchan world' because the First World War and the Depression had discredited Buchan's patriotic upper-class heroes. His thrillers drew on lower social strata; the 'hero' of *A Gun for Sale* comes from the meanest imaginable social depth.

Very conservative in conventions, thrillers are often, like Buchan's, politically conservative in their assumptions. Greene's are not. The capitalist Sir Marcus is the villain of *A Gun for Sale* and his killing, watched with satisfaction by his valet, seems an act of justice or, at least, of appropriate revenge. Greene dislikes and disclaims symbols, but a socialist reader in 1936 might well have seen this character's extreme old age and physical frailty, wheelchair and hoarse whisper, as signs of the current state of capitalism. The title refers to the profits to be made in dealings in metals for arms, from which Sir Marcus profits, as well as to the hired gunman, Raven, whom he employs to kill a foreign statesman and start a lucrative war; its point was missed in the United States where Doubleday changed the title to *This Gun for Hire*. Money and violence are frequently associated: a journalist predicting war urges colleagues to buy armament shares and make a fortune. Greene's essay 'At Home' (1940) expresses a leading idea of his early novels, and especially of the thrillers.

Violence comes to us more easily because it was so long
expected—not only by the political sense but also by the moral
sense. The world we lived in could not have ended any other
way.

Neil McEwan, *Graham Greene* (New York: St. Martin's Press, 1988), pp. 115–16

---

**WILLIAM M. CHACE**      ⟨. . .⟩ the marginality of Greeneland, the
ways in which the sad loneliness of defeated men is mirrored by appropriate
expressionist landscapes, gives considerable prestige to the people living in
those landscapes. They are people separated from the common pursuits of
life. Priests, to be sure, figure in such seedy places, and so do uncertain
travellers in exotic regions as well as petty hoodlums, lepers and their doctors,
mercenaries, smugglers, terrorists, career soldiers and the politically inept.
But no calling is given greater attention in Greeneland than that of the
secret agent. In Greene's world, the spy represents that peculiar mix of
knowledge, estrangement, authority and exceptionality towards which the
novelist's creative instincts seem always to gravitate. Those instincts generated *The Confidential Agent, The Ministry of Fear, The Third Man, The Quiet
American, Our Man in Havana* and *The Human Factor.* Indeed, "spying"—
the act of gaining and holding knowledge surreptitiously, the process of
achieving advantage over others by remaining detached from them and yet
cognizant of their activities, the contest of an emotional relationship in
which one of the parties holds exclusive pieces of covert information about
that relationship—is central to Greene's work.

It is, of course, also central to all works of the creative imagination.
Throughout his career, Greene seems to be suggesting that the novelist
must always be a spy, must apply a superior kind of knowledge to the
situations he creates while he fashions a means of ultimately providing, over
time, full access to that knowledge for the reader. Such an unequal division
of authoritative knowledge is at the root of the kind of literary irony Greene
practices, for by always holding the upper hand with respect to his "secrets,"
he gives pleasure by gradually allowing his reader a larger and larger share
of those secrets and by enabling that reader to understand how those secrets
have been withheld. Thus the pleasures of Greene's plotting, of his character
development and of the consequences of concatenated action in his fictions.
We at last learn most of what the author once knew, but we can never

escape the recognition that the author—the spy—always knew it first and better.

To occupy a position of greater knowledge is to gain a degree of superiority and immunity not available to everyone. That is a truth about life as well as literature, and it is a truth about the need for solace that every human being can feel. ⟨. . .⟩

All writers, Greene included, function as "God's spies," but in Greene's work the authority of God and the authority of the spy are invoked in equal measure. The creative collusion between the omniscient writer and the secret agent lends to his writing a strong element of seductive attraction— we are led to believe that we are in the presence of a mind that knows how destinies can be shaped, or ruined, and is in the very business of powerfully arranging, behind the scenes, those destinies. For all its apparent seediness, then, Greeneland is not a place where God is dead; for the author is God. Indeed, by virtue of the author's magisterial control and domination of events, he is omnipresent, watching how everything has been carefully set in motion to "ebb and flow by th' moon" ⟨Shakespeare⟩.

"The novel," says Jacques Barzun, "has been prurient and investigative from the start . . . from Gil Blas to Henry James' 'observer' somebody is always prying. From Scott to Dreiser we take a course in how some other half lives, how fradulent men and their society really are. The novel is dedicated to subversion; the novelist is a spy in enemy country." Greene reinforces this basic truth about the genre in which he writes by making the entire business of prurience, investigation, fraudulence and subversion the substantively explicit as well as the operationally implicit action of his fiction. From "D" in *The Confidential Agent* (1939) to Maurice Castle in *The Human Factor* (1978), Greene's focus has been on those separated, by the burden of knowledge they bear, from the common turmoil of "who loses and who wins." They must carry on alone, tasting the bittersweet pleasures that solicitude and greater awareness give them.

William M. Chace, "Spies and God's Spies: Greene's Espionage Fiction," *Graham Greene: A Revaluation*, ed. Jeffrey Meyers (New York: St. Martin's Press, 1990), pp. 159–61

---

**ANN PIROËLLE**     My premise has been that Graham Greene was the first and perhaps the only writer so far to understand the possibilities of union that exist between fiction and film. *The Third Man* is an ageless example of that.

The facts surrounding the creation of the film are well-known. The novelist had already made one successful film with Carol Reed—*The Fallen Idol*, an adaptation of his short story, "The Basement Room". They decided to work together again as a team, and from the idea found by Sir Alexander Korda (production chief of London Films), Greene left for post-war Vienna. He started from a fragment he had written twenty years earlier, got stuck for three weeks, then heard about the penicillin racket and discovered the labyrinthine sewage system under the city. From this his story grew.

Greene himself has described the creative process involved. "My approach to writing an original screenplay is to write a *treatment* of a story which is then turned into a script. I cannot do the kind of treatment that is written in the historical present. I write the treatment like a novel. What today is known as the novel of *The Third Man* is really the treatment which I did before writing the script": "One must have the sense of more material than one needs to draw on". So, we learn, it started as a short story, written to serve as raw material for the script he wrote. Just as a script evolves as the film starts to take shape and changes are made by the film director, alone or with his scriptwriter(s)—so the Harry Lime story also evolved. We are a long way from the situation which so often existed on film or television studio sets, where, as one disgruntled novelist has complained, he was always treated like "Banquo's ghost, with B.O. . . ." ⟨Jack Rosenthal⟩. Greene and Reed worked together on every detail of the text and film. Many revisions were made to the original story, but Greene insists that not one was thrust upon him against his will, but that the changes were often his own suggestions. He has said, "The film is in fact better than the story, because it is in this case, the finished state of the story". ⟨. . .⟩

The use of shadow and light, the use of running the water in the chase in the sewers, and once again but above all, the human faces, all of these have become unforgettable. It has been said that *The Third Man* is remembered for two things: one sentence pronounced by Orson Welles about Cuckoo clocks and the Swiss, and the shot of a hand coming through the grating in the street in Vienna. I would like to conclude by suggesting that the real reason for the durability of this masterpiece is the fusing of two real talents in the creation of fiction and film. Two last examples confirm this premise. First, Karas' zither theme accompanying Harry Lime throughout like his shadow, originally conceived by Greene, although the musician was discovered by

Reed, and the blending into the story achieved by both. And the famous controversy concerning the last sequence which, contrary to the myth, was not a sign of discord, but of profound reflexion. Greene wanted a happy ending, Reed insisted on Anna walking past. Greene said the last shot was far too long and that the audience would never sit it out to the end. And when he saw the final version, he was the first to applaud Reed's choice. Their collaboration was complete.

> Ann Piroëlle, "Graham Greene: Fiction and Film," *Graham Greene in Perspective: A Critical Symposium*, ed. Peter Erlebach and Thomas Michael Stein (New York: Peter Lang, 1991), pp. 87–88, 90

# ◈ *Bibliography*

*Babbling April.* 1925.

*The Man Within.* 1929.

*The Name of Action.* 1930.

*Rumour at Nightfall.* 1931.

*Stamboul Train ⟨Orient Express⟩.* 1932.

*It's a Battlefield.* 1934.

*The Old School: Essays by Divers Hands* (editor). 1934.

*England Made Me.* 1935.

*The Bear Fell Free.* 1935.

*The Basement Room and Other Stories.* 1935.

*Journey without Maps.* 1936.

*A Gun for Sale: An Entertainment ⟨This Gun for Hire⟩.* 1936.

*Brighton Rock.* 1938.

*The Lawless Roads: A Mexican Journey ⟨Another Mexico⟩.* 1939.

*The Confidential Agent ⟨The Labyrinthine Ways⟩.* 1939.

*The Power and the Glory.* 1940.

*British Dramatists.* 1942.

*The Ministry of Fear: An Entertainment.* 1943.

*The Little Train.* 1946.

*Nineteen Stories.* 1947.

*The Heart of the Matter.* 1948.

*Why Do I Write?* (with Elizabeth Bowen and V. S. Pritchett). 1948.

*After Two Years.* 1949.

*The Third Man and The Fallen Idol.* 1950.

*The Little Fire Engine.* 1950.

*The Best of Saki* (editor). 1950.

*The Lost Childhood and Other Essays.* 1951.

*The End of the Affair.* 1951.

*The Little Horse Bus.* 1952.

*The Living Room.* 1953.

*The Little Steamroller: A Story of Adventure, Mystery and Detection.* 1953.

*Nino Caffè.* 1953.

*Essais Catholiques.* Tr. Marcelle Sibon. 1953.

*Twenty-one Stories.* 1954.

*Loser Takes All.* 1955.

*The Quiet American.* 1955.

*The Spy's Bedside Book* (editor with Hugh Greene). 1957.

*The Potting Shed.* 1957, 1958.

*Our Man in Havana: An Entertainment.* 1958.

*The Complaisant Love: A Comedy.* 1959.

*A Visit to Morin.* 1960.

*A Burnt-Out Case.* 1961.

*In Search of a Character: Two African Journals.* 1961.

*The Bodley Head Ford Madox Ford* (editor). 1962–63. 4 vols.

*Introduction to Three Novels.* 1962.

*A Sense of Reality.* 1963.

*The Revenge: An Autobiographical Fragment.* 1963.

*Carving a Statue.* 1964.

*The Comedians.* 1966.

*Victorian Detective Fiction* (with Dorothy Glover et al.). 1966.

*May We Borrow Your Husband? and Other Comedies of the Sexual Life.* 1967.

*The Third Man* [film script] (with Carol Reed). 1968.

*Collected Essays.* 1969.

*Travels with My Aunt.* 1969.

*A Sort of Life.* 1971.

*Collected Stories.* 1972.

*The Pleasure-Dome: The Collected Film Criticism 1935–40.* Ed. John Russell
    Taylor. 1972.

*The Virtue of Disloyalty.* 1972.

*The Portable Graham Greene.* Ed. Philip Stratford. 1973.

*The Honorary Consul.* 1973.

*Lord Rochester's Monkey: Being the Life of John Wilmot, Second Earl of Rochester.*
		1974.
*An Impossible Woman: The Memories of Dottoressa Moor of Capri* (editor).
		1975.
*The Return of A. J. Raffles: An Edwardian Comedy.* 1975.
*Shades of Greene: The Televised Stories of Graham Greene.* 1975.
*A Wedding among the Owls.* 1977.
*The Human Factor.* 1978.
*How Father Quixote Became a Monsignor.* 1978.
*Dr. Fischer of Geneva; or, The Bomb Party.* 1980.
*Ways of Escape.* 1980.
*The Great Jowett.* 1981.
*Across the Bridge and Other Stories.* 1981.
*Monsignor Quixote.* 1982.
*J'Accuse: The Dark Side of Nice.* 1982.
*Yes and No and For Whom the Bell Chimes.* 1983.
*The Quick Look Behind: Footnotes to an Autobiography.* 1983.
*Getting to Know the General: The Story of an Involvement.* 1984.
*Victorian Villainies* (editor; with Hugh Greene). 1984.
*The Tenth Man.* 1985.
*Collected Plays.* 1985.
*Collected Short Stories.* 1986.
*Classic Tales of Espionage and Suspense.* 1987.
*The Captain and the Enemy.* Ed. Paul Roberts. 1988.
*Reflections on* Travels with My Aunt. 1989.
*Dear David, Dear Graham: A Bibliophilic Correspondence* (with David Low).
		1989.
*Why the Epigraph?* (editor). 1989.
*Reflections.* Ed. Judith Adamson. 1990.
*The Last Word and Other Stories.* 1990.
*Yours etc.: Letters to the Press.* Ed. Christopher Hawtree. 1991.
*Fragments of Autobiography.* 1991.
*A World of My Own: A Dream Diary.* 1992.
*Conversations with Graham Greene.* Ed. Henry J. Donaghy. 1992.
*A Discovery in the Woods.* 1993.

⊞ ⊞ ⊞

# Dashiell Hammett
## *1894–1961*

SAMUEL DASHIELL HAMMETT was born on May 27, 1894, in St. Mary's County, Maryland, and grew up in Baltimore, where his family moved in 1901. Leaving school in 1908, he drifted from job to job before becoming an operative for Pinkerton's Detective Agency in 1915. His career was interrupted by service with the U.S. Army Ambulance Corps in 1918–19 and by illness; although highly rated by Pinkerton's, he resigned his position in 1922. By this time he had moved to San Francisco and married, and in the following years barely supported himself and his family by writing short stories, book reviews, and advertising copy.

From 1923 Hammett's stories, drawing on his experiences as a detective, appeared in the popular magazine *Black Mask*, where Hammett was soon recognized as the leading exponent of the "hard-boiled" school of writing. His first three full-length novels appeared in *Black Mask* and helped to establish the character of the hard-boiled detective. *Red Harvest* and *The Dain Curse* (both 1929) were assembled from short stories featuring his nameless detective hero the Continental Op, a hired gunman who often steps outside the boundaries of the law to get his job done. In *The Maltese Falcon* (1930) he introduced Sam Spade, an efficient and expedient detective whose morals are nevertheless suspect. Hammett's stories were praised from the outset for their gritty realism and command of underworld jargon.

With his national reputation firmly established, Hammett gave up magazine work and in 1930 accepted an offer to write movie stories. The Hollywood social scene accentuated his already marked habits of heavy drinking, gambling, and womanizing, which a lifelong liaison with Lillian Hellman, whose playwriting career he decisively encouraged, did little to diminish. His fourth novel, *The Glass Key*, was published in 1931, and in 1934 appeared *The Thin Man*, which became the basis for several immensely popular films starring William Powell and Myrna Loy as the debonair detective team of Nick and Nora Charles. Despite many plans, he was unable to complete another novel and spent much of the rest of his life developing film, television, and radio series based on his characters. He also collaborated briefly with cartoonist Alex Raymond, writing plots and dialogue for the comic strip *Secret Agent X-9*.

From 1937 Hammett was increasingly involved in various left-wing causes. In 1940 he was named chairman of the Communist-affiliated Committee on Election Rights; after serving in the Aleutians in World War II, he became president of the Civil Rights Congress in 1946 and began an association with the Jefferson School of Social Science in New York that lasted until 1955. In 1951 he served a six-month jail sentence for refusing to testify about the Civil Rights Congress bail fund, and in 1953 he was interrogated by the House Un-American Activities Committee. His last years were made still more difficult by financial troubles and declining health; he suffered a heart attack in 1955, and died of lung cancer on January 10, 1961.

# ▨ *Critical Extracts*

**HERBERT ASBURY**     It is doubtful if even Ernest Hemingway has ever written more effective dialogue than may be found within the pages of this extraordinary tale of gunmen, gin and gangsters ⟨*Red Harvest*⟩. The author displays a style of amazing clarity and compactness, devoid of literary frills and furbelows, and his characters who race through the story with the rapidity and destructiveness of machine guns, speak the crisp, hard-boiled language of the underworld. Moreover, they speak it truly, without a single false or jarring note, for Mr. Hammett, himself an old-time Pinkerton detective, knows his crime and criminals through many years of personal contact. Those who begin to weary of the similarity of modern detective novels, with their clumsily involved plots and their artificial situations and conversations, will find their interest revived by this realistic, straightforward story, for it is concerned solely with fast and furious action and it introduces a detective who achieves his purposes without recourse to higher mathematics, necromancy or fanciful reasoning. It reads like the latest news from Chicago.

Mr. Hammett's hero, an operative of a private detective agency, who tells the story, is confronted by a mystery when he arrives in Personville, a western town so wicked that its citizens call it Poisonville, but it is a mystery of no particular consequence and he quickly gets to the bottom of it by simply employing common sense and his powers of observation.

Thereafter, he performs no miracles whatsoever. But in a moment of panic, soon regretted, Personville's big political boss hires him to rid the town of its gunmen and gangsters, and he proceeds to do the job by acting as a sort of *agent provocateur* among the criminal cliques, inciting one against the other by superb manoeuvering until in successive bursts of blazing fury they have destroyed themselves. He thus sets the local underworld by the ears and, in one way or another, he is concerned with no fewer than a score of killings. For a considerable period the detective is in doubt about whether he may have committed one of the murders himself, for he awakens from a laudanum-and-gin debauch with the handle of an ice pick clutched in his hand and the steel sliver buried in a girl's breast. The chapter in which this excellent crime occurs is one of the high spots of the liveliest detective story that has been published in a decade.

Herbert Asbury, [Review of *Red Harvest*], *Bookman* (New York) 69, No. 1 (March 1929): 92

---

**DONALD DOUGLAS**          Until the coming of Mr. Dashiell Hammett in *Red Harvest,* and now in *The Maltese Falcon,* the memorable detectives were gentlemen. The ever-delightful M. Lecoq and his copy, Mr. Sherlock Holmes, are fair gods against the gnomes. Their only worthy successor, Father Brown, is a priest. Scratch every other detective and you'll find a M. Lecoq. Now comes Mr. Hammett's tough guy in *Red Harvest* and his Sam Spade in *The Maltese Falcon,* and you find the Pinkerton operative as a scoundrel without pity or remorse, taking his whiffs of drink and his casual amours between catching crooks, treating the police with a cynical contempt, always getting his crook by foul and fearless means, above the law like a satyr—and Mr. Hammett describing his deeds in a glistening and fascinating prose as "American" as Lardner's, and every bit as original in musical rhythm and bawdy humor.

There is nothing like these books in the whole range of detective fiction. The plots don't matter so much. The art does; and there is an absolute distinction of real art. It is (in its small way) like Wagner writing about the gnomes in *Rheingold.* The gnomes have an eloquence of speech and a fascinating mystery of disclosure. Don't get me wrong, bo. It's not the tawdry gumshoeing of the ten-cent magazine. It is the genuine presence of the myth. The *events* of *The Maltese Falcon* may have happened that way in "real" life. No one save Mr. Hammett could have woven them to such a silver-steely mesh.

Donald Douglas, "No One Hoots for the Law," *New Republic*, 9 April 1930, p. 226

**DASHIELL HAMMETT**     Spade had no original. He is a dream man in the sense that he is what most of the private detectives I worked with would like to have been and what quite a few of them in their cockier moments thought they approached. For your private detective does not— or did not ten years ago when he was my colleague—want to be an erudite solver of riddles in the Sherlock Holmes manner; he wants to be a hard and shifty fellow, able to take care of himself in any situation, able to get the best of anybody he comes in contact with, whether criminal, innocent by-stander or client.

Dashiell Hammett, "Introduction," *The Maltese Falcon* (New York: Modern Library, 1934), pp. viii–ix

**RAYMOND CHANDLER**     Hammett wrote at first (and almost to the end) for people with a sharp, aggressive attitude to life. They were not afraid of the seamy side of things; they lived there. Violence did not dismay them; it was right down their street. Hammett gave murder back to the kind of people that commit it for reasons, not just to provide a corpse; and with the means at hand, not hand-wrought dueling pistols, curare, and tropical fish. He put these people down on paper as they were, and he made them talk and think in the language customarily used for these purposes.

He had a literary style but his audience didn't know it, because it was in a language not supposed to be capable of such refinements. They thought they were getting a good meaty melodrama written in the kind of lingo they imagined they spoke themselves. It was, in a sense, but it was much more. All language begins with speech, and the speech of common men at that, but when it develops to the point of becoming a literary medium it only looks like speech. Hammett's style at its worst was as formalized as a page of *Marius the Epicurean*; at its best it could say almost anything. I believe this style, which does not belong to Hammett or to anybody, but is the American language (and not even exclusively that any more), can say things he did not know how to say, or feel the need of saying. In his hands, it had no overtones, left no echo, evoked no image beyond a distant hill.

Hammett is said to have lacked heart; yet the story he himself thought the most of is the record of a man's devotion to a friend. He was spare, frugal, hard-boiled, but he did over and over again what only the best writers can ever do at all. He wrotes scenes that seemed never to have been written before.

> Raymond Chandler, "The Simple Art of Murder," *Atlantic Monthly* 174, No. 6 (December 1944): 58

---

**ANDRÉ GIDE**     And speaking at random, there is one recent author, Dashiell Hammett, who is doubtless not in the same class as the four great figures we began by discussing. Again it was Malraux who drew my attention to him; but for the last two years I have been vainly trying to find a copy of *The Glass Key*, which Malraux specially recommended; it couldn't be procured either in the original or in translation, whether on the Riviera or in North Africa. Hammett, it is true, squanders his great talent on detective stories; they are unusually good ones, no doubt, like *The Thin Man* and *The Maltese Falcon*, but a little cheap—and one could say the same of Simenon. For all of that, I regard his *Red Harvest* as a remarkable achievement, the last word in atrocity, cynicism, and horror. Dashiell Hammett's dialogues, in which every character is trying to deceive all the others and in which the truth slowly becomes visible through the haze of deception, can be compared only with the best in Hemingway. If I speak of Hammett, it is because I seldom hear his name mentioned.

> André Gide, *Imaginary Interviews*, tr. Malcolm Cowley (New York: Alfred A. Knopf, 1944), pp. 145–46

---

**ELLERY QUEEN**     In our considered judgment we would not label Hammett a "realist" and merely let it go at that. We would add an adjective of our own, to fill out the picture, to put the finger on the very heart of Hammett. We would call him a "romantic realist."

Examine the plot of Hammett's most famous story, *The Maltese Falcon*: the 17 years' crusade to win that fabulous, solid-gold, gem-loaded bird; the trail of theft, murder, doublecross, chicanery, blood, sweat, and tears. Can you imagine a more *romantic* theme?

Every incident in the main line of the plot is 20th Century fairy tale. Against this background of sheer melodrama and sensational romanticism, how does Hammett achieve the hard lacquer of realism? What makes critics and readers, one and all, think of *The Maltese Falcon*—and *Red Harvest* and *The Dain Curse* before the *Falcon*—as hardboiled stories?

The secret is in Hammett's method. Hammett tells his modern fables in *terms* of realism. He blends, intermingles, combines extreme romanticism of plot with extreme realism of characterization. His *stories* are the stuff of dreams; his *characters* are the flesh-and-blood of reality. The stories are flamboyant extravaganzas but the characters in those stories are authentic human beings who talk, think, and act like real people. Their speech is tough, earthy, two-syllabled; their desires, their moods, their frustrations, are cut open, laid bare, probed with frank, hard fingers.

The skin of realism hides the inner body of romance. All you see at first glance is that tough outer skin. But inside—deep in the core of his plots and counterplots—Hammett is one of the purest and most uninhibited romantics of us all.

Ellery Queen, "Meet Sam Spade," *A Man Called Spade and Other Stories* (New York: Dell, [1945]), pp. 5–6

---

**DAVID T. BAZELON**     The core of Hammett's art is his version of the masculine figure in American society. The Continental Op constitutes the basic pattern for this figure, which in the body of Hammett's work undergoes a revealing development.

The older detectives of literature—exemplified most unequivocally by the figure of Sherlock Holmes—stood on a firm social and moral basis, and won their triumphs through the exercise of reason. Holmes, despite his eccentricities, is essentially an English gentleman acting to preserve a moral way of life. The question of his motives never arises, simply because it is answered in advance: he is one of the great army of good men fighting, each in his own way, against evil. Who needs a "motive" for doing his duty? (Holmes' love for his profession is never contaminated by any moral ambiguity: he is not fascinated by evil, but only by the intellectual problem of overcoming evil.) With Hammett, the moral and social base is gone; his detectives would only be amused, if not embarrassed, by any suggestion that they are "doing their duty"—they are merely *doing*.

The Op is primarily a job-holder: all the stories in which he appears begin with an assignment and end when he has completed it. To an extent, *competence* replaces moral stature as the criterion of an individual's worth. The only persons who gain any respect from the Op are those who behave competently—and all such, criminal or otherwise, are accorded some respect. This attitude is applied to women as well as men. In *The Dain Curse*, the Op is attracted deeply only to the woman who has capacity and realism— and he fears her for the same reason. So Woman enters the Hammett picture as desirable not merely for her beauty, but also for her ability to live independently, capably—unmarried, in other words.

But the moral question is not disposed of so easily. Hammett's masculine figures are continually running up against a certain basic situation in which their relation to evil must be defined. In *Red Harvest*, for instance, the detective doing his job is confronted with a condition of evil much bigger than himself. He cannot ignore it since his job is to deal with it. On the other hand, he cannot act morally in any full sense because his particular relation, as a paid agent, to crime and its attendant evils gives him no logical justification for overstepping the bounds of his "job." Through some clever prompting by the Continental Op, the gangsters—whose rule is evil in *Red Harvest*—destroy each other in their own ways. But it becomes a very bloody business, as the title suggests. And the Op's lost alternative, of perhaps having resolved the situation—and performed his job—with less bloodshed, grows in poignancy. He begins to doubt his own motivation: perhaps the means by which a job is done matters as much as the actual accomplishment of the job.

David T. Bazelon, "Dashiell Hammett's 'Private Eye': No Loyalty Beyond the Job," *Commentary* 7, No. 5 (May 1949): 469

**JOHN PATERSON**      The Continental Op–Sam Spade saga has no continuation. After the publication of *The Maltese Falcon*, Hammett abdicated the literary scene, perhaps because he had exhausted the possibilities of his subject matter. Certainly the symbolism of his private eye has not since received more thorough exploitation, more vivid statement: alone he has invaded the predatory world of compulsive greed and dispassionate murder and has won what alone remains of victory—the personal victory. What exactly he has gained, even in this sense, is not immediately apparent. Certainly it is neither the certitude of victory nor the rapture of victory. Returned to his desk in the final scene of his career in fiction, he is in fact a bleak, lonely, and unhappy figure, without love, without community, conscious perhaps that his victory is far from final and that it may have cost him far too much.

Dashiell Hammett is, I think, with so many of his literary contemporaries, protesting the horrors of a savagely competitive society, the horrors of an urban-industrial civilization. For when we scrape away the tough exterior of his hero we find not heart of stone and nerves of steel but the tortured sensibility of the Nineteen Twenties, its romantic isolation and its pessimism, its inability to find grounds for action.

John Paterson, "A Cosmic View of the Private Eye," *Saturday Review*, 22 August 1953, p. 32

---

**ERLE STANLEY GARDNER**     When Hammett started writing, there was a dictionary of the underworld which used the word "shamus" as a tag for a private detective. Hammett picked that word up and ran it through all of his stories. Every time one of his detectives would enter on the scene, someone would sneeringly refer to him as a shamus. Since Hammett's time, a whole school of realistic writers have had their characters refer to the private detective as a shamus.

Just where did that word come from? I have made it a point to try and find out, and am completely baffled. The late Raymond Schindler, one of the world-famous private detectives, told me he had never heard of the word. At my request, he had asked private detectives whom he employed, and they had never heard it used. I asked the wardens of various penitentiaries, and they told me they had never encountered the word except in fiction. During the past eighteen years, I have had quite a few contacts with the inmates of penitentiaries; I have asked them about "shamus" and whether they ever heard it applied to a private detective. Not one of them ever had.

Then one day I happened to be discussing the matter with a man who had worked for a Jewish haberdasher, and he told me he *had* heard the word used; it applied not to a private detective but to some sort of phony. No matter; thanks to Dashiell, the *Dictionary of American Underworld Lingo* lists "shamus" as a Jewish-American word meaning a policeman or a prison guard, and the *American Thesaurus of Slang* lists it as applying to a policeman, an informer, or a stool pigeon.

It has been many years since Dashiell Hammett first put the word into circulation. Today the general reading public considers "shamus" a slang term customarily used by the underworld in describing the private detective. It assumes that the writer who uses it knows his way around.

> Erle Stanley Gardner, "Getting Away with Murder," *Atlantic Monthly* 215, No. 1 (January 1965): 73

---

**ROSS MACDONALD**     The contemporary world is the special province of the American hardboiled detective story. Dashiell Hammett, Raymond Chandler, and the other writers for *Black Mask* who developed it, were in conscious reaction against the Anglo-American school which, in the work of S. S. Van Dine for example, had lost contact with contemporary life and language. Chandler's dedication, to the editor of *Black Mask*, of a collection of his early stories (1944), describes the kind of fiction they had been trying to supplant: "For Joseph Thompson Shaw with affection and suspect, and in memory of the time when we were trying to get murder away from the upper classes, the weekend house party and the vicar's rose-garden, and back to the people who are really good at it." While Chandler's novels swarm with plutocrats as well as criminals, and even with what pass in Southern California for aristocrats, the *Black Mask* revolution was a real one. From it emerged a new kind of detective hero, the classless, restless man of American democracy, who spoke the language of the street.

Hammett, who created the most powerful of these heroes in Sam Spade, had been a private detective and knew the corrupt inner workings of American cities. But Sam Spade was a less obvious projection of Hammett than detective heroes usually are of their authors. Hammett had got his early romanticism under strict ironic control. He could see Spade from outside, without affection, perhaps with some bleak compassion. In this as in other respects Spade marks a sharp break with the Holmes tradition. He possesses the virtues and follows the code of the frontier male. Thrust for his sins into the urban inferno, he pits his courage and cunning against its denizens, plays for the highest stakes available, love and money, and loses nearly everything in the end. His lover is guilty of murder; his narrow, bitter code forces Spade to turn her over to the police. The Maltese falcon has been stripped of jewels.

Perhaps the stakes and implied losses are far higher than I have suggested. This worthless falcon may symbolize a lost tradition, the great cultures of the Mediterranean past which have become inaccessible to Spade and his generation. Perhaps the bird stands for the Holy Ghost itself, or for its absence.

The ferocious intensity of the work, the rigorous spelling-out of Sam Spade's deprivation of his full human heritage, seem to me to make his story tragedy, if there is such a thing as dead-pan tragedy. Hammett was the first American writer to use the detective-story for the purposes of a major novelist, to present a vision, blazing if disenchanted, of our lives. Sam Spade was the product and reflection of a mind which was not at home in Zion, or in Zenith.

Ross Macdonald, "The Writer as Detective Hero," On Crime Writing (Santa Barbara: Capra Press, 1973), pp. 14–16

---

**H. H. MORRIS**     Hammett's vision of America was that of a man staring at a vast wasteland. He shared with Sinclair Lewis the belief that the nation's traditional leaders lack integrity, that the balance sheet had replaced ethical codes of conduct. Like F. Scott Fitzgerald, Hammett saw the children of the rich as spoiled seekers after illicit thrills. With Faulkner, he wrote of society's dregs, the misfits condemned to live out a nightmare existence with no hope of escape. Hammett was one more writer of the 1920's and 1930's who took the naturalism of Dreiser and Norris as a received fiction technique and applied it to life around him.

None of these comparisons should suggest that Dashiell Hammett belongs among the giants, that in leaving him out of standard American literature anthologies editors have overlooked a great novelist. His writing is flawed. He fit too well into the Black Mask ambience. His strained metaphors and thieves' argot come across as stylized and artificial, and in the future readers will need the cumbersome network of explanatory footnotes found in most editions of John Gay's *The Beggar's Opera*. Hammett's characters are often flat, distinguished from one another only by colorful nicknames, physical descriptions, and police records. Because pulp fiction demanded lots of action, his plots dominate all other story elements.

H. H. Morris, "Dashiell Hammett in the Wasteland," *Midwest Quarterly* 19, No. 2 (Winter 1978): 197

---

**EDWARD A. NICKERSON**     Through the motives, the dark milieu, and the structure of relations in *The Maltese Falcon*, Hammett has created a myth of early twentieth century capitalism, a world in which self-interested entrepreneurs fiercely compete for a property whose ownership is ambiguous. On the capitalistic model, contracts and the pursuit of wealth hold society together. In the novel, characters give their word, form tempo-rary alliances, talk extensively about "trust," and do what they feel they need to in order to obtain the treasure. The literal murders are less significant than the resultant pervasive killing of human ties and relations. Because of the human isolation, betrayals and obsessive pursuits of false goals, the novel renders a hell-on-earth, a kind of vital death-in-life that brings the outside American world to the test and that finally brought Dashiell Hammett to an independent relation with the Communist Party. In *The Maltese Falcon* Hammett has thus refined, complicated, and made much more precise the world of the individualistic, Hobbesian violence, warfare, and systematic absence of trust he had imagined in *Red Harvest* and the Continental Op stories.

Edward A. Nickerson, " 'Realistic' Crime Fiction: An Anatomy of Evil People," *Centennial Review* 25, No. 2 (Spring 1981): 402

---

**EDWARD MARGOLIES**     Hammett's tough-guy fiction represents the marriage of two kinds of popular writing that had been developing in America since the nineteenth century: the novel of detection derived from Poe, and the western adventure derived from James Fenimore Cooper. The Poe-like puzzle element requiring some kind of intellectual effort on the part of the detective is not altogether absent in Hammett's stories, but it gives way more often than not to suspenseful episodic adventures replete with violence and danger to the hero. One of Hammett's contributions to the genre is that he rendered popular adventure more plausible by making the detection seem more realistic—mental acuteness is preceded by solid plodding investigation. In "The Girl with the Silver Eyes" (1924), for example, the Op tracks down a missing girl by checking out bank statements, taxi trip records, railroad ticket purchases, and even weather reports. Without question Hammett brought his professional experience to bear on this kind of fiction, but he was also one of the rare pulp writers capable of conveying a feeling for a character. It was not simply that he gave murder back to real murderers (to paraphrase Raymond Chandler), but he gave them style, speech, and dress. Their brutality and avarice were a part of their natures and not something grafted onto dull people to surprise the reader.

Edward Margolies, "Dashiell Hammett: Success as Failure," *Which Way Did He Go? The Private Eye in Dashiell Hammett, Raymond Chandler, Chester Himes, and Ross Macdonald* (New York: Holmes & Meier, 1982), p. 24

---

**SINDA GREGORY**     Hammett's own reasons for entering a field of writing that seemed artistically limited can only be speculated upon. It would be easy to see his decision to write detective fiction as the result of circumstances: his experience in the field coupled with the popularity of the subject. Yet such a view fails to account for two important paradoxes. First of all, at the same time that his books are almost universally acclaimed as the best of American detective fiction, they are also among the best examples of the antidetective novel. As Hammett maintained the outward form and pattern of the hard-boiled story, he also infused it with irony, paradox, parody, and humor, so that, like the Maltese falcon, all is not as it seems. Thus, the black-and-white appeal of the detective story—a detective who pursues, a villain who eludes, a mystery created by evil and dissipated by good—is present in Hammett's fiction with disquieting contradictions that keep the reader slightly off balance. Reading a Hammett novel is like trying to put a lid on a box that is too large. You can jam it down by cheating a bit at the corners, but it will never really fit. And for a form whose most common metaphor is a jigsaw puzzle that must be assembled, each clue settling into place with a satisfying little "click," this sort of poor fit seems inconceivable.

The second paradox is the contradiction between Hammett's own philosophy and that of the genre. It is difficult to imagine a literary form more
antithetical to his own beliefs. Traditionally the classical detective story—
a product of nineteenth century empiricism—has stressed the superiority of
reason and the inevitable domination of clear-thinking law over the chaos
of lawlessness. A subsequent discussion of the differences between the classical and the hard-boiled story will show that the latter form did not accept
this blanket certainty that reason will always win out, but both kinds of
popular detective fiction can be interpreted at their most basic levels as
allegories about the individual's search for meaning and structure. This
search presupposes that reason can ferret out and discern order and, more
importantly, that such an order exists in the first place. Hammett's fiction
denies these fundamental assumptions. In his novels reason, just because it
presumes an external order to life, will always fail in the end to explain
fully human conduct and emotions. For Hammett the power of mystery is
absolute because human consciousness is absolutely mysterious.

Sinda Gregory, *Private Investigations: The Novels of Dashiell Hammett* (Carbondale:
Southern Illinois University Press, 1985), pp. 12–13

---

**JASMINE YONG HALL**       The detective story—which in its conventional form promises both to reveal the truth about the world and return
that world to order—becomes, in *The Maltese Falcon*, an arbitrary ellipsis
framed by a corpse, a physical world devoid of meaning or order. In the
middle of the novel, Spade tells Brigid a story which encapsulates this vision
of the world, and demonstrates his knowledge that what he does as a
detective is always meaningless. Spade had been hired to find a missing
person named Flitcraft by Flitcraft's wife. Flitcraft is difficult to trace because
there seems to be no motive for his disappearance; however, Spade eventually
finds him and hears the story behind that disappearance. Flitcraft had led
a very ordinary life: he was a real-estate agent with a wife and two kids
who lived in a suburb of Tacoma. One day, though, he was almost hit by
a beam falling off a construction site, and this near fatal accident revealed
to him that people have no necessary or determined relationship to the
material world. A falling beam could come out of the sky and hit you for
no reason, not because you are good or evil, but just by chance. After this
accident, Flitcraft abandoned his settled and ordered life and drifted from

one place to another. He finally settled in Spokane, where Spade finds him leading pretty much the same life he had lived before the accident—now he is an automobile salesman, with a wife and baby living in a Spokane suburb. This is the part of the story Spade enjoys the most: "He adjusted himself to beams falling, and then no more of them fell, and he adjusted himself to them not falling." Flitcraft organized his life around a story in which he played the main role as father and breadwinner. The physical world intruded and showed him the meaninglessness of that organization. Yet he returns, in the end, to another version of that same story. Similarly, Spade plays his role in the detective story only to confront the meaningless physical world represented by the Falcon, by Iva's presence, and by Archer's body. Yet he, too, returns to his role in the story; he continues to play the detective, an identity as meaningless as being the Falcon's owner.

> Jasmine Yong Hall, "Jameson, Genre, and Gumshoes: *The Maltese Falcon* as Inverted Romance," *The Cunning Craft: Original Essays on Detective Fiction and Contemporary Literary Theory*, ed. Ronald G. Walker and June M. Frazer (Macomb: Western Illinois University, 1990), pp. 117–18

# ◈ *Bibliography*

*$106,000 Blood Money* ⟨*Blood Money*; *The Big Knock-Over*⟩. 1927.

*The Dain Curse.* 1929.

*Red Harvest.* 1929.

*The Maltese Falcon.* 1930.

*The Glass Key.* 1931.

*Creeps by Night: Chills and Thrills* (editor). 1931, 1932 (abridged; as *Modern Tales of Horror*), 1961 (abridged; as *The Red Brain and Other Thrillers*), 1968 (abridged; as *Breakdown and Other Thrillers*).

*Secret Agent X-9* (with Alex Raymond). 1934. 2 vols.

*The Thin Man.* 1934.

*Dashiell Hammett Omnibus: Red Harvest; The Dain Curse; The Maltese Falcon.* 1935.

*The Complete Dashiell Hammett.* 1942.

*The Battle of the Aleutians: A Graphic History 1942–1943.* 1944.

*The Adventures of Sam Spade and Other Stories.* 1944, 1945 (as *A Man Called Spade and Other Stories*).

*The Continental Op.* 1945.

*The Return of the Continental Op.* 1945.

*Hammett Homicides.* Ed. Ellery Queen. 1946.

*Dead Yellow Women.* Ed. Ellery Queen. 1947.

*Nightmare Town.* Ed. Ellery Queen. 1948.

*The Creeping Siamese.* Ed. Ellery Queen. 1950.

*Woman in the Dark: More Adventures of the Continental Op.* Ed. Ellery Queen. 1951.

*A Man Called Thin and Other Stories.* Ed. Ellery Queen. 1962.

*The Big Knockover: Selected Stories and Short Novels.* Ed. Lillian Hellman. 1966.

*The Continental Op.* Ed. Steven Marcus. 1974.

# E. W. Hornung
## 1866–1921

ERNEST WILLIAM HORNUNG was born on June 7, 1866, in Middlesbrough, Yorkshire, to Mr. and Mrs. John Peter Hornung. Upon graduating from Upingham, an Anglican boy's school, at the age of eighteen, the feeble-bodied Hornung emigrated to Australia in search of milder weather. Although Hornung returned to England just two years later, Australia provided the setting for his first novel, a colonial romance entitled *A Bride from the Bush* (1890), and for many of his other early works including *Tiny Luttrell* (1893), *The Boss of Taroomba* (1894), *The Unbidden Guest* (1894), *Irralie's Bushranger* (1896), and *The Rogue's March* (1896), a novel about Australian convicts that revealed Hornung's increasing interest in crime and the moral questions surrounding it. While in Australia, Hornung contributed to the *Sydney Bulletin* and built enough of a reputation as a journalist to be admitted into London's literary society upon his return: in 1891 he became a member of the Idler's Club and the Strand Club, which were organized and frequented by London literati.

On September 27, 1893, Arthur Conan Doyle, author of the popular Sherlock Holmes stories, hosted the wedding of his sister Constance and Hornung at his home in South Norwood. Doyle praised Hornung's character, wit, and literary abilities in speech and print. Hornung, in turn, dedicated *The Amateur Cracksman* to Doyle.

Hornung is best remembered for his creation of Raffles, a raffish and rakish cricketer who courts high society to gain access to their homes and valuables. The Raffles tales—*The Amateur Cracksman* (1899), *The Black Mask* (1901), *A Thief in the Night: The Last Chronicle of Raffles* (1905), and *Mr. Justice Raffles* (1909)—are an inversion of the Sherlock Holmes stories in that Raffles and his assistant Bunny Manders (who narrates the adventures, just as Watson narrates the adventures of Holmes) use their wits to commit, not solve, crimes. Raffles is certainly a scoundrel, but he is also a gentleman and a patriot: he dies in the Boer War after enlisting to serve Queen and country. Raffles was later adapted for the stage by Hornung and others, including Graham Greene. Hornung also adapted his collection of stories entitled *Stingaree* (1905) for the stage in 1908. A fascination with technology can be seen in some of his later writings such as *The Carmera Fiend* (1911), *Witching Hill* (1913), and *The Crime Doctor* (1914).

Despite his poor health, Hornung volunteered for service in World War I. His days as an ambulance driver, rest-station worker, and an officer in the YMCA services is recorded in *Notes of a Camp-Follower on the Western Front* (1919). His experiences in the war also inspired three volumes of war poetry, *The Ballad of Ensign Joy* (1917), *Wooden Crosses* (1918), and *The Young Guard* (1919). In failing health, Hornung retired to France after the war, where he died on March 22, 1921.

# ▣ *Critical Extracts*

**FRANK WADLEIGH CHANDLER**     The most popular literary rogue of recent times owes to the most popular of literary detectives his birth and characteristics. Hornung's *Amateur Cracksman* (1899), dedicated to Conan Doyle, betrays with its sequels, *Raffles* (1901) and *A Thief in the Night* (1905), the distinguishing traits of Sherlock Holmes. Raffles is secretive and taciturn, a non-professional who excels in ability those of the trade, and a gentleman when not engaged in business. He is gifted with analytic powers of no mean order. He has his fastidious specialties,—cricket and Sullivan cigarettes. His cleverness is heightened by contrast with the surprised stupidity of his associate, the narrator Bunny, who reflects Doyle's Watson. Raffles's exploits, like many of Sherlock Holmes's, are chronicled by episodes in short story form, and they make their appeal by similar devices to the same emotions.

The great difference between the two groups of fictions is the reversal of point of view. But in this reversal the rogue is at a disadvantage morally and intellectually. To offset his intellectual disadvantage, Raffles is given peculiar and difficult undertakings, as well as special qualities,—"his high spirits, his iron nerve, his buoyant wit, his perfect ease and self-possession." His cleverness and breeding are meant to blind admirers to his moral disadvantage; but the whole question of right and wrong is blinked. Though he dies as a patriot in the Boer War, he is still the rogue and adventurer, and all his creator's attempts to portray him as a hero, rather than an anti-hero, deservedly fail.

Raffles himself holds to the theory propounded by Fielding. Human nature is a chess-board, a thing of alternate black and white. "Why desire to be all one thing or all the other," he asks, "like our forefathers on the stage or in the old-fashioned fiction? Let us know all squares on the board and enjoy the light the better for the shade." As a matter of fact, he does not know what conscience means. To speak of him as "forever dazzling one with a fresh and unsuspected facet of his character" indicates what his creator wished him to do, rather than what he does. At first, even his skill fails to be convincing. The burglary of the jewelry shop in "The Ides of March" is altogether too simple. When he disguises as a policeman and rescues his pal by apprehending him, Raffles is better; but Mackenzie, the Scotch detective with whom he must frequently contend, is far from the equal of Holmes.

Frank Wadleigh Chandler, *The Literature of Roguery* (Boston: Houghton Mifflin, 1907), Vol. 2, pp. 515–16

---

**UNSIGNED**      Word reached here yesterday of the death on March 22, at St. Jean de Luz, France, of influenza, of E. W. Hornung, the English short story writer and novelist, who created the famous character of the amateur cracksman "Raffles," thereby setting a fashion that has been followed by many other writers of recent years.

Although he was born in England, in 1866, Australia was given the credit for much of his early work, for he had lived there as a youth and had gathered the material for many of his stories, notably *A Bride from the Bush* and the vivid bandit tale, *Stingaree.*

*The Amateur Cracksman* appeared in 1899 and was followed by other adventures of the fascinating lawbreaker, one of these later volumes being *Mr. Justice Raffles.* The play of *Raffles,* in which Kyrle Boilew acted the picaresque hero, was produced with success here and in England.

Mr. Hornung was married in 1893 to Miss Constance Doyle, a sister of Sir Arthur Conan Doyle. Thus the great detective, Sherlock Holmes, and the great thief, Raffles, became in a sense, brothers-in-law. The Hornung home was Midway Cottage, Partridge Corners, Sussex.

Unsigned, [Obituary of E. W. Hornung], *New York Times,* 8 April 1921, p. 13

**SIR ARTHUR CONAN DOYLE**        Willie Hornung, my brother-in-law, is another of my vivid memories. He was a Dr. Johnson without the learning but with a finer wit. No one could say a neater thing, and his writings, good as they are, never adequately represented the powers of the man, nor the quickness of his brain. These things depend upon the time and the fashion, and go flat in the telling, but I remember how, when I showed him the record of some one who claimed to have done 100 yards under ten seconds, he said: "It's a sprinter's error." Golf he could not abide, for he said it was "unsportsmanlike to hit a sitting ball." His criticism upon my Sherlock Holmes was: "Though he might be more humble, there is no police like Holmes." I think I may claim that his famous character Raffles was a kind of inversion of Sherlock Holmes, Bunny playing Watson. He admits as much in his kindly dedication. I think there are few finer examples of short-story writing in our language than these, though I confess I think they are rather dangerous in their suggestion. I told him so before he put pen to paper, and the result has, I fear, borne me out. You must not make the criminal a hero.

Sir Arthur Conan Doyle, Memories and Adventures (Boston: Little, Brown, 1924), pp. 252–53

---

**GEORGE ORWELL**        Nearly half a century after his first appearance, Raffles, "the amateur cracksman," is still one of the best-known characters in English fiction. Very few people would need telling that he played cricket for England, had bachelor chambers at the Albany and burgled the Mayfair houses which he also entered as a guest. ⟨. . .⟩

At this date, the charm of *Raffles* is partly in the period atmosphere and partly in the technical excellence of the stories. Hornung was a very conscientious and on his level a very able writer. Anyone who cares for sheer efficiency must admire his work. However, the truly dramatic thing about Raffles, the thing that makes him a sort of byword even to this day (only a few weeks ago, in a burglary case, a magistrate referred to the prisoner as "a Raffles in real life"), is the fact that he is a *gentleman*. Raffles is presented to us—and this is rubbed home in countless scraps of dialogue and casual remarks—not as an honest man who has gone astray, but as a public-school man who has gone astray. His remorse, when he feels any, is almost purely social; he has disgraced "the old school," he has lost his right to enter "decent society," he has forfeited his amateur status and become a cad. Neither Raffles nor Bunny appears to feel at all strongly that stealing is wrong in itself, though Raffles does once justify himself by the casual remark that "the distribution of property is all wrong anyway." They think of themselves not as sinners but as renegades, or simply as outcasts. And the moral code of most of us is still so close to Raffles' own that we do feel his situation to be an especially ironical one. A West End club man who is really a burglar! That is almost a story in itself, is it not? But how if it were a plumber or a greengrocer who was really a burglar? Would there be anything inherently dramatic in that? No—although the theme of the "double life," of respectability covering crime, is still there. Even Charles Peace in his clergyman's dog-collar seems somewhat less of a hypocrite than Raffles in his Zingari blazer. ⟨. . .⟩

It is important to note that by modern standards Raffles's crimes are very pretty ones. Four hundred pounds' worth of jewelry seems to him an excellent haul. And though the stories are convincing in their physical detail, they contain very little sensationalism—very few corpses, hardly any blood, no sex crimes, no sadism, no perversions of any kind. It seems to be the case that the crime story, at any rate on its higher levels, has greatly increased in blood-thirstiness during the past twenty years. Some of the early detective stories do not even contain a murder. ⟨. . .⟩ The Raffles stories, written from the angle of the criminal, are much less anti-social than many modern stories written from the angle of the detective. The main impression that they leave behind is of boyishness. They belong to a time when people had standards, though they happened to be foolish standards. Their key-phrase is "not done." The line that they draw between good and evil is as senseless as a Polynesian taboo, but at least, like the taboo, it has the advantage that everyone accepts it.

George Orwell, "Raffles and Miss Blandish" (1944), *Dickens, Dali & Others* (New York: Harcourt, Brace & World, 1946), pp. 202–4, 207–8.

---

**COLIN WATSON**        There are certain elements of attraction that the Raffles books have in common with most other successful works of fiction. Flamboyant character and preposterous situation have in themselves an appeal that persists against the grain of logic and even of taste, if that is the best word for what might be otherwise described as literary conscience.

Heoroes do best for themselves when they are cheeky and daring. The memorable ones nearly always have an imbecilic streak that in the real world would render them liable to be shunned and perhaps locked up. Exaggeration is an expected feature of escapist literature—the 'larger than life' requirement. That it reads sometimes like a parody means only that time has shifted our sympathies away from those of the readers for whom a book was originally written. Much of our own fiction will seem to be burlesque in twenty or thirty years.

Hornung's writing has a place. The stories, however ridiculous, carry the readers along briskly. Superfluous description has been avoided and account of action is to the point.

There remain certain peculiar characteristics to be considered.

The atmosphere, the dialogue and many of the events described in the Raffles books are schoolboyish. The excitement is at the level of a dormitory rag or a midnight fest. Even the mutual loyalty of the confederates is expressed in terms more appropriate to the Lower Sixth than to an association of armed criminals. 'Old chaps' in the sense of men mature enough to shave and sufficiently worldly-wise to have a smattering of thieves' argot, if that is what is implied by 'Whitechapel lingo', are not normally in the habit of clasping one another's hands. Nor do we expect a pair of foiled burglars to celebrate their escape from arrest by treating themselves to a cigarette apiece, however choice the brand. But Raffles and Bunny are not subject to the likelihoods of human development. Eternally callow, they mirror from the pages of fiction the reader's inmost desire for happy immutability. ⟨. . .⟩

The supra-legal status of Raffles is possibly a further contribution to the character's popularity. He does not just break the law; he commits crime so frequently and successfully that the impression is created of his being above the law. Now the English, who so seldom do it themselves, love a man who cocks a snook at authority. No myth has been more cherished and expanded than that of Robin Hood. Our national heroes include only one saint (and him dubiously) but a score of pirates and highwaymen. Is Raffles in this company? Certainly he is a lone wolf, or one of a pair anyway. He spends his time fleeing from the police. He robs the rich (whom else could he rob?). Perhaps Hornung calculated that these attributes would be enough to make Raffles a satisfactory embodiment of the Robin Hood tradition. Undiscerning readers certainly have accepted him as such. But what he really personifies is something quite different, something inimical to the principles of justice, of the righting of wrongs, with which the rebel heroes of England have always been associated. Raffles is himself a product of privilege; he is unconcerned with justice; his crimes are mean, his commission of them purely selfish and arrogant. There can scarcely be excluded from any theory of why narration of his exploits sold so well the presumption that it reached some part of the reader's mind that was ready to applaud the success of even a bully and a thug, provided he had estimable credentials.

Colin Watson, *Snobbery with Violence: Crime Stories and Their Audience* (New York: St. Martin's Press, 1971), pp. 47–50

---

**WILLIAM VIVIAN BUTLER**     Obviously, the Raffles-Bunny relationship derives, basically, from the Holmes-Watson one. But, apart from the fact that they were contemporaries, and talked in the same late Victorian style, there are remarkably few real similarities between Sherlock Holmes and Raffles. Raffles is from the very outset a completely new kind of hero, and a far from prepossessing one. The chilling side of him comes across on his first appearance on the printed page. In the first Raffles story, 'The Ides of March', Bunny finds himself in dire financial straits after a card game at Raffles's flat. Later that night, he returns to the flat to appeal to Raffles for help. When this help does not appear to be forthcoming, he whips a pistol from his overcoat pocket and points it at his own temple, resolved on instant suicide. He expects, at the very least, to see a look of horror cross Raffles's face. Instead, all he sees is 'wonder, admiration, and such a measure of pleased expectancy' that he pockets the gun with an oath, saying: 'You devil! I believe you wanted me to do it!' ⟨. . .⟩

There are, of course, many other sides to Raffles than this. Some people have called him a pasteboard, two-dimensional creation. In fact, his character has more facets then any of the diamonds he tries (often so unsuccessfully) to purloin. There is Raffles the cool, cricket-disparaging cricketer. ('Where's the satisfaction of taking a man's wicket when you want his spoons?') There is Raffles the implacably determined criminal. ('A stern chase and a long one, Bunny, but I think I'm well to windward this time.') There is Raffles the schoolboyish taunter. ('You've grown such a pious old rabbit in your old age.') There is Raffles the dignified observer of niceties. ('When we took old Lady Melrose's necklace, Bunny, we were not staying with the Melroses, if you recollect.') There is Raffles the passionate romantic about the one real love of his life, a simple Italian maiden called Faustina. ('Only to look at her—only to look at her for the rest of my days—I could have lain low and remained dead even to you! And that's all I'm going to tell you about that, Bunny; cursed be he who tells more!') There is the vulnerable Raffles, the very opposite of the durable desperado, ageing twenty years when his Faustina is killed by a Mafia-type gang; even his hair turns white at a stroke. And finally—a side of him usually forgotten—there is Raffles the patriot, who celebrates Queen Victoria's diamond jubilee by sending Her Majesty a priceless gold cup which he has just stolen from the British Museum. He makes quite a stirring speech into the bargain. ('My dear Bunny, we have been reigned over for sixty years by infinitely the finest monarch the world has ever seen. The world is taking the present opportunity of signifying the fact for all its worth. Every nation is laying of its best at her royal feet; every class in the community is doing its little best except ours. All I have done is to remove a reproach from our fraternity . . .')

William Vivian Butler, *The Durable Desperadoes* (London: Macmillan, 1973), pp. 35–37

---

**OWEN DUDLEY EDWARDS**     Conan Doyle's brother-in-law Ernest William Hornung produced in Raffles and Bunny an imitation of Holmes and Watson which is very obviously homosexual, and a mawkish, cloying, stifling business it is. This is particularly evident in the narrator, Bunny, who becomes very jealous whenever Raffles looks at girls, and fairly tense when any male rival for Raffles's attention is present also. Bunny is represented as having been in love with a woman when he became Raffles's assistant in the amateur cracksman business, but Raffles quite effectively drives that out of his mind. In any case the lady receives her first mention in the third book of the series which suggests that Hornung thought his original version needed some cosmetic treatment. The relationship between Raffles and Bunny has begun in public-school, with Bunny as Raffles's fag, or conscript batman from a junior class, and this is constantly stressed as basic to all of their subsequent proceedings. Graham Greene very reasonably made the homosexuality explicit in his light-hearted play *The Return of A. J. Raffles*, but even his genius could not quite sustain the atmosphere of schoolboy "crush" which radiates from Bunny. Curiously, the initial effort to sweeten the Raffles saga from the moralists' standpoint, when it was serialised, in *Cassell's* in 1898, resulted in a title *"In the Chains of Crime"*, subtitled "Being the Confessions of a late prisoner of the Crown, and sometime accomplice of the more notorious A. J. Raffles, Cricketer and Criminal, whose fate is unknown". This may have reminded everyone that Crime Did Not Pay And Was Wrong rather better than Hornung would succeed in doing, but it carried with it a picture, repeated each month, showing Bunny wearing evening-dress and chained by the neck being dragged by a skeleton in a monk's habit, possibly towards a pit but actually into the arms—and not very skeletal arms—of the skeleton who holds in his hand farthest from Bunny a confused bunch of leather possibly intended for punitive purposes.

Leaving this picture aside as a mere curiosity, the contrast between Holmes-Watson and Raffles-Bunny asserts itself most notably at the outset because of Conan Doyle's confidence in describing such a relationship and Hornung's wallowing in public-school sentimentality. To say this is not to question Hornung's artistry; if such a partnership as Raffles and Bunny were to exist, prolonged public-school idolisation was about the most likely basis for it. In any case, Hornung can claim much credit in facilitating the return of Sherlock Holmes. If Raffles owed much of his existence to the example of Holmes, Holmes owed much of the renewal of his to the example of Raffles.

Owen Dudley Edwards, *The Quest for Sherlock Holmes: A Biographical Study of Arthur Conan Doyle* (Totowa, NJ: Barnes & Noble, 1983) pp. 110–11

---

**JEREMY LEWIS**     The truth of the matter is that Raffles is a good deal more interesting and less predictable than the stereotype of the light-fingered, amiable toff. He is also a good deal less gentlemanly than he's usually assumed to be, not least in his sometimes caddish treatment of the dogged, devoted Bunny (who, to be fair, must have presented him with temptation of the sorest kind). As Orwell pointed out, Raffles is accepted in upper-crust society but is not of it; he is only too aware that he is there on suffrance, that 'the gentlemen of England would scarcely have owned me as one of them', and is fiercely resentful of the fact that he is invited for his sporting abilities rather than in his own right. 'Society is like rings in a target, and we were never in the bull's eye, however thick you may lay on the ink,' he informs Bunny: 'I was asked for my cricket. I haven't forgotten it yet.' Country-house owners who take liberties and treat him like a 'professional'—the ultimate insult in a society in which amateur status was jealously guarded—might well find themselves in for an unpleasant shock: 'As a general rule nothing would induce me to abuse my position as a guest. I've never done it, Bunny. But in this case we're engaged like the waiters and the band, and by heaven we'll take our toll!'

Nor is Raffles merely a simple-minded sportsman with a taste for crime. Bunny believed that 'the man might have been a minor poet instead of an athlete of the first water', and while visiting Raffles's rooms in the Albany he is struck by the 'absence of the usual insignia of a cricketer's den. Instead of the conventional rack of war-worn bats, a carved oak bookcase, with every shelf in a litter, filled the better part of one wall; and where I looked for cricketing groups I found reproductions of such works as "Love and Death" and "The Blessed Damozel".' No doubt Raffles was a keen subscriber to the *Yellow Book,* and sneaked off to the Café Royal to drink champagne with unwholesome poets when Bunny wasn't looking. Like Sherlock Holmes, his artistry often manifests itself in the form of impenetrable disguises. In his school days, Raffles was much given to stealing out at night and 'parading the town in large checks and a false beard'; like Holmes with Watson, he occasionally stupefies the simple-minded Bunny by looming up disguised as a particularly repellent and odoriferous tramp or even—when rescuing his companion from the flashy St. Johns Wood mansion belonging to the South African diamond magnate, Reuben Rosenthall—as a member of the Metropolitan Police. (The helmet is 'one of a collection I made up at Oxford'—an agreeably Woosterish touch.) Given his weakness for Sullivans, Raffles's insistence on using a particularly foetid tobacco in order to put the finishing touches to an utterly baffling impersonation represented, for the awestruck Bunny, 'the last, least touch of the insatiable artist'. (Judging by the remarkable powers of disguise displayed by the likes of Raffles, Holmes and Carl Peterson, there must have been an astonishing number of insatiable artists clipping on false beards and applying soot stains in the great days of English crime.) Raffles prides himself on an impressive range of regional accents, and Hornung's own attempts at the demotic have a comically stilted, antique flavor to them: 'No sperrits—no, thank'ee—not yet!' insists a fellow-burglar, refusing Raffles's kindly offer of a drink. 'Once let me loose on lush, and, Lord love yer, I'm a gone coon!'

Jeremy Lewis, "Introduction," *The Collected Raffles* (London: J. M. Dent & Sons, 1985), pp. xii–xiii.

# ✦ *Bibliography*

*A Bride from the Bush.* 1890.

*Under Two Skies: A Collection of Stories.* 1892.

*Tiny Luttrell.* 1893. 2 vols.

*The Boss of Taroomba.* 1894.

*The Unbidden Guest.* 1894.

*Irralie's Bushranger.* 1896.

*The Rogue's March.* 1896.

*My Lord Duke.* 1897.

*Some Persons Unknown.* 1898.

*Young Blood.* 1898.

*The Amateur Cracksman* ⟨*Raffles, the Amateur Cracksman*⟩. 1899.

*Dead Men Tell No Tales.* 1899.

*The Belle of Toorak* ⟨*The Shadow of a Man*⟩. 1900.

*Peccavi.* 1900.

*The Black Mask* ⟨*Raffles: Further Adventures of the Amateur Cracksman*⟩. 1901.

*At Large.* 1902.

*The Shadow of the Rope.* 1902.

*Denis Dent.* 1903.

*No Hero.* 1903.

*Stingaree.* 1905.

*A Thief in the Night: The Last Chronicle of Raffles.* 1905.

*Mr. Justice Raffles.* 1909.

*The Camera Fiend.* 1911.

*Fathers of Men.* 1912.

*The Thousandth Woman.* 1913.

*Witching Hill.* 1913.

*The Crime Doctor.* 1914.

*"Trusty and Well Beloved": The Little Record of Arthur Oscar Hornung.* 1915.

*The Ballad of Ensign Joy.* 1917.

*Wooden Crosses.* 1918.

*Notes of a Camp-Follower on the Western Front.* 1919.

*The Young Guard.* 1919.

*Old Offenders and a Few Old Scores.* 1923.

*Raffles: Raffles; Mr. Justice Raffles; A Thief in the Night; The Shadow of the Rope.* 1929.

*E. W. Hornung and His Young Guard, 1914.* Ed. Shane R. Chichester. 1941.
*The Complete Short Stories of Raffles, the Amateur Cracksman.* 1984.
*The Collected Raffles.* 1985.

# John D. MacDonald
## *1916–1986*

JOHN DANN MACDONALD was born on July 24, 1916, in Sharon, Pennsylvania. An only child, he moved with his family to Utica, New York, in 1926 while recovering from a life-threatening bout with scarlet fever. He enrolled as an undergraduate at the Wharton School of Finance at the University of Philadelphia in 1932, but dropped out in the spring of his sophomore year. That fall, he began attending the Syracuse School of Business Administration, from which he received a B.S. degree in 1938. That same year he married Dorothy Prentiss and entered the Harvard Graduate School of Business Administration, which awarded him an M.B.S. in 1939.

Following several short-lived business positions MacDonald enlisted in the armed services in 1940, receiving a commission as first lieutenant and working as a branch commander in Ceylon for the Office of Strategic Services. He sold his first piece of fiction to *Story* magazine upon his return to the United States in 1945 and began writing professionally in 1946. In the years that followed he wrote in a variety of genres for the pulp fiction magazines, but became best known for his work in the mystery/detective field. His first novel, *The Brass Cupcake* (1950), was originally intended as a novella for magazine publication, but MacDonald expanded it on the advice of his agent and sold it to Fawcett Gold Medal Books, initiating a lifelong relationship as the publisher's best-known author.

Between 1950 and 1963, MacDonald wrote forty-two novels, most paperback originals such as *The Damned* (1952), *The Deceivers* (1958), and *Last Monday We Killed Them All* (1961), which helped to establish his reputation as a writer of "hard-boiled" crime fiction, albeit one whose work reflected an atypical streak of social consciousness. In 1962, the year he was elected president of the Mystery Writers of America, his 1958 novel *The Executioners* was adapted as the critically acclaimed film *Cape Fear*.

In 1964 MacDonald overcame his longstanding resistance to series characters by creating Travis McGee, a salvage expert who lives on a boat off the coast of Florida, in the novel *The Deep Blue Good-By*. A detective hero whose casework invariably serves as a springboard for commentary on the cultural and political problems of the day, McGee proved a popular success and dominated the rest of MacDonald's career. The first four McGee novels appeared that year, and the next three over the next two years. Twenty-one Travis McGee novels appeared in MacDonald's lifetime, but only one, *Darker Than Amber* (1966), was filmed.

MacDonald was awarded the American Book Award in 1980 for Best Hardcover Mystery for the nineteenth Travis McGee novel, *The Green Ripper*. His other honors included the University of Illinois's Ben Franklin Award for the best magazine short story of 1955, the Mystery Writers of America Grand Master Award in 1972, and the institution of the John D. MacDonald Conference on Mystery and Detective Fiction at the University of South Florida. He died on December 28, 1986, following complications during bypass surgery.

# ◈ *Critical Extracts*

**JOHN D. MacDONALD**      It is, of course, entirely possible to write a successful mystery wherein the characters are merely symbols—two-dimensional personifications of virtues and vices to be moved about within a puzzle plot until by the final page they fit the pattern of solution as neatly as the flat pieces of a completed jigsaw puzzle. But today this sort of mystery is the exception rather than the rule—as it was a few years ago. Raymond Chandler's classic article in the *Atlantic*, "The Gentle Art of Murder," covers this shift of emphasis thoroughly and definitively.

Today a less patient republic requires more suspense than mystification, more action than cerebration. Purists will not recognize the novel of action and suspense as a mystery. Indeed, they will be content with flatness of character, so long as there is a carefully interwoven web of clue and counterclue. Unfortunately the purists do not form a sufficiently large market.

That leads us directly to my point. There is nothing more dreadful than the "mystery" novel of action and suspense wherein the characters have that peculiar woodenness characteristic of the English school of the mystery story, genus 1925. We can see, therefore, that as the mystery story becomes less dependent on intricacy of plot and detection, it becomes ever more dependent on the depicting of characters "in the round." And as the characters in mystery fiction become ever more fully realized, the dividing line between the mystery and the straight novel becomes constantly more vague (e.g., the work of Margaret Millar).

Thus, insofar as lead protagonists are concerned, the rules of depicting character—if indeed we can affirm that any rules exist—differ in no significant way as between the straight novel and the mystery.

John D. MacDonald, "How a Character Becomes Believable," *The Mystery Writer's Handbook*, ed. Herbert Brean (New York: Harper & Brothers, 1956), pp. 113–14

---

**ANTHONY BOUCHER**      *The Executioners* tells of a successful lawyer, leading a contented suburban life with wife and three children, who was responsible, thirteen years ago, for the conviction of a G. I. rapist. Now the released criminal appears, clearly intent upon revenge yet shrewd enough to permit no overt evidence of his intentions.

What do you do when you know your family is threatened with destruction by a sadist and yet have no proof that you can offer to the law? And, moreover, you respect that law too much to take the direct course of removing the threat yourself? MacDonald not only tells with quiet realism a powerful and frightening story; he takes a deeper look than most suspense novelists at the problem of private and public justice—even if his ending does avoid some of the questions he has raised.

Anthony Boucher, "Criminals at Large," *New York Times Book Review*, 1 June 1958, p. 17

---

**FRANCIS M. NEVINS, JR.**      One crucial reason why it is so difficult to use the formal deductive problem as a vehicle for serious literary intent is the artificiality of a genre in which the destruction of a human being serves as a pretext for a display of logical acumen. This obstacle does not exist where an author adopts a looser structure and avoids the creation of intellectual puzzles, as JDM has done since the beginning of his career. Thereby he won the freedom to work, within the crime-novel form, at his intensely personal evocations of the times we live in, with their powerful images of the inhuman.

What makes one of our kind treat one another as something less than human? In JDM's novels, the answer is generally greed. The acquisitiveness with which we indoctrinate our children before we throw them into the maw of some huge corporation like the one that uses us has its logical culmination in a Junior Allen, a Bayard Mulligan, or a Gary Santo. For love of money, we mutilate not only others but ourselves, as Staniker did in *The Last One Left.*

Francis M. Nevins, Jr., "JDM's Images of the Inhuman," *JDM Bibliophile* No. 13 (April 1968): 6

**MICHAEL J. TOLLEY**     MacDonald likes to place his hero in steamy situations that are calculated to arouse the drooling envy of the average male reader, and then to have McGee behave with superior virtue. A typical scene is that in which McGee hovers near wench in bathtub, while stoically refraining from plunging in with her. Such righteousness could seem intolerably smug to the said reader (who might think that the essence of the problem lay in getting into such situations), were it not that these victories over lust cost McGee more than he likes to admit. In situations such as these, where McGee behaves with implausible but exemplary virtue, MacDonald rescues his hero from self-righteousness and invests him with a much more plausible and persuasive mantle of virtue, that of Quixote.

The Quixote is one of the few acceptable hero types for this cynical age. The Quixote is a Romantic (so far so bad) doomed to perpetual failure (which reassures our sense of the cynical disposition of the world and so is good). We sneer at the impossible idealist who tilts at windmills and we laugh as he suffers his deserved comeuppance, while we secretly respect his sincerity and courage and so half take seriously the ideals that generate his admirable stoicism. I am talking, of course, about a debased and secondhand notion of the character created by Cervantes, because the popular cliché is all that MacDonald needs to use, and indeed, all that he can use if he is to work upon the imaginations of his chosen audience. But MacDonald's subtle and varied use of the Quixote image should be distinguished from its ordinary use by thriller writers. It is quite common for a hero in thrillers to characterize an action of his own as quixotic, by which he usually means "chivalric, supererogatory, foolish, brave, and unaccountable"; his tone is self-critical, yet the reader is usually inclined to congratulate him on his action, on his quixotry (which may, of course, be a successful action, despite the label—in which case, the action is termed quixotic because it ought to have failed). What seems a temporary aberration in some heroes is an essential characteristic of the early McGee. Again, MacDonald's hero should be distinguished from modern Quixotes who do not know that they are Quixotes, such as Arthur Peabody Goodpasture, the hero of Richard Powell's hilarious *Don Quixote, U.S.A.* McGee usually knows when he is behaving quixotically and this complicates our response. McGee's self-consciousness can turn obvious disadvantages of the Quixote type into strengths. One disadvantage of the Quixote is that he is an intelligent man exhibited as behaving with crass folly, which may be more irritating than amusing to the reader (as is the case, I think, with some actions of Powell's hero, in his early phase). Such irritation could be near fatal to MacDonald's purposes, but McGee's awareness that he has a choice of action between the selfish or cynical line and the principled or quixotic line, can only enhance our impression of his intelligence and sensitivity. Another disadvantage of the Quixote is that sometimes we may laugh merely at him, not with him, because his downfall is merely absurd and we are conscious of our own superiority. By getting in first, as it were, and laughing at himself, McGee can induce us to laugh with him; more interestingly, McGee's laughter can at times itself be superior, a laughter at an inferior image of himself, which may be dangerously close to the reader's own image of himself.

Michael J. Tolley, "Color Him Quixote: MacDonald's Strategy in the Early McGee Novels," *Armchair Detective* 10, No. 1 (January 1977): 7

**DAVID A. BENJAMIN**　　The success of ⟨MacDonald's⟩ formula over the span of 16 books is due to more than simplicity. One obvious factor is the characterization of Travis McGee: a bundle of contradictions, brutal yet likable, fairly honest, with a Marlovian sense of humor and honor. Another ingredient is MacDonald's peculiar genius in creating with several swift sure strokes highly believable and interesting subsidiary characters, who take on a real life of their own and interract convincingly with Travis, whether for him or against him. Perhaps John D. had subconsciously registered the complaint in Edmund Wilson's essay on "Why do People Read Detective Stories?" (1944):

> . . . you cannot become interested in the characters, because they
> never can be allowed an existence of their own even in a flat two
> dimensions but they have always to be contrived so that they can
> seem either reliable or sinister, depending on which quarter, at
> the moment, is to be baited for the reader's suspicion.

MacDonald displays equal skill in creating fascinating vignettes of the towns and cities where these adventures take place (often sociological documents in their own right), and equally interesting details concerning whichever con is being played, from stamp collecting (*The Scarlet Ruse*, 1973) to the old badger game (*Darker Than Amber*, 1966) played for deadly stakes, to pornographic blackmailing in Hollywood (*The Quick Red Fox*). Finally there is the writer's Poeish knack for creating an atmosphere of elemental night-marish terror, in generating the "smell of fear," as Chandler put it in discussing *Black Mask* writers, a magazine for which MacDonald wrote several short stories.

This smell of fear relates directly to MacDonald's ability to create believ-able characters with whom we can identify as victims and equally convincing and frightening villains. Although Travis himself is as indestructible as most mythic heroes, we realize that his friends are less immortal. Often we meet them first after they have already been victimized, and are fully aware of how much they have suffered, and how cruel and destructive any further suffering would be. We are therefore almost as psychologically vulnerable as they are themselves to the idea of further pain, and we cringe when such violence recurs. In *Bright Orange for the Shroud* (1965), Vivian Watts is raped by the animalistic yet shrewd Boone Waxwell. She is ravaged not only sexually, but psychically, a cruel abasement that leaves her no choice but suicide.

The McGee novels (and in fact almost everything written by MacDonald) are morality plays: Travis engaged in an endless struggle on behalf of defense-less victims, a force of Good against the multifarious evil rampant in our harsh society. Though protean in their form the MacDonald villain is generally greedy, sexually twisted and amoral; in short, a sociopath, total madness only a flicker away. MacDonald's moral vision is conservative and Manichean: McGee strives to preserve traditional values which he honors as an act of social good.

David A. Benjamin, "Key Witness," *New Republic*, 26 July 1975, pp. 30–31

**GEOFFREY O'BRIEN**     MacDonald's narrative mastery gives him the advantage of being able to digress as much as he likes. So sure is his control over the basic impetus of the story that he can throw in a grab bag of extras, discourse on his somewhat courtly sexual philosophy, analyze the decline and fall of Plymouth Gin, give practical tips on anything from caulking a houseboat to stopping a killer dog in its tracks to doctoring a set of books without breaking the law.

Through all this, there flutter traces of a political philosophy which remains (perhaps mercifully) indistinct. Early in his career, MacDonald perpetrated a few startlingly banal anti-Communist thrillers such as *Murder for the Bride* and *Area of Suspicion* (the latter now available only in an edition "specially revised by the author") but many of his later books (notably *A Flash of Green, Pale Gray for Guilt, The Only Girl in the Game, A Key to the Suite, Condominium*) explore the vagaries of laissez-faire capitalism far more convincingly than most Marxist writers. MacDonald's magnates, racketeers, and crooked politicians are not fundamentally different in characters from Hammett's or Chandler's, but we learn a great deal more about how they actually achieve and maintain their power. *Condominium* might almost serve as an instruction manual for aspiring land sharks. MacDonald is, after all, a graduate of the Harvard Business School, and all told he has probably taught more people the rudiments of capitalist economics than Milton Friedman and Paul Samuelson rolled together.

No use putting him in a category; MacDonald has created his own identity, more garrulous than Cain, more full of color and joie de vivre than the monochrome paranoid worlds of Goodis or Cornell Woolrich. Not to say it's all cheerful going; readers of *The End of the Night* and *One Monday We Killed Them All* know how rough MacDonald's sociopaths can play. The violence is fully comparable to that of any writer in the field. But there is always an element of measure, each book designed to contain a well-balanced set of ingredients as one would balance the ingredients of a meal, implying that MacDonald is not an obsessed man impelled to spell out the horrors of his vision; he is a professional, whose obsession is Narrative.

Geoffrey O'Brien, *Hardboiled America: The Lurid Years of American Paperbacks* (New York: Van Nostrand Reinhold, 1981), pp. 124–25

---

**DAVID GEHERIN**     Although it is difficult to generalize about the overall accomplishment of a body of work as large and varied as MacDonald's, one can isolate the basic qualities that have contributed so much to his enormous success.

First of all, MacDonald seldom fails to tell interesting stories and tell them well, one of his greatest strengths in this regard being the knack of getting a story moving quickly, grabbing the reader's attention immediately. *The Empty Trap* (1957), for example, begins with a dramatic scene in which Lloyd Westcott is pushed off a mountain in his car by three men hired to kill him. Miraculously, he is thrown from the car and survives. The incident raises a multitude of questions which only reading the rest of the novel can answer. In *You Live Once* (1956), Clint Sewell is awakened by the police, who want to question him about the disappearance of Mary Olan, a friend of his. After they leave he showers and, opening his closet to get some clothes, is shocked to find her body there. MacDonald has honed his narrative skills by writing for the pulps, and one of the things he had learned best was how to control the pace of a story, how to narrate with economy while at the same time generating tension, suspense, and mystery.

But if openings are his strength, endings are sometimes his downfall. Either because he lost interest in his story, or rushed to finish, or his material simply proved intractable, the resolution of many promising plots is disappointing—a weakness of which MacDonald himself is not unaware: "I tend to neaten things up too carefully at the end," he has confessed. "Many of my solutions are too glib." In *Soft Touch* (1958), the murderer is dramatically exposed when he gets amnesia after suffering a blow to the head and unwittingly digs up the body of his wife (whom he had murdered), thinking he was recovering loot he had buried. The impending takeover of the Harrison Corporation by entrepreneur Mike Dean in *A Man of Affairs* (1957) is averted at the last moment when he suddenly drops dead of a heart attack.

Furthermore, MacDonald also strains to provide what Thomas Doulis, in an interesting study of the formulaic elements of these early novels, calls "terminal reassurance." The villain is invariably punished, the good guy always amply rewarded, usually in the company of the beautiful woman he meets during the course of the novel. Even when the villains appear to have triumphed, as in *April Evil* (1956), retribution awaits them: one is killed when her car rams into a speeding train; the other, who has escaped in a boat with hundreds of thousands of dollars, perishes at sea, a victim of exposure and lack of water. When the plot of a novel requires victims, it is seldom the innocent who are sacrificed. In both *Cry Hard, Cry Fast*

(1955), about a multiple traffic accident, and *Murder in the Wind* (1956), about a hurricane, it is an escaping convict and his girlfriend who are killed off. Darby Garon is punished for his infidelity by being killed by a stray bullet in *The Damned* (1952); he is where he shouldn't be, having temporarily abandoned his wife and children for a quick fling in Mexico with a woman he had just met. Most of the female characters who die in these novels are either hookers, like Tony Rasselle in *A Bullet for Cinderella* (1955), or in some way morally damaged, like Lucille Branson, who, in *The Price of Murder* (1957), has been unfaithful to her devoted husband. One of the most blatant examples of MacDonald's compulsion for "terminal reassurance" occurs in *The Beach Girls* (1959), which concludes with a letter written several years after the events of the story, bringing the reader up-to-date concerning the various rewards and punishments doled out to each of the characters.

David Geherin, *John D. MacDonald* (New York: Ungar, 1982), pp. 13–14

---

**T. FREDERICK KEEFER**     In the Travis McGee novels we find also that evil does exist and there are two types. One originates in the nature of the universe, in "how things are." Natural disasters, the aging process, the vulnerability of the human body to damage from within and without—all make suffering and death an inescapable evil. In these novels, for instance, cancer, which claims many victims, has a role much like that of the bubonic epidemic in Camus' book ⟨*The Plague*⟩.

The second source of evil is man, or rather some men, for McGee too sees people as inherently more good than bad; one could compile a long list, starting with Meyer, of decent people, and McGee acknowledges (*A Deadly Shade of Gold*) that he sees only the underside, the worst of mankind. But what explains the monsters who victimize the innocent? Looking within himself, McGee recognizes, beneath the civilized surface of his personality, the "curiously deadly" qualities, "the ancient shrewdness" of his predator ancestors. Atavism, then, explains the awesome destructiveness of the mass murderer, Wally McLeen, supposedly the most civilized of beings, a retired businessman from Youngstown, Ohio (*Dress Her in Indigo*). He is, admittedly, insane, but that dementia has only released the killer in him.

In other instances, the factor that creates monsters is the domination of a whole personality by that all too common human trait, the need to obtain pleasure by causing suffering in others. Junio Allen tortures the innocent and helpless to "feed his own emptiness" (*The Deep Blue Goodbye*), and Wilhelm Vogel, the Nazi war criminal and master torturer (*One Fearful Yellow Eye*), likes best "to create those moments of ultimate hopeless horror when his companion (the victim) experiences damage she knows cannot be undone, cannot be mended, and then begins to wonder how long she will be forced to sustain the burden of consciousness and of life itself." A third factor that unleashes savagery into the world is a personality defect, the total lack of an ability to experience normal human feeling that produces the sociopath. He has no sense of right or wrong, no conscience, no capacity for empathy. Such a person is a worse menace than the sadist, since the whole world, not just the helpless, is his hunting territory and he, a machine, cannot be hindered by emotions. The best example is Paul Dissat in *A Tan and Sandy Silence*, whose utter coldness gives him the unlimited capacity for evil that almost overwhelms McGee's survival instincts. Another is Howard Brindle, who killed people who annoyed him (*The Turquoise Lament*).

There are a number of other examples of men like these—perhaps born without the power to feel, perhaps with personalities damaged in their early years—and sometimes one cannot distinguish between the sociopath, the sadist and the psychopath. Boone Waxwell, the rapist-murderer in *Bright Orange for the Shroud*, Terry Ansel, the cold-blooded cruise-ship killer of *Darker Than Amber*, "Dirty Bob" Grizzel, the certifiably insane rapist, sadist and serial murderer who terrifies Meyer so badly that he betrayed McGee (*Freefall in Crimson*), and Cody Pittler, the man who murdered a series of women for their money and to assuage his own demons (*Cinnamon Skin*)— all inhabit the world of Travis McGee, depopulating it, brutalizing the weak, often so physically strong, quick and treacherous that they come close to terminating the matchless McGee himself.

T. Frederick Keefer, "Albert Camus' American Disciple: John D. MacDonald's Existentialist Hero," *Journal of Popular Culture* 19, No. 2 (Fall 1985): 42–43

---

**ROBERT G. SHOEMAKER**     Hemingway's heroes found their way through nothingness or meaninglessness and held tightly to courage, honor, nobility, compassion, ritual, family and passion. As trivialized as it has now become, the word "fine" expressed a technical and earnest ethical and aesthetic judgment. It *mattered* to oppose cruelty, war, superstition and vanity. And most of all it mattered that one faced death and dying with all the composed dignity the human spirit could muster.

Contrast this with Travis McGee, who seems at best to be terribly confused and ambivalent concerning normal human interaction, commitment and the moral categories of virtue and nobility, and at worst to have no inkling of these matters whatsoever. He vaunts friendship, but does little to maintain it. He cannot fathom socially responsible behaviors. He cannot sacrifice enough of himself to sustain a companionship. He approaches a relationship with a woman with the fear, rather than the hope, that it might turn into love. He carefully grooms a rough-and-ready, careless and fearless appearance, but the moment he is alone he reveals an adolescent fussiness about quite silly things and a less-than-admirable tendency to simper about the effects of age on his physical prowess. To even the casual observer this poor schmuck is quivering in his sandals over the prospect of death. It is not a pretty picture.

After the tenth or twelfth McGee adventure, I began wondering why the series is so popular. Or perhaps most readers can only take a dozen or so, but not necessarily the same dozen, so there is the statistical mirage that a large group of readers followed each new tale, until production stopped. I cannot force myself to believe that our culture has become so amoral, so decadent, so axiologically vacant or schizophrenic that Travis McGee could actually serve as any kind of hero, even in escapist literature. I prefer to think, instead, that readers project themeselves—and their values—into the void and then proceed to fantasize through the plot as written. McGee is not a character to identify with, but a place-marker, to be filled in by the reader. McGee-as-written, especially in bed, is only comic relief. He is a poor, misguided fool, compared to whom virtually any reader comes out the wiser, the more successful, the happier, the braver, and the better.

Robert G. Shoemaker, "Travis McGee: A Fit But Empty Jaundiced Shell," *Clues: A Journal of Detection* 13, No. 1 (Spring–Summer 1992): 64–65

---

**RICK LOTT**      From the beginning, Travis McGee has been that most cynical of people, the disillusioned romantic. His is "a world of plausible scoundrels and psychopathic liars," where horrific and senseless violence may erupt at any moment, where if you "lift the wrong rock . . . something is going to come out from under it as fast as a moray, aiming right for the jugular." An earned and tempered cynicism is necessary for survival in such a fearful world, and McGee's serves him well. Beginning, however, with *A Tan and Sandy Silence* and continuing until the final book, *The Lonely Silver Rain*, MacDonald's world view, as revealed in the mind of Travis McGee, grows increasingly pessimistic, and sometimes desolate.

In the novels of the seventies, McGee's malaise crops up so often it becomes part of the series' pattern. His depression and self-loathing can be relieved only by another adventure, an excuse to endure pain and injury in selfless service to another, or through a new love affair and its attendant human interaction. In *The Empty Copper Sea* (1978), malaise is pervasive. Discussing his mental state with friend and confidant Meyer, McGee speculates that he suffers "Some kind of culture shock [that] manifests itself in an inability to see a reality untainted by" apocalyptic imagination, and the provenance of this disorder seems to be both the chaotic times and more personal influences. Meyer's response suggests that one cause may be Mac-Donald's own sense of mortality: "You have felt that horrid rotten exhalation, Travis, that breath from the grave, that terminal sigh. You've been singing laments for yourself."

*The Lonely Silver Rain* was written near the end of MacDonald's life; it is suffused with a dirge-like quality and filled with images of death and decay. The death of Millis Hoover's rooftop garden appears emblematic of MacDonald's own intimations of mortality: ". . . the cold in the night killed my whole garden. Everything is black and sagging and ugly. Like some kind of message." McGee feels old and tired, emotionally and spiritually bankrupt. Drinking alone one night to the accompaniment of Edye Gorme on the stereo, a voice of the past, McGee peels away layers of self-deceit in search of his "essential self" and finds: "Nothing! . . . McGee, the empty vessel . . . at one time . . . packed full of juice and dreams. Promises. Now there was a little dust at the bottom." The connection between MacDonald's sense of mortality and his broader vision of apocalypse is evident in McGee's recurrent feeling of premonitory dread: " 'Okay, Meyer . . . Life is full of signs and portents . . . You aimed a finger at me a while back and said "Bang, you're dead." It is so unlike you to do a thing like that, I get the feeling something was trying to talk to me through you.' " The chill shadow cast by MacDonald's imminent death is depicted even more poignantly near the novel's end when McGee, lying next to a vital, beautiful young woman on a boat laden with partying friends, has a sudden vision: "In a momentary flash of panic I believed the gaudy boat, noisy people, everything is dead and gone, imagined long ago and forgotten."

McGee resolves his existential crisis in a traditional way upon discovering that he has fathered an illegitimate daughter with former lover Puss Killian. This sudden, new relationship forces upon McGee some of the mundane obligations and duties he has spent his life avoiding. But it also provides a sense of continuity beyond the grave. Jean Killian becomes for McGee "A promise of light. A Way to continue."

This surprising development brings MacDonald's remarkable series to a singular height of maturity and realization, but does little to counter the book's overall tone of despair. Apocalyptic literature provides a solace in times of crisis, ensuring transition to a more orderly age, if not to a new Jerusalem or a Golden Age. Because MacDonald's apocalyptic vision, however, sees nothing beyond the cataclysm, it is perhaps ultimately nihilistic. In his typology of apocalypse ⟨*Toward a New Earth: Apocalypse in the American Novel* (1972)⟩, John May delineates the modes of American literary apocalypse and observes that contemporary literature tends to employ traditional symbols to express the despair traditional apocalyptics was designed to mitigate. Thus the apocalyptics of much modern American literature is nontraditional because it rejects the possibility of re-creation. May terms this mode "apocalypse of despair." This nihilistic despair is the reason for McGee's periodic spiritual bankruptcy and his attempts to find renewal in heroic action and love.

Rick Lott, "Signs and Portents: John D. MacDonald's Apocalyptic Vision," *University of Mississippi Studies in English* 10 (1992): 183–85

# Bibliography

*The Brass Cupcake*. 1950.
*Wine of the Dreamers* ⟨*Planet of the Dreamers*⟩. 1951.
*Judge Me Not*. 1951.
*Murder for the Bride*. 1951.
*Weep for Me*. 1951.
*The Damned*. 1952.
*Ballroom of the Skies*. 1952.
*Dead Low Tide*. 1953.

*The Neon Jungle*. 1953.

*Cancel All Our Vows*. 1953.

*All These Condemned*. 1954.

*Area of Suspicion*. 1954, 1961.

*Contrary Pleasure*. 1954.

*A Bullet for Cinderella* ⟨*On the Make*⟩. 1955.

*Cry Hard, Cry Fast*. 1955.

*April Evil*. 1956.

*Border Town Girl* ⟨*and Linda*⟩: *Two Novellas* ⟨*Five Star Fugitive*⟩. 1956.

*Murder in the Wind* ⟨*Hurricane*⟩. 1956.

*You Live Once* ⟨*You Kill Me*⟩. 1956.

*Death Trap*. 1957.

*The Empty Trap*. 1957.

*The Price of Murder*. 1957.

*A Man of Affairs*. 1957.

*Clemmie*. 1958.

*The Executioners* ⟨*Cape Fear*⟩. 1958.

*Soft Touch* ⟨*Man-Trap*⟩. 1958.

*The Deceivers*. 1958.

*The Beach Girls*. 1959.

*The Lethal Sex: The 1959 Anthology of the Mystery Writers of America* (editor).
    1959.

*The Crossroads*. 1959.

*Deadly Welcome*. 1959.

*Please Write for Details*. 1959.

*The End of the Night*. 1960.

*The Only Girl in the Game*. 1960.

*Slam the Big Door*. 1960.

*One Monday We Killed Them All*. 1961.

*Where Is Janice Gantry?* 1961.

*A Flash of Green*. 1962.

*The Girl, the Gold Watch & Everything*. 1962.

*A Key to the Suite*. 1962.

*The Drowner*. 1963.

*On the Run*. 1963.

*I Could Go On Singing*. 1963.

*The Deep Blue Good-by*. 1964.

*Nightmare in Pink*. 1964.

*A Purple Place for Dying.* 1964.

*The Quick Red Fox.* 1964.

*A Deadly Shade of Gold.* 1965.

*Bright Orange for the Shroud.* 1965.

*The House Guests.* 1965.

*Darker Than Amber.* 1966.

*One Fearful Yellow Eye.* 1966.

*End of the Tiger and Other Stories.* 1966.

*The Last One Left.* 1967.

*Three for McGee* ⟨*Nightmare in Pink, The Deep Blue Good-by, A Purple Place for Dying*⟩. 1967, 1975 (as McGee).

*Pale Gray for Guilt.* 1968.

*No Deadly Drug.* 1968.

*The Girl in the Plain Brown Wrapper.* 1968.

*Dress Her in Indigo.* 1969.

*The Long Lavender Look.* 1970.

*Seven.* 1971.

*A Tan and Sandy Silence.* 1972.

*The Scarlet Ruse.* 1973.

*The Turquoise Lament.* 1973.

*The Dreadful Lemon Sky.* 1975.

*Condominium.* 1977.

*Other Times, Other Worlds.* 1978.

*The Empty Copper Sea.* 1978.

*The Green Ripper.* 1979.

*Free Fall in Crimson.* 1981.

*Nothing Can Go Wrong* (with John H. Kilpack). 1981.

*Cinnamon Skin: The Twentieth Adventure of Travis McGee.* 1982.

*The Good Old Stuff: 13 Early Stories.* Ed. Martin H. Greenberg, Francis M. Nevins, Jr., Walter Shine, and Jean Shine. 1982.

*One More Sunday.* 1984.

*More Good Old Stuff.* 1984.

*The Lonely Silver Rain.* 1985.

*John D. MacDonald, a True Bibliophile.* Ed. Walter Shine and Jean Shine. 1985.

*Barrier Island.* 1986.

*A Friendship: The Letters of Dan Rowan and John D. MacDonald 1967–1974.* 1986.

*Reading for Survival.* 1987.

# Ross Macdonald
## *1915–1983*

ROSS MACDONALD is the pseudonym of Kenneth Millar, who was born on December 13, 1915, in Los Gatos, California, the only child of Canadians John and Anne Millar. In 1919 the family moved to Vancouver, British Columbia, where John Millar abandoned his wife and son. Millar and his mother were left so poor that Kenneth had to beg for money and food. Anne Millar took her son to Ontario, where they lived intermittently in rented quarters and with relatives. Throughout his youth Kenneth was shuttled between his mother, maternal grandmother, and two aunts; the instability and poverty of his home life left a lasting impression upon him. Kenneth received a spotty education at St. John's School, a semimilitary academy in Winnipeg, and at the Kitchener-Waterloo Collegiate and Vocational School in Kitchener, Ontario. During this period Kenneth, always a voracious reader, stumbled upon Dashiell Hammett's *The Maltese Falcon* and was electrified by it.

The death of John Millar in 1932 provided Kenneth with the money to attend the University of Western Ontario the next year. He graduated in 1938, after spending a year traveling through Europe to recover from the death of his mother in 1935. At the university he met Margaret Sturm, a high school classmate; they married in June 1938. In 1939, when the Millars' only daughter, Linda, was born, Kenneth Millar taught at Kitchener-Waterloo while striving to become a professional writer. In 1941 he received a fellowship at the University of Michigan at Ann Arbor; that same year his wife published her first mystery novel, *The Invisible Worm*, and went on to become a distinguished author of psychological mysteries.

Kenneth Millar published his first novel, *The Dark Tunnel*, in 1944. In that year he was sent by the U.S. Naval Reserve to the Pacific as a communications officer, remaining on duty until 1946. By this time Margaret and Linda had settled in Santa Barbara, California, and the Millars remained there for most of the rest of their lives. Millar wrote several other novels under his own name, and in 1948 he began a novel, *The Moving Target*, about the private detective Lew Archer. Unsure about its quality, he published it the next year under the pseudonym John Macdonald (the first and middle names of his father). The detective writer John D. MacDonald complained about the possible confusion caused by Millar's pseudonym, and—after several novels published as by John Ross Macdonald—Millar settled on Ross Macdonald as his pseudonym in *The Barbarous Coast* (1956).

In 1949 the Millars returned to Ann Arbor, where Kenneth finished his Ph.D. in 1952, writing a dissertation on Coleridge. While there he wrote two more Lew Archer novels. The Millars returned to California, where their family life was shaken in 1956 when Linda was involved in a vehicular homicide and was forced to undergo psychiatric treatment; Millar himself went into therapy, and from this time on his work changed character, becoming heavily psychological and autobiographical. *The Galton Case* (1959) is a watershed book in this regard, and it also marks the beginning of Millar's increasing recognition as a serious crime novelist. His novels of the 1960s cemented his reputation, and his popularity soared when *The Moving Target* was filmed in 1966 as *Harper*, starring Paul Newman.

Kenneth Millar continued writing successfully into the 1970s, despite the death of his daughter in 1970. In 1974 he received the Grand Master Award from the Mystery Writers of America. A film version of *The Drowning Pool* (1950) and a television adaptation of *The Underground Man* (1971) appeared, as well as a series based on Lew Archer stories. But in the late 1970s Millar was found to have Alzheimer's disease; his condition steadily deteriorated, and he died on July 11, 1983. In all, Kenneth Millar published seventeen novels and two short-story collections involving Lew Archer, along with seven other novels. Ralph Sipper collected his autobiographical essays in *Self-Portrait: Ceaselessly into the Past* (1981).

# ◈ *Critical Extracts*

**STEVEN R. CARTER**     Human justice cannot function without administrators, but modern misuses of authority by entire regimes like Stalinist Russia and Nazi Germany have given us a heritage of mistrust for everyone in power. This heritage is reflected in all of Macdonald's work. In *The Dark*

*Tunnel,* his first novel, the professor-hero and a Nazi spy debate the relation of morality to the state. The professor asserts that the individual conscience provides the only check on the dictates of the state and applauds the action of a German girl who tried to protect an old Jewish doctor from government authorities. Later, the professor is framed for murder and flees, rather than trust the local government. He decides to avoid even Chet Gordon, the F.B.I. agent. Yet he eventually develops a half-trusting alliance with Gordon and almost becomes reconciled to the police, as he reaches a balance between total acceptance and total rejection of authority. ⟨. . .⟩

Macdonald clearly recognizes that men in authority are subject to the same pressures as the rest of mankind. Both *The Drowning Pool* and *Find a Victim* show representatives of the law torn between their public duties and their private ones. Both Chief of Police Knudson and Sheriff Church have worked honestly and vigorously all their lives and both betray their professions to protect their loved ones. Knudson destroys the suicide note of his dead mistress and attempts to force Archer to leave town. He also tries to cover up the fact that his daughter has committed murder, but he has enough integrity left to resign from his job and to devote the rest of his life to raising his daughter properly. Sheriff Church lets a highjacker pass through a roadblock in order to conceal his wife's responsibility for several murders, but he also tries to lock her in their house so that she won't be able to repeat her crimes. Archer believes that both men were wrong to betray the law, but that their mistakes are understandable. Officials must be judged as flexibly as ordinary human beings.

Yet public office can be used for private ends, and the official who misapplies his authority must be condemned. Sheriff Ostervelt in *The Doomsters* is willing to hush up a murder in return for the political influence of a wealthy man. Until the murder, he has been facing exposure for his regular pay-offs from the local houses of prostitution. After the murder, he is easily re-elected to his office and no one can touch him. Later, he uses both the knowledge of this particular incident and the power of his office to force Mildred Hallman to become his mistress. Macdonald suggests that under the cover of his office Ostervelt has killed several men who might have found out too much about him. Otto Sipes in *The Far Side of the Dollar* uses his job with the police to obtain money through bribes. After he is dismissed from the force, he eventually becomes a house detective and blackmailer at a second-rate hotel. Jack Fleischer in *The Instant Enemy* waits until his retirement as deputy Sheriff before making the further investigation of a case which will enable him to collect blackmail, but he too has relied on his office for a criminal purpose. Ostervelt's power is finally undermined and both Sipes and Fleischer are murdered, but not one of the three officers deserves compassion, though they do deserve our utmost attention. Men with power can only be curbed in their excesses by ordinary men who watch them closely. ⟨. . .⟩

Archer's own ideals are closely linked to justice; for this reason he cannot finally reject authority. In *The Zebra-Striped Hearse*, he goes to a lot of trouble to make a citizen's arrest of the suspected murderer Burke Damis, but he questions him afterwards in conjunction with the police official Captain Royal. When Damis then accuses both Captain Royal and Archer of being "storm troopers," Archer gets red in the face and feels "a growing solidarity with Royal." In a later conversation with Damis, Archer tells the rebellious young painter that his cop-hater attitude is foolish and that he could have saved himself a lot of discomfort by trusting other people. Archer points to himself specifically as a person worthy of trust and states that Captain Royal also qualifies. Again he has identified himself with Captain Royal, the official representative of the law. Yet Archer more truly represents the conscience of the individual which must provide a check on the dictates of the state.

Steven R. Carter, "Ross Macdonald: The Complexity of the Modern Quest for Justice," Mystery and Detection Annual, 1973, pp. 70–73

---

**PETER WOLFE**     The novels magnify rather than imitate or copy. Highly compressed, they are metaphors for stress. The characters stand larger than life, and the crises that claw them would wreck most of us. According to Ross Macdonald, his novels do not break away from reality so much as give a poetic documentary: "They are related to what goes on in the world, not in factual terms but in imaginative terms. They are halfway between a sociological report and a nightmare." Their working-out of philosophical principles and their poetic symbolism give them a strong intellectual thrust. But they are not modernist in their irony: Ross Macdonald's irony, unlike that of Joyce and Eliot, is not epistemological. Reality is not only given; it also has shape, laws, and meaning. The problem is not how to find it, but how to cope with it. Though living in the twilight of faith, Ross Macdonald's characters believe certain truths worth living and fighting—even, sometimes, worth killing—for. These truths are given in everyday experience. Nor are they described in night language, dream symbolism, or hallucination. Though the novels use the same filial-sexual materials as Joyce in the Circe ("Nighttown") section of *Ulysses*, Ross Macdonald writes objective narratives in straightforward prose. His style obeys the natural controls of conventional syntax and word choice. The inner world of his characters is intelligible. His plots, though full of strange meanings, are continuous. Without trivializing the complex process of causation, the plots transcribe bizarre events accurately.

But, crackling with ingenious twists and turns, they do not develop simply. While their complex symmetry recalls Dickens, it also summons up the eighteenth-century musical mode called the Invention. The Invention fused mathematical precision of design with effortless drive. The fluid formality of the Archer novels, like the best of Mozart and Haydn, rests on stronger undergirding than a Rococo dexterity. A relentless interior logic and a carefully regulated tempo controls the novels. At the same time, the energy building from their robust style, Archer's moral sympathy, and the mood of desperation cast by murder make them human dramas rather than technical diversions. Their strength stems chiefly from their dramatic force—an intensification of existence. Their gyrating plots mesh well with the larger-than-life impressions created by the characters and their crises. The abundance in each book imparts a sense of peopled space, even, in view of the pent-up energies driving the characters on, of overflowing life. The conjunction of Ross Macdonald's plots with the human drives impelling them also dramatizes today's leading concept, in psychology as well as in literature, of the city as maze.

Peter Wolfe, Dreamers Who Live Their Dreams: The World of Ross Macdonald's Novels (Bowling Green, OH: Bowling Green State University Popular Press, 1976), p. 5

---

**JERRY SPEIR**     Macdonald never suggests that women are completely faultless or that they lack their own sense of alienation. Roughly half his killers are women. But, characteristically, they are the victims of years of psychological oppression at the hands of the patriarchy. Mrs. Snow, in *The Underground Man*, sees her first murder as a blow for justice against the tyrannizing, womanizing Leo Broadhurst. Mildred Hallman's murdering ways, in *The Doomsters*, are the result of the combined pressures of Dr. Grantland and Senator Hallman and the grotesque abortion at the gunpoint of Alicia Hallman, herself a victim of generations of male domination. The primary instance of reversal of this theme comes in *The Chill*. Tish Macready's obsessively possessive love defines the insensitive, consuming evil of that book and she is assisted in her ruse by two other women, her sister and Mrs. Hoffman. But even in this instance, the values expressed (the sense that money can buy happiness) are values imbibed at the knee of a powerful, materialistic father. A portrait of the great patriarch hangs prominently in each sister's residence. Such women are what they are largely as a result of the socializing forces operative in the modern masculine world. Nevertheless, a woman's sense of alienation and isolation may still spark a violent eruption since, as Archer says, "girls can do about anything boys can do when they set their minds to it."

But the alienation which fosters the split between men and women and which finds its clearest expression in war is not limited to violence between the sexes or politically opposed nations. It extends to an alienation from other people, from nature, and finally from the continuum of time and human experience—particularly, in Macdonald's works, an alienation from the past. This latter, especially, would revoke the continuity of history and human development to leave man adrift and a stranger even to himself.

Jerry Speir, *Ross Macdonald* (New York: Ungar, 1978), pp. 129–30

---

**ROSS MACDONALD**      "Hardboiled" is rather a misnomer for this kind of story. Its distinctive ingredient is a style which tries to catch the rhythms and some of the words of the spoken language. While the essential features of its plot are a crime and a solution, there is room in the form for complexities of meaning which can match those of the traditional novel. It is a form which lends itself to the depiction, at the same time energetic and disenchanted, of the open society which California in the years just after the war was struggling to become.

I needed time, and deeper personal knowledge of that society, before I could make it entirely my own in fiction, or make the California detective novel my own. Raymond Chandler was and remains a hard man to follow. He wrote like a slumming angel, and invested the sun-blinded streets of Los Angeles with a romantic presence. While trying to preserve the fantastic lights and shadows of the actual Los Angeles, I gradually siphoned off the aura of romance and made room for a completer social realism. My detective

Archer is not so much a knight of romance as an observer, a socially mobile man who knows all the levels of Southern California life and takes a peculiar wry pleasure in exploring its secret passages. Archer tends to live through other people, as a novelist lives through his characters.

In the course of the first three Archer novels, I tried to work out my own version of the "hardboiled" style, to develop both imagery and structure in the direction of psychological and symbolic meaning. In the fourth, *The Ivory Grin* (1952), I extended the range of the form beyond California, touching on Boston and Montreal, Chicago and Detroit; and doing a portrait of a gangster family which was unblurred by any romantic admiration. But it took me five more novels, and seven more years, to work out within the limits of this rather difficult craft the kind of story that I was aiming at: a story roughly shaped on my own early life, transformed and simplified into a kind of legend, in *The Galton Case*.

Even here I approached my life from a distance, and crept up on it in disguise as one might track an alien enemy; the details of the book were all invented. But there was personal truth in its broad shape, as I have explained elsewhere. In crossing the border from Canada and making my way in stages to my birthplace in California, I had learned the significance of borders. They make the difference between legitimacy and fraudulence, and we cross them 'as a ghost passes through a wall, at the risk of our own reality.'

Perhaps *The Galton Case* validated my journey, and made it possible for my mind to look both north to Canada and south to Mexico and Panama, in later books like *The Zebra-Striped Hearse* and *Black Money*. At any rate it thawed my autobiographical embarrassment and started a run of somewhat more personal fiction which has, for better or worse, gone on unabated ever since. Of my twenty-three books, the three I have just named are among my favorites. They have a certain intensity and range.

But one writes on a curve, on the backs of torn-off calendar sheets. A writer in his fifties will not recapture the blaze of youth, or the steadier passion that comes like a second and saner youth in his forties, if he's lucky. But he can lie in wait in his room—it must be at least the hundredth room by now—and keep open his imagination and the bowels of his compassion against the day when another book will haunt him like a ghost rising out of both the past and the future.

Ross Macdonald, "Kenneth Millar/Ross Macdonald—A Checklist," *Self-Portrait: Ceaselessly into the Past*, ed. Ralph B. Sipper (Santa Barbara, CA: Capra Press, 1981), pp. 27–28

**JULIAN SYMONS**    In England Macdonald has received little serious critical regard, being viewed as a rather faint carbon-copy of Hammett
and Chandler. Yet the differences are greater than the similarities, how
much greater may be seen by comparing Philip Marlowe with Lew Archer.
Marlowe "is the hero, he is everything", in Chandler's words. Archer, as
Macdonald says here ⟨in *Self-Portrait: Ceaselessly into the Past*⟩ more than
once, is not the central character, nor the main object of interest, in the
books where he appears. He is simply the man to whom people talk, the
surveyor discovering the crack in the family's apparently irreproachably
sound building. This was not always true. If one looks at early and late
Archer it is plain that Macdonald has consciously tried to reduce the
detective's importance and eliminate him as a personality, so that he shall
not stand between the reader and the books' real subject, the rediscovery
of the past.

It would be foolish not to admit that there have been losses, as well as
gains, in Macdonald's single-minded pursuit of the past during the thirty-
odd years that he and his wife the crime novelist Margaret Millar have
spent in the haven of Santa Barbara. The early books do show debts to
Hammett and Chandler, but they have a verve and an audacity in the use
of simile and metaphor that is restricted, almost placed in cold storage, in
the later ones. *The Way Some People Die* and *The Ivory Grin* are particularly
exciting and enjoyable. But as Macdonald has said himself, the blaze of
youth does not last, "one writes . . . on the backs of torn-off calendar sheets",
and the later stories are immensely more subtle and serious. At times the
symbolism is too insistent, like the forest fire in *The Underground Man*,
"much like the Coyote Canyon fire that threatened Santa Barbara", Mr
Sipper tells us, that is reflected in the purgative fire burning out the secrets
of the Broadhurst family. Yet the opening of *The Blue Hammer*, which
casually mentions "the towers of the mission and the courthouse half sub-
merged in smog", most delicately suggests the mists and confusions through
which Archer will look for the truth about Richard Chantry's missing
painting.

This last, or most recent, novel is in some ways the peak of Macdonald's
achievement, bringing to the unravelling of past guilts much of the sparkle
in the early work. A choice of books that suggest his range as crime writer
and novelist might include the early ones already mentioned, together with
*The Zebra-Striped Hearse* and *Black Money*, two of his own favourites, plus
*The Far Side of the Dollar* and *The Blue Hammer*. When one sees the increasing

skill, subtlety and sense of purpose shown in the course of Macdonald's writing, it is obvious that he has had in England much less than his due of praise. He stated his intentions with clarity in an interview given several years ago: "I've been trying to put into my books the same sorts of things that a reader finds in a general novel, a whole version of life in our society and in our time. Of course, my books are somewhat limited by the kind of structure and subject matter that is inherent in the contemporary detective novel. I seem to work best within such limitations."

> Julian Symons, "In Pursuit of the Past," *Times Literary Supplement*, 2 April 1982, p. 369

**MATTHEW J. BRUCCOLI**      W. H. Auden was a visiting professor at the University of Michigan in the fall of 1941; Millar enrolled in his English 135, Fate and the Individual in European Literature, an undergraduate course with thirty-two required books. Millar had admired Auden's verse and leftist politics for years, and English 135 expanded his grasp of literature, introducing him to Kafka and Kierkegaard. A notable mystery-fiction buff, Auden knew and liked Margaret's work. (When he came to visit, his voice upset two-year-old Linda, who had to be pacified with marshmallows.) Millar has perhaps over-generously identified Auden as "the most important single influence on my life." Auden "set fire to me . . . simply by being exposed to a first rate writer who read my stuff and kindly advised me to cut the crap out of it was, I suppose, one of the four or five crucial events in my life." Despite his own preference for the murder-in-the-village school, Auden "legitimized" the writing of detective fiction for Millar.

> Both Margaret and I were writing mysteries at this time. He was most encouraging to us. That kind of push is unbelievably important to a young writer. Auden was the greatest poet in the English speaking world at that time. It gave us a shove in the direction in which we were going anyway. It just couldn't have been equaled in any other way. It marked a point in my life where I chose to become a fiction writer rather than a man who writes about other people's writings as a scholar; that's where I was headed. I would have done both, actually, but this straightened me out and put me on the creative path.

Auden offered to introduce him to his New York literary friends, but Millar thought it would be a mistake to go there under the auspices of a homosexual.

Matthew J. Bruccoli, *Ross Macdonald* (New York: Harcourt Brace Jovanovich, 1984), pp. 11, 13

---

**EUDORA WELTY**      The Macdonald novel begins as a rule at the point of discovery of a crime. The question is not simply, Who did it?—not by a long shot. Where, and from how long ago, out of what human fissure, did this crime start, and why at this moment did it erupt? What connections will lead us back to the source? The identity of the man or woman there to be found can be reached only through following this network of connections. It's the connections that absorb the author and magnetize his plots into their intricate and daunting patterns. In the brilliant, shapely designs of their construction, in their motions, in their timing, in their only seeming coincidences ("There are no coincidences," says Archer), in their evolving whole of moral significance, in their depth of irony, the plots are keyed and attuned to human beings as human beings. The novels' central concern is human relationships—i.e., human beings in trouble.

It is not illogical that Ross Macdonald, a novelist absorbed by character and working through structure, should have found the detective story responsive and flexible to his needs. The mystery and its solution are twin constructions in his hands, based on the same secret, which is always one of serious human import. This secret is often buried in a family past, and it needs to be made known *now*—urgently, in order to save a life, often a child's or a young person's. Thus Archer is driven headlong on his search. To this private detective, spinning through time and the generations as he spins through the hills of California, it is a search for comprehension as well, for understanding. And Macdonald, at the eventual success of the tracking down, lets us see further: uncover the secret and it goes back as far as Sophocles.

Macdonald plots, set on a course of discovery, are strewn—without seeming for an instant to lose momentum—with might-have-beens. For characters, major and minor, are given their due. All, givers and takers, killers and victims, the lost and the found, are qualified participants whom we are to see joined at the meeting point of their lives, lit up and exposed and brought to speak by the sudden flare of crisis. Though the novels carry through the search for the killer, and finally name the killer with strong, often chilling impact, the reader is aware (through Archer's experiencing the story) that the ending is not resolved in a passing of judgment. Character, rather than deed in itself, is what remains uppermost and decisive to Macdonald as a novelist. In the course of its being explained, guilt is seldom seen as flat-out; it is disclosed in the round, and the light and shadings of character define its true features. The history of more than a single character will surface before a crime's true nature is understood, and before the full reach of the crime is comprehended and its roots in the past and the legends they've traveled lie unearthed.

Eudora Welty, "Finding the Connections," *Ross Macdonald: Inward Journey*, ed. Ralph B. Sipper (Santa Barbara, CA: Cordelia Editions, 1984), pp. 155–56

---

**T. R. STEINER**      Writer and trained critic, "Anglo"-American, a modern trafficking in classical myths, Ross Macdonald was in many ways the hardboiled's T. S. Eliot. The critical apotheosis of his novels in the 1970s signalled not only notice of their quality but also that detective fiction was being widely accepted as mainstream literature. Its adventure, innocent realism, play, and innovation within convention always have attracted the popular audience. Since the 1940s, however, self-conscious European and Latin American detective fiction and parallels in literary theory have developed our sense of the genre. Criticism now recognizes that its conventions and stylizations present greatly, largely untapped, potential for metaphor, symbolism, and generic self-exploration. The unceasing imperative of a competitive market, "Make it new," has been augmented by the demand, "Make it meaningful."

In the context of such literary sophistication, Macdonald's novels—intended by him to be judged by demanding standards—often disappoint. If their narrowness and thinness could be regarded as mimetic—say, imitation of the desiccated world or consciousness of the narrating Private Eye—these apparent limitations could be justified. But I haven't been able to read them that way, and that does not seem to have been the author's intent.

At his best, Macdonald fulfilled something of his stated ideal for serious detective fiction, and his best stuff endures. We have been told, even by admirers like Auden, that detective novels cannot be read a second time.

They are (to use the dichotomy in Kenneth Burke's "Psychology and Form") works of "information," not "form." Once we learn whodunit, we have exhausted the interest. This is true enough of many mysteries. It is for me a measure and index of Macdonald's achievement that *The Chill* and *The Goodbye Look* easily have borne several readings. Neither book much enlightens the reader about the human condition or even, as Macdonald intended, about "technological" man. Despite the design to be current by representing "today's youth" or "ecological crime" in *The Underground Man* or *Sleeping Beauty*, Macdonald feels more old fashioned than the kaleidoscopic Chandler and certainly more than the typical postwar hardboiled writer. What sustains his best novels is not just "narrative unity" but "form" in Burke's sense, the satisfying narrative rhythm, the sensed rightness of design and placement, especially as the books work up essential conventions of detective story. As the detection narrative weaves and unravels tangled histories, the texture and weight of social interconnection becomes almost palpable. As the plot sinuates toward an ever more clearly indicated goal, we feel the inexorability and chill of destiny.

To the ongoing dialogue of detective fiction in the hardboiled tradition, Macdonald contributed the insistence in word and deed that writers and critics labor with form. In this, he perpetuated the thoroughness of Golden Age detective stories. Although his chief ambition was to present a valid, intense image of the time, his successes seem to me primarily "technical" within the tradition: shorter, tighter, cleaner narrative; more threads interwoven without absurdity; the placement of scenes and the relatively unobtrusive amassing of information; the coherent denouement. *The Goodbye Look* encourages me to ask for such formal virtues in realistic detective fiction, even as I seek moral, historical, symbolic weight greater than that of the Lew Archer novels.

T. R. Steiner, "The Mind of the Hardboiled: Ross Macdonald and the Roles of Criticism," *South Dakota Review* 24, No. 1 (Spring 1986 [Ross Macdonald Issue]): 50–52

---

**BERNARD A. SCHOPEN**     Clearly Macdonald changed the possibilities for the art for both writers and readers of the American detective novel. For writers he not only demonstrated, as ⟨Dennis⟩ Lynds testifies, that the genre was not limited to stories of professional crime, but he also proved that the form could be what he said in his "manifesto" ("Farewell, Chandler") he wanted it to be—literate and adult. This in itself changed the American detective novel for those who would practice it, for by writing literate and adult novels Macdonald eventually attracted a different audience—the literate and adult—for whom these new writers could write. For these new readers, on the other hand, he provided a fiction that produced a double effect, combining the pleasure that comes from the detective story and the satisfaction that comes from the novel.

He did this in two ways. First, he developed the human aspect of the "hard, logical structure" of the detective novel, transforming it from the presentation of a logical puzzle into "a vehicle of meaning," expanding plot from a narrated sequence of events into a mode of emotional and intellectual apprehension. As George Grella has astutely observed, "the books seem, at times, to consist entirely of plot, to be about their plots, to be in fact all plot." And all meaning. So integrated are these plots that those of us who would summarize or encapsulate them for purposes of critical discussion must to some extent falsify them. In the best of Macdonald's novels, plot is action that defines character, and character is attitude that qualifies action, so that the work develops in patterns that alter and reinforce meaning.

The other way Macdonald changed the art of the detective novel was to bring to it the techniques developed in and normally reserved for other kinds of novels. I have tried in this study to point out how Macdonald's rhetorical practices, his careful manipulation of the reader's response, employs the traditional suspense of the detective novel to bring the reader to a deeper view of certain basic human situations. His success in this enterprise results to a considerable extent from his use of the specific point of view he created through the use of Lew Archer as narrator, as well as his effective employment of structural, spatial, and symbolic devices more commonly found in serious fiction.

Bernard A. Schopen, Ross Macdonald (Boston: Twayne, 1990), pp. 128–29

# ▨ *Bibliography*

*The Dark Tunnel*. 1944.
*Trouble Follows Me*. 1946.
*Blue City*. 1947.

*The Three Roads.* 1948.

*The Moving Target.* 1949.

*The Drowning Pool.* 1950.

*The Way Some People Die.* 1951.

*The Ivory Grin ⟨Marked for Murder⟩.* 1952.

*Meet Me at the Morgue ⟨Experience with Evil⟩.* 1953.

*Find a Victim.* 1954.

*The Name Is Archer.* 1955.

*The Barbarous Coast.* 1956.

*The Doomsters.* 1958.

*The Galton Case.* 1959.

*The Ferguson Affair.* 1960.

*The Wycherly Woman.* 1961.

*The Zebra-Striped Hearse.* 1962.

*The Chill.* 1964.

*The Far Side of the Dollar.* 1965.

*Black Money.* 1966.

*Archer in Hollywood ⟨The Moving Target, The Way Some People Die, The Barbarous Coast⟩.* 1967.

*The Instant Enemy.* 1968.

*The Goodbye Look.* 1969.

*Archer at Large ⟨The Galton Case, The Chill, Black Money⟩.* 1970.

*The Underground Man.* 1971.

*Sleeping Beauty.* 1973.

*On Crime Writing.* 1973.

*Great Stories of Suspense* (editor). 1974.

*The Blue Hammer.* 1976.

*Lew Archer, Private Investigator.* 1977.

*Archer in Jeopardy ⟨The Doomsters, The Zebra-Striped Hearse, The Instant Enemy⟩.* 1979.

*A Collection of Reviews.* 1980.

*Self-Portrait: Ceaselessly into the Past.* Ed. Ralph Sipper. 1981.

*Early Millar: The First Stories of Ross Macdonald and Margaret Millar* (with Margaret Millar). 1982.

# ⊠ ⊠ ⊠

# Jim Thompson
## *1906–1977*

JAMES MYERS THOMPSON was born on September 27, 1906, in Anadarko, Oklahoma. In 1919 his family moved to Forth Worth, Texas, where Thompson's father made and lost a fortune during the oil boom. Upon graduating from high school, Thompson himself worked in the oil fields, an experience he would later document in his semi-autobiographical novels *Bad Boy* (1953), *Roughneck* (1954), and *South of Heaven* (1967). He enrolled in the University of Nebraska in 1928 and married Alberta Hesse in 1931. With the need for steady employment following the birth of his first child in 1932, Thompson traveled around the Southwest between 1933 and 1935, working as a hotel doorman and freelance writer for newspapers and pulp magazines.

Thompson began selling crime stories to true detective magazines such as *Master Detective* and *True Detective* in 1935. In 1936 he was hired as a nonrelief worker on the Oklahoma Writer's Project, an offshoot of the WPA. He was eventually promoted to Guide Book editor and contributed to *The Economy of Scarcity: Some Human Footnotes* (1939), a publication of the project, before resigning from his position in 1939. He received a one-year fellowship from the Rockefeller Foundation in 1940 to write a labor history of Oklahoma, which was never completed.

In 1941 Thompson traveled to New York and, staked to an advance by a publisher, wrote his first novel, *Now and On Earth* (1942), in two weeks. At the same time he began drinking heavily. He enlisted in the Marines in 1944, but was discharged for medical reasons after only twelve weeks. His second novel, *Heed the Thunder* (1946), and his first crime novel, *Nothing More Than Murder* (1949), met with lukewarm critical reception. Undaunted, Thompson moved his family to New York and embarked on a career as a writer of paperback originals.

Between 1952 and 1955 Thompson wrote thirteen novels, most in the crime-suspense genre. With his fifth novel, *The Killer Inside Me* (1952), he established himself as a master of the *roman noir*, a hard-boiled style of fiction focused on characters leading dead-end lives in an unjust world. Told from the point of view of a murderous police officer, the novel was the first of many in which Thompson explored the psyche of people who live outside the boundaries of conventional morality. Thompson developed his bleak vision through later novels such as *The Getaway* (1959), *The Grifters* (1963), and his masterpiece, *Pop. 1280* (1964), which Bernard Tavernier filmed in 1982 as the Academy Award–nominated *Coup de Torchon*.

Film director Stanley Kubrick approached Thompson to write the screenplay for *The Killing* in 1955. Thompson later worked on the screenplay for Kubrick's *Paths of Glory*, which was nominated by the Writer's Guild for best screenplay adaptation in 1957. His attempts to write for film and television, many of them unsuccessful, and his growing dependence on alcohol decreased his output as a novelist. Three of his last six books were novelizations of films or television shows. When Thompson died on April 7, 1977, of complications from a stroke, not one of his twenty-nine novels was in print; but his work has experienced a considerable revival in the last decade.

# ▨ Critical Extracts

**WILL CUPPY**      Mr. Thompson ⟨in *Nothing More Than Murder*⟩ is so cagey with his clews that the reader may find it difficult to guess what is going on at the moment, a serious fault in an item that struck us as a puzzle or nothing and thus requiring the usual mystery guidance, although it is billed as "a novel of suspense." At the same time, the author appears to be aiming up James M. Cain's alley, a perilous feat for the novice. Joe Wilmot, his scheming wife and a girl are the principals and you might want to know who started the fire, who was killed, by whom, and why. Interest bogs down rather early in details of the movie business of a town of 7,500 souls, an undertaking that must be a dreadful bore. Written in spots in a pseudocolloquial style that doesn't pan out any too well—or, in fact, at all.

Will Cuppy, "Mystery and Adventure," *New York Herald Tribune Weekly Book Review*, 27 March 1949, p. 16

**JIM THOMPSON**     The deputy stood up, looked around and saun-
tered into the tool shed. Some fifteen minutes later he came out, wiping
his mouth with the back of his hand.

"Like to have some chow?" he called. "A little water?"

"You kidding?" I croaked.

"I'll find a pail. You can pull it up on the rope."

He started for the toolshed again. In spite of myself, I laughed.

"Let it go," I said, "I'm coming down."

He was a good-looking guy. His hair was coal-black beneath his pushed-
back Stetson, and his black intelligent eyes were set wide apart in a tanned,
fine-featured face. He grinned at me as I dropped down in front of him on
the derrick floor.

"Now that wasn't very smart," he said. "And that's—"

"And that's a fact," I snapped. "All right, let's get going."

He went on grinning at me. In fact, his grin broadened a little. But it
was fixed, humorless, and a veil seemed to drop over his eyes.

"What makes you so sure," he said softly, "you're going anywhere?"

"Well, I—" I gulped. "I—I—"

"Awful lonesome out here, ain't it? Ain't another soul for miles around
but you and me."

"L-look," I said. "I'm—I wasn't trying to—"

"Lived here all my life," he went on softly. "Everyone knows me. No
one knows you. And we're all alone. What do you make o' that, a smart
fella like you? You've been around. You're full of piss and high spirits. What
do you think an ol' stupid country boy might do in a case like this?"

He stared at me, steadily, the grin bearing his teeth. I stood paralyzed
and wordless, a great cold lump forming in my stomach. The wind whined
and moaned through the derrick. He spoke again, as though in answer to
a point I had raised.

"Don't need one," he said. "Ain't nothin' you can do with a gun that
you can't do a better way. Don't see nothin' around here I'd need a gun
for."

He shifted his feet slightly. The muscles in his shoulders bunched. He
took a pair of black kid gloves from his pocket, and drew them on, slowly.
He smacked his fist into the palm of his other hand.

"I'll tell you something," he said. "Tell you a couple of things. There
ain't no way of telling what a man is by looking at him. There ain't no

way of knowing what he'll do if he has the chance. You think maybe you can remember that?"

I couldn't speak, but I managed a nod. His grin and his eyes went back to normal.

"Look kind of peaked," he said. "Whyn't you have somethin' to eat an' drink before we leave?"

I paid my fine. I also paid for a bench warrant, the deputy's per diem for two days and his mileage. And you can be sure that I made no fuss about it.

I never saw that deputy again, but I couldn't get him out of my mind. And the longer he remained the bigger the riddle he presented. Had he been bluffing? Had he only meant to throw a good scare into a brash kid? Or was it the other way, the way I was sure it was at the time? Had my meekness saved me from the murder with which he had threatened me?

Suppose I had hit him with that block of wood. Suppose I had razzed him a little more? Suppose I had been frightened into grabbing for my hatchet?

I tried to get him down on paper, to put him into a story, but while he was very real to me I could not make him seem real. Rather, he was too commonplace and innocuous—nothing more than another small-town deputy. Put down on paper, he was only solemnly irritated, not murderous.

The riddle, of course, lay not so much in him as me. I tended to see things in black and white, with no intermediate shadings. I was too prone to categorize—naturally, using myself as the norm. The deputy had behaved first one way, then another, then the first again. And in my ignorance I saw this as complexity instead of simplicity.

He had gone as far as his background and breeding would allow to be amiable. I hadn't responded to it, so he had taken another tack. It was simple once I saw things through his eyes instead of my own.

I didn't know whether he would have killed me, because he didn't know himself.

Finally, as I matured, I was able to recreate him on paper—the sardonic, likeable murderer of my fourth novel, *The Killer Inside Me*. But I was a long time in doing it—almost thirty years.

And I still haven't gotten him out of my mind.

Jim Thompson, *Bad Boy* (1953), rpt. in *Hardcore: 3 Novels* (New York: Donald I. Fine, 1986), pp. 387–89.

**R. V. CASSILL**        My experience in recommending *The Killer Inside Me* (1952) has convinced me that most readers will try to have done with by assigning it a place in the multitudinous ranks of painted devils by which our eyes are decoyed away from the thicket where the Old Fellow hides and pants and laughs and waits for us. Among caste-minded readers this misprision can be ridiculously easy if not automatic; for this novel bears considerable internal and external evidence of its origin among "paperback originals."

It was hastily written. (According to Arnold Hano, the editor of Lion Books who commissioned it, it was written in two weeks. Hano also told me once, not very convincingly, that the "plot" of the whole thing was his contribution, implying that Thompson merely "wrote it up." The truth of that confidence seems to me irrelevant in view of the way the plot has been integrated and caught up to serve the unified vision and statement of the novel as a whole. Nevertheless, some of the text does have the mangy discoloration that shows haste, some of it is pocked with the formular, hard-breathing clichés of literature for the working man, and a few episodes have the stale cigar smell of editor-author collaboration—"I think you could clarify it on page 80, Jim, if you . . .") I see no more point in denying the irrelevant warts than in affirming them. We know the novel is an impure art, and we had better be guided by Ransom's axiom that we "remember literature by its noblest moments." One needs a goat's stomach to hold out long enough for the noblest moments in Balzac and probably Dostoevsky, too.

The reader of *The Killer Inside Me* will have some obligation to spit out the indigestible bones and husks that are part of the literary mode in which this novel was born. Whoever wishes can give it up at the first token of low birth and retire to the comfort of the notion that only a "hardcover author" who takes a lot of time with his work and has been authenticated by the reviewing and critical media can successfully "paint EEE-VILL."

But what I would like to declare is that in Thompson's hands, the mode of the paperback original, husks and all, turns out to be excellently suited to the objectives of the novel of ideas. (See Balzac on Stendhal for definition thereof.) Using the given idiom—and for all I can be sure of, a given plot as well—Thompson makes a hard, scary, Sophoclean statement on American success.

That statement can be tentatively paraphrased thus: Even if you are a rotten, murderous piece of astral excrement and know it, you're supposed to go on and succeed.

Succeed at what?

Well, the society expects you to succeed at something socially valuable, of course, but it gives you the momentum toward success in any cause. And your nature splits between this momentum and the inertia of the heart, however vile or sublime that heart may be. The American dream (conscious, unconscious or merely fatal as it may be) makes no provision for an asylum for failures. Among a decent, godless people those who are—and that which is—hopeless from the start find no repose in the bosom of the author of their inadequacy.

> R. V. Cassill, "*The Killer Inside Me*: Fear, Purgation, and the Sophoclean Light," *Tough Guy Writers of the Thirties*, ed. David Madden (Carbondale: Southern Illinois University Press, 1968), pp. 232–33

---

**NICK KIMBERLEY**      Perhaps paralleling his own experiences, the typical Thompson family unit is in disarray, truncated or shattered: the nuclear family in fission. Indeed, in *South of Heaven* the family is literally exploded when Tommy Burwell's grandparents, who had brought him up, are blown to pieces while trying to dynamite a plot for their new privy; while in *Pop. 1280* Nick Corey's family consists of husband, wife and wife's idiot brother, who may or may not be her lover too: incest is never far away with Thompson. As an extension of the problem family, the women in these novels are secondary, sketchily portrayed for the most part, as if their role is merely that of a disruptive threat, pushing the male characters over the edge into a traumatic loss of control. As if in some overwrought Oedipal force, these women are mothers, substitute mothers, or even absent mothers. In *King Blood*, the hero is sensually aroused in the act of beating his mother over the bare backside with a belt. In *The Grifters* Roy Dillon confuses, to his own cost, his mother and his fiancée/accomplice, while Nick Corey's mother died giving birth to him. These women are incomplete, fragmentary (". . . the way she stretched her clothes, it was kind of a case of the parts being greater than the whole": *South of Heaven*).

But the most striking, and the most troubling, aspect of this fiction is its sadism, sometimes so powerfully evoked that it's hard to escape the conclusion that Thompson is enjoying it. Nick Corey kicking a dying man, Lou Ford stripping and tying up a woman (a prostitute . . .) before taking a belt to her as foreplay; Rudy Torrento (*The Getaway*) giggling as he disembowels his bank-robbing accomplice: these are the men Thompson writes about most convincingly. The more demented their behaviour, the more in tune they are with this world gone haywire. We might try to dismiss them as painted devils from some primeval past, but Thompson knows better. As he says in *The Killer Inside Me*, "all of us started the game with a crooked cue". This is a godless world (south of heaven . . .) in which sadistic psychopaths for whom murder is a casual chore, can say "I'm the Saviour himself, Christ on the Cross come right here to Potts County, because God knows I was needed here" (Nick Corey in *Pop. 1280*). This may not be the world we think we know, but it's not very far from it; we'd all do well to heed the road-signs in *The Killer Inside Me*: "WARNING! WARNING! Hitch-hikers may be escaped LUNATICS!" And so might the rest of us.

Nick Kimberley, "Introduction," *4 Novels by Jim Thompson* (London: Zomba Books, 1983), pp. viii–ix

---

**BARRY GIFFORD**     The French seem to appreciate best Thompson's brand of terror. *Roman noir*, literally "black novel," is a term reserved especially for novelists such as Thompson, Cornell Woolrich and David Goodis. Only Thompson, however, fulfills the French notion of both *noir* and *maudit*, the accursed and self-destructive. It is an unholy picture that Thompson presents. As the British critic Nick Kimberley has written, "This is a godless world," populated by persons "for whom murder is a casual chore."

The most intriguing aspect of Thompson's work is that he often exposes himself as being more than a stylist. He can be an excellent writer, capable of creating dialogue as crisp as Hammett's, descriptive prose as convincing as Chandler's. But then, all of a sudden, there will come two or three successive chapters of throwaway writing more typical of the paperback original Trash & Slash school of fiction. Thompson's male leads are almost always schizophrenics, plagued by erratic behavior, haunted by an unpredictable demon; this split personality emerges as well in the writing itself, marking the author as recognizably as he marks his confused characters.

Barry Gifford, "The Godless World of Jim Thompson," *Nothing More Than Murder* by Jim Thompson (Berkeley, CA: Black Lizard/Creative Arts, 1984), p. vii

**LUC SANTE**       Murder is an enjoyable, if compulsive activity in Thompson's books, like eating potato chips. Yet his novels are thoroughly devoid of either the macho posturing or the righteous pretext of duty to be found in most pulp violence. His heroes are usually cheerful and thoroughly psychotic. As Barry Gifford notes in his introduction to the Black Lizard editions, Thompson's writing mirrors the schizoid duality of his characters, veering sharply between carefully stylized prose and penny-a-word sensationalizing. Similarly, he seems to be cheering on his protagonists, making them sympathetic, their confusion understandable, even as their killings pile up, but he cannot resist meting punishment at the end, reserving for them the most agonizing fates. Novelists are often accused of playing God, but few have wallowed in the conceit as lustily as Thompson.

*Pop. 1280* (1964) could almost be taken as his statement of purpose. Nick Corey is sheriff of the smallest county in Texas. He likes to sleep, eat, drink, and screw, and dislikes any kind of exertion. Most people think he is simple-minded, or at least malleable. Nevertheless, when people annoy him, he kills them, and pins the deed on someone else he doesn't like. He remains ostensibly good-natured and without a speck of doubt or remorse. Throughout the book there are scattered hints that he is considerably more canny than he makes out. These parallel an increasingly blasphemous suggestion, unveiled at the end: because it was all so clear to me, Christ knew it was clear: love one another and don't screw no one unless they're bending over, and forgive us our trespasses because we may be a minority of one. For God's sake, *for God's sake*—why else had I been put here in Potts County, and why else did I stay here? Why else, who else, what else but Christ Almighty would put up with it? This is satire with a bludgeon, but Nick Corey is nevertheless the only one of Thompson's killer-heroes who goes unpunished.

*Pop. 1280* seems to be a farcical recasting of Thompson's earlier *The Killer Inside Me* (1952). Sheriff Lou Ford shares many of Nick Corey's traits, but he is a more straightforward version of the serial killer case history, and the ironies are more obvious. The off-hand candor of the first person narration is a particularly convincing rendition of mass-murderer talk. *A Hell of a Woman* (1954) plays with James M. Cain's patented fatal-woman theme, sticking all the misogyny up top, where it can be seen, and pawing through it with hilariously definitive overkill. *The Getaway* (1959) sets up a winsome male-female pair of crooks and chases them to, literally, hell. It is the best of the four because it so thoroughly camouflages itself as a routine crime book that its aberrant qualities don't strike the reader until nearly the end, the end being a horrific fantasy that jumps the genre altogether. Thompson's books are palpably evil. They can be as revolting as Mexican vampire movies, but with a suggestion of personal meaning that is hardly laughable. His professional deployment of likable characters, emblematic locales, and tried-and-true situations functions much like the cornball skits and platitudes of his heroes: to mask the ooze and suck of disease inside.

> Luc Sante, "The Gentrification of Crime," *New York Review of Books,* 28 March 1985, p. 19

---

**GEOFFREY O'BRIEN**     *No familiar thing to cling to.* The phrase describes perfectly the unnerving atmosphere of these novels. The hero of one of his last books declares: "I had tried to do right, whenever and wherever I could. But right and wrong were so intertwined in my mind as to be unidentifiable, and I had had to create my own concepts of them." More than one reader has finished *The Killer Inside Me* or *A Hell of a Woman* with a sense of having intruded on a personal struggle almost too painful for fiction. The narrator is not dramatizing the struggle between good and evil—he's living it, and the author is living it with and through him. Such naked internal conflict doesn't normally pertain to the literature of macho escapism. We are closer to the mentality of a Doestoevsky: the compulsion to expose moral ulcers, to acknowledge evil impulses, to seek some kind of redemption. But while Dostoevsky could come to rest in an image of religious orthodoxy, however self-delusive, Jim Thompson remains out on a limb. There is no salvation, no point. Even when he tacks on a happy ending for the sake of the genre—as in *Recoil* and *The Golden Gizmo*—nobody is likely to be fooled. The pain underlying this work was not to be abolished by the stroke of a pen.

I am not proposing that *A Swell-Looking Babe* and *Wild Town* be enshrined alongside *Crime and Punishment* and *The Possessed.* Thompson wrote rapidly and for money; his handling of plot and character grew increasingly perfunctory; he cheated on more than one ending. Yet what endures in his work is a relentless questioning, a moral intensity unable to settle for an easy answer. We are always on the edge. Thompson might be, then, a low-budget Dostoevsky in a distinctly American mode, our very own underground man, choking on industrial fumes, blinded by neon bar signs, eking out a living as a door-to-door salesman or third-rate con man. A poverty of the imagination pervades his depleted, spiritless world: "The whole place had a decayed, dying-on-the vine appearance . . . There was something sad about it, something that reminded me of baldheaded men who comb their side hair across the top." Least of all is there any love. Sexuality consists entirely of violence, sometimes implied, usually acted out: hideous marriages begin in alcoholism and end in murder, joyless prostitutes fall prey to obsessive sadists. Rarely has an American writer—especially a mass market writer like Thompson— portrayed such hopeless ugliness, so unadorned a dead end.

The temptation is to read his books simply as testimonials of his own compulsions. Indeed, the recurrence of certain images—the murderous mother, the helpless father, the termagant wife, the terminally alienated, often impotent husband—invites such a reading. Yet although Thompson's specific obsessions are personal, their *tone* belongs to the culture at large. His plot materials derive from the atrocities of the daily papers—he was, after all, a reporter and a regular contributor to *True Detective*—and his settings distill a lifetime's worth of highways and railroad yards and hotel lobbies. It's all too clear that, far from being objective fantasies, Thompson's books faithfully reflect a mentality that seethes all around us, as American as the next mass murder.

Geoffrey O'Brien, "Jim Thompson, Dimestore Dostoevsky," *Savage Night* by Jim Thompson (Berkeley, CA: Black Lizard/Creative Arts, 1985), pp. 153–54

---

**RODERICK THORP**     Thompson's vision makes him like nobody else. His is a world peopled with psychopathic killers, expensive sluts, crooked cops, moronic publishers (talk about literary risks!), filthy-minded doctors, cretins, perverts, obsessives—well, read today's paper. Thompson's novels don't have good guys, just anti-heroes and the women who deserve them. In *The Nothing Man*, Deborah Chasen is so horny for Clinton Brown that she tells him she's glad his wife has died. Clinton Brown doesn't have a penis. Then he kills Deborah Chasen. Or he thinks he does. Thompson is *always* like that. Most of us want to forget that the government tolerates a certain amount of insect parts and rodent feces in our wedding cakes. For Thompson, that information is essential to finding a meaning of life—and some meaning it is. Thompson's characters enjoy picking their noses. Why? Thompson won't buy into the lies we tell ourselves.

If Thompson's vision sentenced him to the low rent district of original paperback publication, that marketplace doomed him to an out-of-hand critical rejection that helped stifle his voice. Yet what was wrong with original paperback publication was right for Thompson, too. It gave him an otherwise unavailable opportunity to keep going, and found him the readers who would later encourage others to read his books: writers like R. V. Cassill, Barry Gifford and Stephen King, and the moviemaker Stanley Kubrick.

Paperback originals brought a writer a top price of two or three thousand dollars. John D. MacDonald, Elmore Leonard and Louis L'Amour were at the top in their genres, but Jim Thompson was the master of the field, not submitting to the plot formulas editors were looking for, but very much constrained by the peculiar censorship of the period. The joke in those days was that sex was all on the lurid covers that were designed to catch the buyer's eye. Inside, it was, "And so I kissed her, and kissed her again," followed by a new paragraph that began, "Later . . ." Thompson's books smolder anyway. He studied humanity, and understood the meaning of a downcast eye or stammer. There is always a second level of experience below the surface action of a Thompson novel, just like life itself.

Most of the time he wrote cleanly, moving his story quickly, sparing us the self-indulgence of the florid prose the second-rater thinks is *style*. And Thompson remembers that the best novelists are always good reporters: setting the scene in *The Nothing Man*, he delivers as clear an account of the doings in the small daily newspaper as I have ever read. And finally, he *experiments: The Kill-Off* shifts point of view, which editors regard as dangerous because they think readers want somebody to root for. In *The Kill-Off*, Thompson is not only shifting point of view, he's advancing the story with every shift, a story that revolves fascinatingly around an old woman who refuses to get out of bed. Think about it for a moment: how can *anybody* write a novel like that?

Roderick Thorp, "Introduction," Hardcore: 3 Novels by Jim Thompson (New York: Donald I. Fine, 1986), p. viii

---

**PETER S. PRESCOTT**       The first thing to be said about Thompson is that his fiction resembles no one else's. The distinguishing marks of his novels are a high degree of death, a varying degree of comedy, some astonishing play with psychology, and—most important—the absence of any moral center at all. Hammett, Chandler and Macdonald, the so-called hard-boiled writers, were crusading moralists: cynical though their private eyes may be, they restore moral order to their twilight worlds. In Thompson's novels, morality is replaced by ambition. His protagonists are incompetent, usually psychotic, carnivores; like the people they kill, they're losers—they just leave more of a mess before they go. Whatever order obtains at the end of one of his stories is a writer's order, not a moralist's.

Peter S. Prescott, " 'The Cirrhosis of the Soul,' " *Newsweek*, 17 November 1986, p. 90

---

**JAMES SALLIS**     Now, it is quite unsettling to open the pages of a cheap paperback novel and find yourself staring into Satan's calm face, or Christ's troubled one. Genre conventions themselves are supposed to protect you, holding forth a world parallel to your own but sealed off from it and, whatever the wrath and wreckage, somehow safe. But Jim Thompson's work is one long assault on the words supposed to, and Thompson rarely submitted to the plot formulas editors expected. In fact, he methodically destroys those clichés—not by transcending them as a more "literary" writer might, but by sinking so thoroughly, so unremittingly into them that they're stood on their heads. Finally, as Polito and McCauley note, Thompson's "nods to hard-boiled conventions do not so much toughen Thompson's novels as humanize them—they're all we have to hang onto in the ferocious down-draft."

R. V. Cassill, in his fine appreciation of *The Killer Inside Me*, makes much of the same point. Democratic man, he writes, uses the fiction of violence for its purgative effect but does not want to be purged forcefully. At every level we find "novels of protest and violence affirming the indissoluble contiguity of the democratic mass, the adequacy of received ideas, and the justice of our aspirations toward a Better World," and the writer who chooses crime and violence as his theme yet wishes to go beyond neutralizing conventions may be setting himself quite apart from his readers.

Certainly, Thompson's refusal to play by rules and his dark vision condemned him to the ghetto of original paperback publication, thereby assuring the anonymity and critical disregard that eventually helped stifle his voice. (Gagged by the silence of others, in Sartre's phrase.) But just as certainly, original paperback publication allowed him what otherwise could not have been possible: it let him go on writing, go on exploring the borders of a world uniquely his. "Jim Thompson breaks most of the rules of crime fiction, or indeed any kind of genre fiction," Geoffrey O'Brien points out in his afterword for the Black Lizard reprints. "With his drawling raconteur's voice, his beautifully-modulated storytelling rhythms, and his endless stock of anecdote and naturalistic color, he sets us up for a sucker punch in which the bottom drops out of everything: location, narrative, personality, narrative itself."

That perception seems to me central to understanding Jim Thompson's work. Beginning with the subversion of genre conventions and clichés, slowly and insidiously Thompson progresses to a subversion of character, and finally, of existence itself. One thinks of those cartoon beasts who, going about their destined business, pause to look down and only then discover that the ground beneath their feet—for how long?—no longer exists. But in Thompson's work there is no restoration: in the following frame the coyote remains scorched and smoldering, stripped of hide and hair, foreshortened, legless, transformed.

Again and again, in whatever formulation, this basic truth struggles to light in commentary on Thompson's work: "We are always on the edge," "undercutting any sense of stability to get to the heart of his nightmare," "There's no point of goodness in his books to refer to."

Relentless, unregenerative, beyond redemption: the world of Jim Thompson. Sexuality is synonymous with violence, sometimes implicit, more often manifest; grotesque marriages begin in alcoholism and flight and end in murder; driven, characters circle and stalk one another without quite knowing why. Rarely has an American writer, and a resolutely commercial writer at that, given forth so bleak and damning a vision. One drops his dime into this peek-show nickelodeon and, fitting eyes to the view piece, finds himself peering into the abyss.

> James Sallis, "Jim Thompson: Dime-Store Dostoevski" (1990), *Difficult Lives: Jim Thompson, David Goodis, Chester Himes* (Brooklyn, NY: Gryphon Books, 1993), pp. 23–25

---

**LAWRENCE BLOCK**     Thompson's characters are holdup men and small-time grifters, corrupt lawmen, punch-drunk fighters, escaped lunatics.

They lead horrible lives, do awful things and come to bad ends. Typically, there are no winners in a Thompson novel. Even the innocent are guilty, and no one gets out alive.

In *The Nothing Man* (1954), the narrator is a reporter emasculated in the war and permanently embittered. In the course of the book he thinks he has murdered three people, only finding out at the end that he hasn't killed anyone: one was killed by another character, one committed suicide, one died accidentally. Even in acts of violence, he proves impotent.

In *The Getaway*, bank robbers turn on one another as a matter of course. Two survive, a husband and wife, who reach sanctuary in Mexico. But the place turns out to be hell, they can't leave, and the need to betray each other in order to stay alive destroys their love.

Perhaps we're more ready to listen to Thompson's message than we were 30 years ago. Perhaps his vision, relentlessly bleak, fits our times better than his own. Or maybe any generation is more willing to accept such a message from a distance.

> Lawrence Block, "A Tale of Pulp and Passion: The Jim Thompson Revival," *New York Times Book Review*, 14 October 1990, p. 37

---

**JAMES ELLROY**     Social realism/soap opera verging on horror—Jim Thompson's second novel, *Heed the Thunder*, stands out as a testament to the former, a coming attraction for the latter. More than anything else it shows his roots—both georgraphical and literary—and displays the incuba‐ tion process of his relentless desire to go too far.

> James Ellroy, "Introduction," *Heed the Thunder* by Jim Thompson (New York: Arm‐ chair Detective Library, 1991), p. i

---

**MICHAEL J. McCAULEY**     It might seem odd that the author of *The Killer Inside Me* was so shaken by tales of murder, but everyone that knew him agrees that Thompson actually was like that.

Thompson seemed to have had almost no filter or distancing ability when it came to violence—he was always terribly affected by it. Every day we hear stories of violence and death, note them but do not dwell on them unless something has happened to someone close to us. Thompson evidently reacted to every act of violence he heard about as if it had occurred to someone he knew personally.

Upon reflection this character trait seems to hold the answer to exactly why his novels seem so violent. There's more murder and violence in almost any other crime novel one might pick up, but they lack Thompson's powerful obsessive mix of fascination and revulsion. One feels every punch and kick to Amy Stanton's body in *The Killer Inside Me*—not in the service of some over-the-top, lurid exercise in pulp writing, but because Thompson imparts exactly what it must be like to kill, and be killed.

If Jim Thompson himself seemed to have no "sanitary distance" from the violence of the world, his novels offer the flip side of sanitized violence. You read *The Killer Inside Me* and come away feeling unclean, like you just murdered Amy Stanton or Joyce Lakeland yourself. This from the man who was aghast at secondhand tales of true-life murder.

Michael J. McCauley, *Jim Thompson: Sleep with the Devil* (New York: Mysterious Press, 1991), pp. 51–52

---

**MAX ALLAN COLLINS**     If the world were fair (and it isn't—if it were, Thompson would have had little to write about), Jim Thompson would today be as well known and as highly thought of as his literary progenitor, James M. Cain. It might be said that, roughly, Thompson is to Cain as Chandler is to Hammett. Like Chandler, Thompson's talent and skills are worthy of his predecessor, but like Chandler he brings them to bear on areas his predecessor did not explore. And, like Chandler, Thompson's voice, his shading, is unique his own. Thompson, however, wasn't as limited an artist as Chandler (who, good as he was, wrote one book seven times) and at times outstrips even Cain. This is not to suggest that Thompson is "better" than Cain (or Chandler or Hammett). It is, however, a suggestion that he is worthy of similar attention—and respect.

Max Allan Collins, "Jim Thompson: The Killers Inside Him," *Scream Factory* No. 11 (Spring 1993): 31

# ◈ *Bibliography*

*Now and On Earth*. 1942.

*Heed the Thunder*. 1946.

*Nothing More Than Murder*. 1949.

*Cropper's Cabin*. 1952.

*The Killer Inside Me*. 1952.

*The Alcoholics*. 1953.

*Bad Boy*. 1953.

*The Criminal*. 1953.

*Recoil*. 1953.

*Savage Night*. 1953.

*A Swell-Looking Babe*. 1954.

*The Golden Gizmo*. 1954.

*A Hell of a Woman*. 1954.

*The Nothing Man*. 1954.

*Roughneck*. 1954.

*After Dark, My Sweet*. 1955.

*The Kill-Off*. 1957.

*Wild Town*. 1957.

*The Getaway*. 1959.

*The Transgressors*. 1961.

*The Grifters*. 1963.

*Pop. 1280*. 1964.

*Texas by the Tail*. 1965.

*Ironside*. 1967.

*South of Heaven*. 1967.

*The Undefeated*. 1969.

*Nothing But a Man*. 1970.

*Child of Rage*. 1972.

*King Blood*. 1973.

*4 Novels* ⟨*The Getaway, The Killer Inside Me, The Grifters, Pop. 1280*⟩. 1983.

*Hardcore: 3 Novels* ⟨*The Kill-Off, The Nothing Man, Bad Boy*⟩. 1986.

*More Hardcore: 3 Novels* ⟨*The Ripoff, The Golden Gizmo, Roughneck*⟩. 1987.

*Fireworks: The Lost Writings of Jim Thompson*. Ed. Robert Polito and Michael
McCauley. 1988.

# Cornell Woolrich
## *1903–1968*

CORNELL GEORGE HOPLEY-WOOLRICH was born on December 4, 1903, in New York City. The family moved to Mexico in 1907. When Woolrich's parents separated shortly afterward, he stayed with his father until he was a teenager, traveling extensively through Mexico and Central America. Woolrich returned to live with his mother and attended Columbia University. Strongly influenced by the work of F. Scott Fitzgerald, he wrote his first novel, a portrait of the Jazz Age, *Cover Charge* (1926), during a six-week convalescence from a foot infection. His second novel, *Children of the Ritz* (1927), won a $10,000 prize from *College Humor* magazine and brought him to the attention of First National Pictures, who invited him to Hollywood. His career as a screenwriter was disastrous, as was his 1930 marriage to Marian Blackton, which went unconsummated and forced him to confront his homosexuality.

Woolrich returned to New York and began living an introverted life, sharing a hotel room with his mother. He found that the publishing climate had changed in the wake of the stock market crash, and that he was no longer able to sell the type of fiction he had been writing for almost a decade. In 1934 he sold his first mystery story, "Death Sits in the Dentist's Chair," to the pulp magazine *Detective Fiction Weekly*. Woolrich began contributing prolifically to such pulp magazines as *Black Mask* and *Dime Detective*, which in 1942 would publish "It Had to Be Murder," the story Alfred Hitchcock adapted for the award-winning film *Rear Window*.

In the 1940s Woolrich began to concentrate on writing novels and produced so many that it became necessary for him to publish several under the pseudonyms George Hopley and William Irish. His "Black" series—consisting of the novels *The Bride Wore Black* (1940), *The Black Curtain* (1941), *Black Alibi* (1942), *Black Angel* (1943), *The Black Path of Fear* (1944), and *Rendezvous in Black* (1948)—was praised for its atmospheric blend of mystery and horror that compensated for occasionally far-fetched plots and weakly developed characters. In 1948 the Mystery Writers of America gave him the Edgar Allan Poe award for lifetime achievement.

Woolrich's stories attracted the attention of many distinguished filmmakers, including Hitchcock, Jacques Tourneur, François Truffaut, and Rainer Werner Fassbinder. Adaptations of his novels *Phantom Lady* (1942), *I Married a Dead Man* (1948), and *Night Has a Thousand Eyes* (1949) played a role in shaping the look and texture of *film noir* in the 1940s and '50s. His work was also adapted extensively for radio, particularly the CBS series "Suspense," and for television.

The death of his mother in 1957 left Woolrich devastated. His drinking increased and aggravated his diabetes. In 1967 an infected leg was amputated. Woolrich never recovered from the stress of the operation and died of a stroke on September 25, 1968. His unfinished novel *Into the Night* was completed by Lawrence Block in 1987. *Blues of a Lifetime*, Woolrich's informal autobiography, was published in 1991.

# ❖ *Critical Extracts*

**RAYMOND CHANDLER**      I have just been reading a book called *Phantom Lady*, by William Irish, whoever that is. It has one of those artificial trick plots and is full of small but excessive demands on the Goddess of Chance, but it is a swell job of writing, one that gives everything to every character, every scene, and never, like so many of our overrated novelists, just flushes the highlights and then gets scared and runs. I happen to admire this kind of writing very much. I haven't seen the book advertised anywhere and such reviews as I have seen of it show a complete unawareness of the technical merits of the book. So what the hell.

Raymond Chandler, Letter to Blanche Knopf (22 October 1942), *Selected Letters of Raymond Chandler*, ed. Frank MacShane (New York: Columbia University Press, 1981), p. 22

**RAYMOND CHANDLER**      William Irish is a man named Cornell Woolrich, an author under his own name, and one of the oldest hands there are at the pulp detective business. He is known in the trade as an idea writer, liking the tour de force, and not much of a character man. I think his stuff is very readable, but leaves no warmth behind it.

Raymond Chandler, Letter to Alfred A. Knopf (8 February 1943), *Selected Letters of Raymond Chandler*, ed. Frank MacShane (New York: Columbia University Press, 1981), p. 24

**JAMES SANDOE**    All of these writers ⟨Margaret Millar, Lenore Glen Offord, Mabel Seeley, Dorothy B. Hughes, Elisabeth Sanxay Holding⟩ are concerned, if very differently, with the tale of terror; but their methods are nearly diverse as their capacities. Cornell Woolrich is in some ways the most superb and garish literary juggler of the lot and his special capacity has been to perform a series of variations on what will be remembered as the puzzle of the vanishing lady.

You will recall the story of the girl and her mother who arrived in Paris one afternoon during the year of the Exposition, went to a crowded hotel and were assigned to different rooms, whereupon the mother vanished completely as if she had never existed while all the world seemed bent upon denying to the frantic girl that she had ever existed.

The theme is common property and its variations nearly as many as those of the equally celebrated puzzle of the locked room. The essence of this sort of tale is the discovery of the inexplicable within the circle of the ordinary. One of Cornell Woolrich's most facile variations was the one he called *Phantom Lady* and published under the name William Irish.

Woolrich has sought and found terror not where one has been led to expect it—in the graveyard at midnight, in the deserted haunted house— but in the streets of the city. He shows fear stalking the subway and walking along Broadway, fear all the more striking for making its way boldly through crowds into the light of day.

But while his skill in contriving variations is staggering, his stories are inclined in retrospect to seem more than a little absurd. To seem, that is, as staged as they are. Woolrich has a facility for catching the reader's attention with a striking situation and then bustling him from shock to shock with a kind of numbing swiftness. The mere facility is apparent only after the last page has been turned and then if one is so unwise as to glance back, the tale itself vanishes into incredibility, very much as Eurydice vanished when Orpheus forsook his vow and turned to look at her before she crossed the threshold of Hell.

James Sandoe, "Dagger of the Mind," *The Art of the Mystery Story*, ed. Howard Haycraft (New York: Simon & Schuster, 1946), pp. 259–60

---

**ANTHONY BOUCHER**     By sober critical standards there is just about everything wrong with much of Woolrich's work. This collection of six stories ⟨Nightmare⟩ illustrates most of the flaws: the "explanation" that is harder to believe than the original "impossibility," the banal and over-obvious twist of "irony," the casual disregard of fact or probability (the Los Angeles Police Department so understaffed that only a single investigator of low rank can be spared to handle the murder of a film star!). However, critical sobriety is out of the question so long as this master of terror-in-the-commonplace exerts his spell. It is an oddly chosen collection, representing neither the best nor the least familiar of Woolrich (or William Irish, as some of these stories have been previously by-lined), but it is characteristic, and I do not envy the hard-hearted reader who can resist its compulsive black magic.

Anthony Boucher, "Criminals at Large," *New York Times Book Review*, 2 September 1956, p. 15

---

**FRANK GRUBER**     Cornell Woolrich was not at the *Black Mask* party, but he was one of the leading contributors to the magazine, as well as other leading pulps of the time. Woolrich was an introvert who lived with his mother at the Hotel Marseilles on upper Broadway and left the hotel only when absolutely necessary. He shunned parties and social gatherings, but Steve Fisher and I got him out to a party one night. The next day I got a call from Fanny Ellsworth ⟨editor of *Black Mask*⟩. "What did you fellows do to Cornell Woolrich last night?" she asked.

"Nothing," I replied. "We got him to take a couple of drinks, that's all."

Fanny went on: "He came tearing in here this morning yelling that I was paying Gruber, Fisher and Torrey four cents a word and he was getting only one and a half cents and he was never going to write for the magazine again!"

I didn't recall that we had told Woolrich that little fib about our word rates, but we *could* have done so.

Later, when I was well established at Rinehart, the company brought out a book by Cornell Woolrich and I asked Stanley Rinehart what he thought of him. Stanley said that he never met him, all the negotiations had been done by mail—although Woolrich lived in New York City!

Frank Gruber, The Pulp Jungle (Los Angeles: Sherbourne Press, 1967), pp. 100–101

---

**STEVE FISHER**     I can best describe his unique ability as "time and place projection". No other writer has ever been able to project the reader *into* the story so completely that all surroundings are totally obliterated. He is living another life, at another place, right along with the creatures that Woolrich is describing. He feels the same emotions, hopes, and fears that they feel. This phenomenon requires a genius of the very highest order, and Cornell Woolrich was the only one able to accomplish it so successfully.

Steve Fisher, "Immortals Do Die: Cornell Woolrich (1903–1968), A Memoriam,"<br>Armchair Detective 2, No. 3 (April 1969): 161

---

**MARTHA FOLEY**     Usually, writers bringing manuscripts to the office asked for me, either because they thought Whit ⟨Burnett⟩, being a man, was too important, or because people with a problem often find it easier to talk to a woman than to a man. Cornell Woolrich was one. I had never heard of him. A thin, shabby, shaking, hungry-looking man, he asked me, almost imploringly, "If I send you a story, will you please read it?"

"Of course," I told him. "That's why I'm an editor. To read manuscripts."

Reassured, he told me about himself. In 1927, when he was twenty-four years old, he had won first prize—$10,000—in a short story contest held by *College Humor*, then a large circulation magazine. (Writing as I am now about Cornell makes me wish, as I have countless times, that I had kept a journal!) As far as I can remember, he said that there was a long hiatus in his writing after winning the prize, and that when he resumed writing his work was rejected. I remember his telling me of how his father had left his mother, and of how as a boy, he had spent years with her roaming around the country in search of his father. I have never forgotten his leaning forward to me and saying earnestly, "A search for a father is a search for God."

The story I promised to read, which Cornell sent me, was the wonderful "Good-By New York," a skin-prickling tale of two people who have committed a crime; desperate to leave the big city, their stratagems to avoid detection, their near-captures and their terror, are told in writing far superior to that of the usual thriller. The praise given the story when it appeared provided Cornell with the renewed impetus he craved. He went on to achieve lifelong publishing success and is best remembered (popularly) for the movie "Rear Window." He wrote many mystery novels and short stories, using both the name Woolrich and William Irish. He won the Poe Award in 1949.

Martha Foley, "*Story in America*," *The Story of* Story *Magazine*, ed. Jay Neugeborgen (New York: W. W. Norton, 1980), pp. 209–10

---

**GEOFFREY O'BRIEN**      Cornell Woolrich (who also wrote under the names William Irish and George Hopley) is another of the writers whom the French have helped salvage from oblivion, and whom Truffaut has filmed with varying success in *The Bride Wore Black* and *Mississippi Mermaid* (adapted from *Waltz into Darkness*). Woolrich has in fact been a gold mine for movie directors: *Rear Window, Phantom Lady, The Night Has a Thousand Eyes, Street of Chance* (from *The Black Curtain*), *The Black Angel*, and perhaps a dozen other films have been based on his novels and stories. Truth to tell, the films are often more effective than the originals, because although Woolrich had a genius for inventing extraordinary situations (Raymond Chandler called him "the best idea man"), he wrote in a bloated purple prose that thuds like overemphatic movie music:

> Death has begun. Darkness has begun, there in the full jonquil-
> blaze of the dinner-table candles. Darkness. A spot no bigger than
> that spilled drop of consommé. Growing, steadily growing, by the
> days, by the weeks, by the months, until it has blotted out
> everything else. Until all is darkness. Until there is nothing *but*
> darkness. Darkness and fear and pain, doom and death. (*Night Has
> a Thousand Eyes*)

It might be tolerable in small doses, but Woolrich writes this way the whole time. Yet through the crudities of style and excesses of melodrama something in his work fascinates. He is quite simply the premier paranoid among crime writers. His is the realm of the impossible coincidence, perceived as a cosmic joke at the expense of man. Even if he writes of thugs and dives and dark city streets, he is miles away from any kind of naturalism; in his world there are magical correspondences between things rather than logical relations.

The perennial unanswered question of his protagonists is: Why me? Why should my husband of five minutes be shot dead on the church steps? Why should my angelic bride turn out to be a vicious murderer? The hero of *Phantom Lady* quarrels with his wife, steps out to a neighborhood bar, and strikes up a conversation with a beautiful woman. He returns home to find his wife dead and himself accused of her murder. He offers his bar encounter as an alibi, but the woman cannot be found, and the people who were in the bar at the time—a demonstrably random assortment of human beings—all deny having seen her.

This comes close to being the classic Woolrich situation. Although the solution is necessarily disappointing (the witnesses have been bribed to keep silent by the real murderer), there remains one further revealing stroke of plotting: the phantom lady is not found, and does not step forward to clear the hero, because she is a hopeless lunatic who on that one evening, in a rare spell of lucidity, had wandered out by herself. This is another of the million-to-one chances that are the essence of Woolrich's stories, like the stray bullet that kills the groom on the church steps in *The Bride Wore Black* or the arbitrary bits of evidence that combine to falsely convince the returning soldier of his wife's infidelity in the cruel story, "The Light in the Window."

For Woolrich, these disasters are meaningless pranks of the gods, and it is always the innocent who are singled out as victims. His work offers testimony of a life lived in fear, a life such as many live but few have described. He himself (as described by Michael Avallone) "lived some forty years of his time in a hotel room; he had no close personal friends and the Big Romance always eluded him; some of his most memorable works are dedicated to such lifeless things as hotel rooms, typewriters, and the utter sadness of the human condition; later on in life he discovered John Barleycorn and the empty days and nights of his withdrawal from society echoed and re-echoed with the typical alcoholic *miseria* of broken appointments, paranoiac harangues and self-lashing which ended in the usual weeping haze of '*Where did I go wrong?*' "

His hero is such a man as himself, whose exactness of perception serves only to intensify an overwhelming sense of impotence and doom. It is strange to think that this prolific and wealthy author of popular thrillers was really offering his readers nothing but despair and the longing for extinction. It cannot be said that he exploited paranoia as a literary device; it was in all sincerity his way of perceiving the world.

Woolrich is an extreme case, but an interesting one because his paranoia so well accorded with the mood of the time. His best books were written between 1940 and 1948, and this was the period in which, concurrent with the Second World War and its aftermath, a great change came over the American consciousness. In many of its aspects, it can be perceived as a morbid gloom which even prosperity and political hegemony could not dispel. This change was to be reflected in phenomena as diverse as the post war *film noir* and the overtly paranoid anti-Communist crusade, and not least in the changing tone of paperback novels.

Geoffrey O'Brien, *Hardboiled America: The Lurid Years of Paperbacks* (New York: Van Nostrand Rinehold, 1981), pp. 91–93

---

**CHARLES CHAMPLIN**      Woolrich is indeed a first-rate storyteller, a master at creating suspense: the against-the-clock race to clear an innocent man of murder, as in *Phantom Lady*, or an urgent quest by the innocent man to discover who he was and what he didn't do during the month he was an amnesiac (*The Black Curtain*).

His novels are thickly atmospheric, and *Black Alibi* is, for example, really a series of free-standing pieces in which we meet, and then await the grisly deaths of the victims of a madman masquerading as an escaped jaguar in a Latin-American city. The whole thing is improbable in a way that nothing in Hammett or Chandler—not the mayhem of Hammett's *Red Harvest*, not the blinding plot intricacies of the Chandler stories—is improbable.

If Hammett and Chandler were men writing out of their close and often discouraged knowledge of the real world, Woolrich was a man writing out of his private nightmares of shadowy but inescapable fates, doomed loves and unbearable anguish.

Charles Champlin, "Dark Fiction by an Invisible Author," *Los Angeles Times Book Review*, 2 January 1983, pp. 1, 5

**JULIAN SYMONS**      Cornell George Hopley-Woolrich (1903–1968), who wrote as Cornell Woolrich, William Irish and George Hopley, is at present a cult figure in America, 'one of the greatest suspense writers in the history of crime fiction', as one enthusiast mistakenly puts it. Woolrich wrote for *Black Mask* and many other magazines, but his work was only loosely associated with that of more typical pulp writers. His best writing is in the novels he produced at great speed in the early forties, including *The Bride Wore Black* (1940) and one of the Irish books, *Phantom Lady* (1942), but the melodramatic silliness and sensationalism of many of his plots, and the continuous high-pitched whine of his prose—seen at its worst in the collection of stories *Nightwebs* (1971)—preclude him from serious consideration.

> Julian Symons, *Bloody Murder: From the Detective Story to the Crime Novel* (New York: Viking/Penguin, 1985), p. 129

---

**FRANCIS LACASSIN**      Cornell Woolrich does not scorn the technical resources of the investigation. Without it, his narratives would be nothing but love stories disturbed by death. But he relies for its execution (sorting out miscellaneous clues, deductions, inquiries and examinations of witnesses) upon the interested principal—that person who everything indicates to be guilty (*Deadline at Dawn*, *The Black Curtain*, "The Dog with the Wooden Leg")—or upon those who do reconaissance for the victim, and not without reason: his wife (*The Black Angel*), or his friend and his mistress (*Phantom Lady*). Why such a strange choice of hero? Because of the dramatic and psychological richness offered by the ambiguity of this criminal/victim situation.

The investigation, conventional in method, but unusual because of the personality of the investigator, sees its inspiration radically modified. In other detective fiction, dramatic progress is marked by the discovery of elements that unlock the mystery concealing the truth; in Woolrich, one follows a psychological progress where the climax is servant to the analysis, as the mystery gives way to the anguish of the investigator.

The latter figure is no longer a salaried functionary searching for a criminal so that the law can retain its force; the investigation is not conducted out of professional conscience, to solve a mystery. The investigator is either a person who is struggling to save his own skin—or one of the relatives, who are attempting to prevent his execution. The investigation: elsewhere, it is a search for the truth; here, it is a race against death. The heightening and alleviation of anguish.

Francis Lacassin, "Cornell Woolrich: Psychologist, Poet, Painter, Moralist," tr. Mark T. Bassett, *Clues: A Journal of Detection* 8, No. 2 (Fall–Winter 1987): 43–44

---

**RICHARD RAYNER**     Woolrich understood better than any other writer in the crime genre that the creation of suspense is a playful, even sadistic process. The point is not to have a bomb explode under a bed, but to tell everyone that there is a bomb and pose some questions. Will it go off? When? And will it hurt the small child asleep in the other room?

Woolrich was an expert in this kind of manipulation, but his writing was never cold-blooded. When he plunged a character into situations where everything was off-key, unexpected, dangerous, it was not simply to create atmosphere and tension. For Woolrich, paranoia was not just a way of teasing the audience, but a way of perceiving the world. He found life to be terrible and terrifying, and he believed he could do nothing about it.

The paranoia is reflected always in the relationships he allowed his male and female characters. In Woolrich sex is at best an ambivalent experience. More often, it involves death, or fear, or (at least) humiliation. Small wonder that when Alfred Hitchcock read "Rear Window" he recognized the current of male sexual terror which runs through Woolrich's work, and gave the disabled voyeuristic photographer a fear of marriage to contend with as well as a fear of being hunted by the man who he believes to have committed a murder. For Hitchcock, like Woolrich, was another superb craftsman who made a career by fashioning entertainment from a deep-rooted sexual anxiety.

Perhaps that's why the stories of Cornell Woolrich, like the films of Hitchcock, have aged well. They touch a contemporary nerve. They are also written in a style that is easy and colloquial, with characters who are always believable and plots that hurtle forward like a runaway lorry. And *then* there's the suspense. Pulp writer Frank Gruber recalls that Woolrich once tried to write an entire novella in a single evening. This was in the 1930s when *Black Mask* paid Woolrich one and a half cents a word. He always delivered more than anyone bargained for.

Richard Rayner, "Introduction," *Rear Window and Other Stories* by Cornell Woolrich (London: Simon & Schuster UK, 1988), pp. x–xi

**GARY INDIANA**     Like Hollywood films, Woolrich's narratives exist primarily because they kill time. The vision is pitch black, but it is also patently unreal. For the fastidious reader, Woolrich's prose is full of irritations. The lyricism of his endless descriptive passages is deep purple, yet weirdly effective in creating atmosphere. His plots are ridiculous, overdetermined by a corny fondness for "ironic twists." After a book's worth of detective work hunting down evidence that would free his condemned best friend, a good guy turns out to be the real killer. Having killed off a number of people she thinks were responsible for her husband's murder, a woman learns they were all innocent. A recovered amnesiac believes that he killed someone when he didn't know who he was, but then it turns out he only witnessed the crime, and then—and so forth. ⟨. . .⟩

Woolrich's florid style undoubtedly persuaded scores of pulp editors in the '30s that they were witnessing a class act: crime stories written in an overtly literary way. That much of Woolrich's word music was pathologically squandered on trivia (and generated because pulps paid by the word) didn't matter in a genre desperate for respectability. The crime novelists whose works have endured are stylists of a completely different sort: Chandler, Hammett, and Cain wrote the lean, abstemious senstences American literature has favored since Hemingway. This style has taken root as the American version of convincing exposition. Woolrich, whose sentences have accurately been termed elephantine, uses a much more sadistic technique to convince readers that something is really happening. He slows down the narration to a crawl and describes every nuance of the visual world in obsessive detail. One reason Woolrich's books were so readily bought by Hollywood must have been that nobody had to bother with a shooting script: "In the light of the full-bodied moon the flower garden at the back of the house was a bright as noon . . . The sanded paths that ran around it foursquare, and through it like an X, gleamed like snow, and her shadow glided along them azure against their whiteness. The little rock-pool in the center was polka-dotted with silver-disks . . ." (*I Married a Dead Man*)

The settings came camera-ready, and so did the characters. "The beauty of her face was expressed in its proportions, in the width of her brow, in the wide spacing of her eyes, in their limpid candor, in the honesty and character already already fully expressed in her chin . . . There was no paint or other marking on her face . . . Her hair, which was of the shade where dark blonde meets light brown, fell in soft disorder . . . she had on a dress of dark cloth, without a single ornament . . ." (*Night Has a Thousand Eyes*)

That was a nice girl. Here is a floozy: "A pair of artificial eyelashes, superimposed on her own with no regard for nature, stuck out all around her eyes like rays in a charcoal drawing of the sun . . . Her hair was frizzy to the point of kinkiness . . . She had a pair of untrue blue eyes, which probably deepened to green when she hated." (*Into the Night*)

Woolrich organizes players into "decent" and "corrupt" characters by way of these irksome judgmental pictures. "Corruption" encompasses all forms of life outside the bourgeois family. A typical Woolrich story is set in motion by a rupture of the family order: a husband's infidelity in *The Black Angel*, the intrusion of a psychic's predictions into the blissful home life of an upper-class father and daughter in *Night Has a Thousand Eyes*. While Woolrich's decent people are frequently ruined by contact with corruption, it's fair to say that no one in any Woolrich novel has a discernible inner life until the corruption is wheeled into place. Once it is, the characters become carefully segregated responses to an escalating emergency, tricked out with little visual and verbal reminders that this one is a sympathetic decent female, that one a resolute protective male, someone else a paranoid obsessive concussion victim, and so on. Their lives before and after their encounters with suspense are insubstantial and static.

Gary Indiana, "Man in the Shadows," *Voice Literary Supplement*, May 1989, p. 26

---

**FRANCIS NEVINS, JR.**      He was the greatest writer of suspense fiction that ever lived. His two dozen crime novels and the best of his more than two hundred short stories and novelettes strike at us with the same wrenching impact, the same resonances of terror and anguish and loneliness and despair, as one finds in the darkest films of his cinematic counterpart, Alfred Hitchcock. He spent most of his creative life as a recluse, living with his mother in an uptown residential hotel. When she died, he cracked, and began his own slow descent to the grave. He had the most wretched life of any American writer since Poe. His funeral was attended by exactly five people. He left no survivors but a rich legacy of fiction. This book is about his life, as much as we can know of it, and about the doom-haunted world he created on the printed page, and about the impact of that world on the nonprint media of movies, radio and television.

No full-scale biography of Woolrich is likely to be written. Too much of his life was spent inside his shell, too much of what he said and wrote about himself was lies. We can penetrate through layers of deception and reach what we think is the truth, but it's just as likely to be a layer of deception that is impenetrable. "I've never lied in all my life," he wrote in his unpublished autobiographical manuscript, "not to anyone else, and not to myself." In fact, he never *stopped* lying. When we try to reconstruct his life we are forced to make educated guesses and to use words like "apparently" and "seems" and "probable" again and again. But the more we explore his fictional nightworld, the more connections we find not only among his novels and stories but between his fiction and his unenviable life, so that writing about his world becomes indistinguishable from writing about him.

Francis Nevins, Jr., "Introduction," *Cornell Woolrich: First You Dream, Then You Die* (New York: Mysterious Press, 1989), pp. vii–viii

---

**CORNELL WOOLRICH**        I started out with one line, as I said. Well, any writer does, any story or any book does. Then the line became a paragraph, the paragraph a page, the page a whole scene, the scene a whole chapter. But this stood alone, by itself, in the middle of nowhere. A scene without a story to go with it, in other words.

I wrote out from it in both directions, forward toward the ending and backward toward the beginning. Finally, I'd stretched it out backward as far as I could, and the thing was suddenly over, finished.

"So that's how you write a book!" I marveled, hardly able to believe it myself.

But the whole thing was still formless anyway; it had no plot progression, no dramatic unity, no structural discipline. There was a great deal of such writing being done at the time, it was called "slice-of-life," I think, and it deliberately avoided plot and structure. But the big difference between it and my own effort was this: these others had something to write about, at least. I didn't. They knew something about life, even if it was only one small segment, one infinitesimal microcosm of it, and they were writing about the part they knew. I knew nothing about any part of it, so therefore I was writing about something I knew nothing about.

What I was actually doing was, not writing autobiographically, which every beginner does and should, but writing objectively, which should come along only a good deal later. What saved it from being any worse than it was, was a facility with words, which probably had been latent in me all along.

But I came to realize later, as I grew a little, that it was far better to be short on words, scantily supplied, poor in them, so long as you could sprinkle the few words you had over a damn good basic situation (which could carry you along by itself, almost without words), than to be able to work them into a rich weave, make them glitter, make them dance, range them into vivid descriptions and word pictures, and in the end have them covering nothing but a great big hole.

> Cornell Woolrich, "Remington Portable NC69411," *Blues of a Lifetime: The Autobiography of Cornell Woolrich*, ed. Mark T. Bassett (Bowling Green, OH: Bowling Green State University Popular Press, 1991), pp. 10–11

# Bibliography

*Cover Charge*. 1926.

*Children of the Ritz*. 1927.

*Times Square*. 1929.

*A Young Man's Heart*. 1930.

*The Time of Her Life*. 1931.

*Manhattan Love Song*. 1932.

*The Bride Wore Black* ⟨*Beware the Lady*⟩. 1940.

*The Black Curtain*. 1941.

*Marihuana: A Drug-Crazed Killer at Large* ⟨with *Cover Painting* by Bill Fleming⟩. 1941.

*Black Alibi*. 1942.

*Phantom Lady*. 1942.

*The Black Angel*. 1943.

*I Wouldn't Be in Your Shoes* ⟨*And So to Death; Nightmare*⟩. 1943.

*The Black Path of Fear*. 1944.

*After-Dinner Story* ⟨*Six Times Death*⟩. 1944.

*Deadline at Dawn*. 1944.

*Night Has a Thousand Eyes*. 1945.

*The Dancing Detective*. 1946.

*Borrowed Crime and Other Stories*. 1946.

*Waltz into Darkness*. 1947.

*Rendezvous in Black.* 1948.

*I Married a Dead Man.* 1948.

*Dead Man Blues.* 1948.

*The Blue Ribbon ⟨Dilemma of the Dead Lady⟩.* 1949.

*Fright.* 1950.

*Savage Bride.* 1950.

*Somebody on the Phone ⟨The Night I Died; Deadly Night Call⟩.* 1950.

*Six Nights of Mystery: Tales of Suspense and Intrigue.* 1950.

*You'll Never See Me Again.* 1951.

*Strangler's Serenade.* 1951.

*Eyes That Watch You.* 1952.

*Bluebeard's 7th Wife.* 1952.

*Nightmare.* 1956.

*Violence.* 1958.

*Hotel Room.* 1958.

*Death Is My Dancing Partner.* 1959.

*Beyond the Night.* 1959.

*The Best of William Irish ⟨Phantom Lady, After-Dinner Story, Deadline at Dawn⟩.* 1960.

*The Doom Stone.* 1960.

*The 10 Faces of Cornell Woolrich.* 1965.

*The Dark Side of Love: Tales of Love and Death.* 1965.

*Nightwebs: A Collection of Stories.* Ed. Francis M. Nevins, Jr. 1971.

*Angels of Darkness.* 1978.

*Fantastic Stories.* Ed. Charles G. Waugh and Martin H. Greenberg. 1981.

*Rear Window and Four Short Novels.* 1984.

*Darkness at Dawn: Early Suspense Classics.* Ed. Francis M. Nevins, Jr., and Martin H. Greenberg. 1985.

*Vampire's Honeymoon.* 1985.

*Blind Death with Death.* 1985.

*Into the Night* (with Lawrence Block). 1987.

*Rear Window and Other Stories.* Ed. Maxim Jakubowski. 1988.

*Blues of a Lifetime: The Autobiography of Cornell Woolrich.* Ed. Mark T. Bassett. 1991.